SWINBURNE

From the portrait by G. F. Watts, in the National Portrait Gallery

ALGERNON CHARLES SWINBURNE

SWINBURNE

BY SAMUEL C. CHEW

I am but a voice;
My life is but the life of winds and tides,
No more than winds and tides can I avail.

HYPERION

Visionary power
Attends the motion of the viewless winds,
Embodied in the mystery of words.

THE PRELUDE

WITH ILLUSTRATIONS

BOSTON 1929

LITTLE, BROWN, AND COMPANY

Published March, 1929

PRINTED IN THE UNITED STATES OF AMERICA

To

THOMAS JAMES WISE,

Scholar and Friend of Scholars,

Bibliographer of Swinburne,

In Memory of many pleasant

Hours in his Library

PREFACE

The appearance of the definitive Bonchurch Edition of Swinburne's Works (London: William Heinemann, Ltd.; New York: Gabriel Wells) makes this an appropriate time to publish a new estimate of the poet's genius and achievement. The present study dates, however, in its original form from more than a decade ago. It was set aside deliberately to await the publication, long announced, of the definitive edition; and consequently, while I have, I hope, profited by the various estimates that have appeared in recent years, my impressions and opinions were formed independently of all critical studies of later date than Sir Edmund Gosse's biography, the primary source of information on the poet's life and character. That I have devoted so much space to the tragedies and prose writings is due to the fact that heretofore these departments of Swinburne's work have been very strictly subordinated by critics to his lyrical, meditative and narrative verse. The chief emphasis remains, however, and must always remain upon Swinburne, the lyric poet.

To the authors of all but two of the works mentioned in my bibliography I wish to express my obligations. The exceptions are the two volumes by M. Georges Lafourcade which, I regret to say, appeared too recently to be made use of in my text. Mr. Thomas J. Wise, by his admirable "Bibliography of the Writings of Swinburne" and by the long series of privately printed pamphlets in which he placed the poet's posthumous writings beyond the reach of destruction, has put all students deeply in his debt. My sense of obligation to him is expressed in my dedication. To Messrs. William Heinemann, Ltd. I am indebted for permission to quote from copyright material. I am under the following obligations for permission to reproduce the illustrations: to the Reverend Mother Superior of the Order of the Sacred Heart at Bonchurch, Isle of Wight, for the photograph of East Dene, which is now a convent; to the Director of the National Portrait Gallery for the portrait of Swinburne by George Frederick Watts; to the authorities of the National Gallery for Whistler's "The Little White Girl"; to Cav. Alinari of Florence for the photographs of San Gimignano, of Delphi, and of Il Sodoma's "Cristo alla Colonna"; to Signor Brogi of Florence for the photograph of Florence; and to Messrs. G. P. Putnam's Sons for the photograph of Swinburne at the age of sixty-five, taken from "The Life and Letters of Theodore Watts-Dunton." The facsimiles of Swinburne's letter to J. C. Hotten are from the original in my own possession.

S. C. C.

Bryn Mawr, Pennsylvania
December, 1928

CONTENTS

ILLUSTRATIONS

SWINBURNE

CHAPTER ONE

"The Youngest Singer that England Bore"

In "Thalassius" Swinburne wrote his spiritual autobiography; the poetic truths which lie beneath the accidents of fact are recorded in this poem; and that is why Edward Thomas, risking the adverse effect which its heady vaporous riot of imagery is bound to have upon the neophyte, advised that it be read first of all Swinburne's poems. Remarkable is the consciousness expressed in it of a divine endowment with the gift of song. Remarkable, too, is the sense of kinship with elemental forces; he is, in Landor's words, what suns and winds and waters have made him; he is Thalassius, child of the sea, a sea-mew borne on the wind above the waste of waters. The image of the sea bird here and in various other poems implies an awareness not only of his physical frailty — "so birdlike slight and light" — but of his isolation from ordinary ways of life — "a fosterling and fugitive on earth." Throughout his poetry the Sun or the Sun God stands as a symbol of Reason and Art and Song; and the Sea, even when celebrated for its own sake, is the symbol of Liberty. Swinburne is the child of Sun and Sea. But it is through a human foster father that knowledge of his divine parents, Light and Freedom, comes to him; and this foster father, "grey with glories", who finds "a babe with flower-soft face" by the margin of the April sea, is Walter Savage Landor. From Landor Swinburne learned to love intellectual and political freedom; to hate injustice and tyranny; and to trust in man's dignity and future.

The poem is as significant for its omissions as for what it records. Of the poet's human parents not a word. Yet from his father, Admiral C. H. Swinburne, he inherited his courage and independence and love of the sea; and from his mother, Lady Jane Swinburne, a woman of delicate taste and culture, his love of poetry and the fine arts. To both he was indebted for their patience and counsel during his riotous years, and to both he paid elsewhere tributes of affection and gratitude. Even more remarkable is the lack of any allusion to Joseph Mazzini in this spiritual autobiography. It cannot be due to any oversight and can be accounted for only on the ground that "Thalassius" tells of the development not of the republican but of the poet. Even so, the narrative of his "renunciation" and return to his early ideals is incomplete as it stands, for Swinburne's repudiation of the rebellious nihilism of his early manhood was directly due to the personal influence of Mazzini. With no word on Mazzini, it is not surprising that the poet is silent as to other personal influences.

It would be uncritical and unsympathetic to look for well-defined allusions or for any record of the routine of daily life in a highly symbolic poem. Otherwise the silence of "Thalassius" with regard to the great struggles in the world of ideas which were enacted in Swinburne's youth would indicate a blank insensitivity to the "fierce intellectual warfare" of the period. All the "practical" movements of his time seem, if we scan too closely the narrative of his soul's development, to have passed him by while he lived in a radiant but amorphous world of sunlight and wide ocean. The vague and grandiose allusions to love of Liberty and hatred of oppression must serve as indications of his sympathy with the forces of progress. We cannot accept literally the poet's account of his spiritual growth, nor did he intend that we should do so. The renunciation and *vita nuova* recorded in "Thalassius" are aspirations rather than accomplished facts. An unsympathetic and unimaginative reading of the poem reduces it, as a like reading reduces the "Epipsychidion", to grotesque absurdity. All that the poet would have us know is this: that he was bred by the sun and the waters; that he learned to love Love and Liberty and to hate Tyranny; that love first and then lust led him astray into disillusionment, satiety and scepticism; and that escaping thence he returned to his first ideal.

Swinburne's admiration for Victor Hugo, though

not recorded in "Thalassius", can be traced back to his boyhood. Until recently there were persons alive who remembered him as a flame-haired boy riding upon his pony across the Northumbrian moors and chanting as he rode the verses from "Gastibelza":

Dansez, chantez, villageois! la nuit gagne
Le mont Falû.
— Le vent qui vient à travers la montagne
Me rendra fou!

and he has told us that he loved Hugo from a time when, as a youth, his own "young song took flight towards the great heat and light" shed on him from the "far splendour" of the French poet.

Landor he did not meet in the flesh till 1864, and the celebrated visits at Florence took place in circumstances not so romantic as, to be poetically satisfying, they should have been. Hugo he did not meet till much later in life, and then in circumstances which were at once pathetic and almost ludicrous. But meetings with two other and very different "elder singers" — differing as much from each other as either did from Landor or Hugo — left a permanent impression upon a sensitive boy who felt stirring within him a sense of "dedication" to poetry. In 1849 Lady Jane Swinburne took her twelve-year-old son to see the aged Wordsworth at Rydal Mount; and being told that the boy was already acquainted with his poetry, Wordsworth remarked that "there was nothing in his writings that would do him harm and there were some things that might do him good." When they took their leave Algernon was in tears. Two years later Lady Jane conducted her son into the presence of another member of the hierarchy of poets, one not so illustrious as Wordsworth but even more venerable: Samuel Rogers, the author of "Italy." She told the old man that they had come "because Algernon thinks more of poets than of any other people in the world"; and Rogers, equal to the occasion, laid his hand upon his head, saying, "I prophesy that you, too, will be a poet." Thus was Swinburne inducted into the apostolic succession of poets. The High Priest of contemporary poetry took no part in the rite. Tennyson, "into whose church", as Swinburne was later to admit, "I and all my generation were baptized", he did not meet until he was one-and-twenty; and on that occasion there was no ceremony of initiation. For though "baptized into his church" Swinburne was not of the line of Tennyson. How quaint is the fact that in after years it was the meeting with Rogers which Swinburne remembered as confirming him in his vocation! Yet though deserving to be chronicled among the curiosities of literature, it does not seem quite so strange when we remember that, however few qualities there were in common between the author of "Jacqueline" and the author of "Faustine", Swinburne possessed a strong sense of the hereditary tradition in poetry. Rogers was the friend of Wordsworth and Byron; a contemporary of Coleridge; older than Shelley and Keats. In comparison with the hieratic distinction which Rogers shared with Landor, Tennyson was a *parvenu*. Throughout his life Swinburne claimed for himself a place in the line royal; he was the youngest of Apollo's sons. Sappho was his "sister"; Villon his "brother"; Marlowe his "brother"; Hugo his "master and father and lord"; Baudelaire his "brother." He delighted to pay homage even to those survivors who had attained an accidental glory through association with the poets of the Romantic Generation: Trelawny, because of his friendship with Byron and Shelley; Wells, because he had known Keats; Kirkup, because he had known Blake; Dobell, because he had known Lamb. It is therefore not extravagant to suppose that a sense of dedication, quite as sincere if not of such mystical intensity as that which Wordsworth experienced in the mountains, may have been imparted to the boy when the old banker-poet laid his withered hand upon the fresh young forehead and flaming hair.

> I made no vows, but vows
> Were then made for me; bond unknown to me
> Was given, that I should be, else sinning greatly,
> A dedicated spirit.

Among the blessings which the Sun God bestowed upon Thalassius was the promise that he should possess "the sound of song that mingles north and south." The allegory is here close to actuality. Though born in London (April 5, 1837), Swinburne's associations were for many years with the extreme north and extreme south of England. Much of his childhood and youth was passed in ranging at will over two dissimilar but equally delightful countrysides: the wild moors of Northumberland around the home of his grandfather, Sir John Swinburne, and the meadows, forests and cliffs of the Isle of Wight. Capheaton in the north and East Dene in the south have equal shares in his life and in his verse. "The white wandering waste of sea far north" and the softer beauty of the southern ocean inspire an equal love; and very often in his poetry there is, as has often been remarked, a commingling of these two influences.

Traditions of the Border country, acting upon a poetic temperament, fixed in the boy's mind an ardent loyalty to the memory of the House of Stuart, strangely at variance with the liberal and republican principles of his mature years, yet continuing to exist side by side with these principles though almost wholly unsupported by any basis of fact in the annals of his family. Mary Stuart was the "red star of boyhood's fiery thought", the queen for whose house his fathers fought and fell. "Born of exiles," he calls himself, and hails

> Mine own twice-banished fathers' harbour-land,
> Their nursing-mother, France, the well-beloved.

Elsewhere he writes of France as "the great nation which twice, in two successive centuries, was the savior and foster mother of my house when driven out of England into exile by civil war." In "Bothwell" he includes the Swinburnes by name among the supporters of Mary Stuart; but actually his "house" never suffered exile; their share in the Stuart misfortunes is the poet's invention, founded apparently upon a distorted remembrance of the marriage of a relative into a distinguished French family. This "Charlie-over-the-Waterism" would be mentioned, if at all, merely as an example of the poet's eccentricity had it not determined the subject of his most ambitious dramatic works and inspired the group of Jacobite songs in which there is more of genuine pathos than is to be found anywhere else in Swinburne's poetry. Older traditions of the North country led to the composition of his "Border Ballads."

He rode his pony upon the northern moors and climbed the Land Slip on the Isle of Wight (a feat of which he was, not unreasonably, proud), swam in the Solent and the North Sea, and read — read omnivorously, through the whole range of English literature, save Byron, whose poems, in obedience to his anxious mother's behest, he did not open till he came to college. He possessed the freedom of the great library of his uncle, the Earl of Ashburnham, a privilege which doubtless did much (as can be proved in particular instances) to fashion his

EAST DENE

tastes in literature, for there is nothing in his lineage on either side to foretell the coming of a great poet. Before coming to Eton he was thoroughly familiar with French and had read Italian with his mother. He himself told Sir Edmund Gosse that he had read Ariosto before ever hearing of "The Faerie Queene"; and when in old age he wrote his tragedy of "Rosamund" he remembered that he had read Alfieri's tragedy on the same theme beside his mother's knee. He of course knew much of Tennyson's verse by heart; many years later he recalled "the joy of the heart-struck boy" upon whose ears first sounded the Tennysonian music. This particular "joy" came and went fitfully throughout his life, alternating with periods of disapproval and distaste. A little later came a passion for Shelley which was lasting and then an enthusiasm for Arnold which did not endure so uninterruptedly. He formed a taste for Scott and Dickens which gave him intense pleasure all his life. At Eton he made the acquaintance of Shakespeare's fellow-dramatists, first in Campbell's "Specimens of the British Poets", then in Lamb's "Specimens of the Dramatic Poets", and presently in "Dodsley's great old plays."

The biographer of a poet looks eagerly for the first signs of budding genius. There is no evidence, apart from his unusual devotion to poetry and his mother's gratification of his desire to make "a first acquaintance with poets", that Swinburne was abnormal or precocious. It is not known when he began to write verses. In the celebrated "Dedication" to the "Poems and Ballads" of 1866 he says of his poems that

> Some sang to me dreaming in class-time
> And truant in hand as in tongue;
> For the youngest were born of boy's pastime,
> The eldest are young;

and elsewhere he has a charming one-line vignette picturing himself as a small boy "reining his rhymes into buoyant order" in the keen northern air. At Eton he attempted a drama in imitation of Cyril Tourneur, but he had the good sense to destroy this piece, together with all, as he thought, of his Etonian and pre-Etonian *juvenilia*. Of the lyric quality of these lost pieces we may well have our doubts, judging by the sole surviving specimen.[1] This is "The Triumph of Gloriana; or, The Temple of Loyalty. On the Queen's Visit to Eton." This copy of verses is as unpromising a beginning as any of Shelley's *juvenilia*. Written in stiff pedestrian couplets of the "closed" variety, it celebrates the glory of the day when myriads flocked with upraised hearts to greet their sovereign. "A virgin train of youthful loveliness" passes forth from the

[1] Certain poems published in *Frazer's Magazine* in 1849 were claimed for Swinburne by Mr. Wise on the ground of the initials "A. C. S." appended to them and were privately printed by the same bibliographer, who afterwards accidently discovered that they were by some one else with the same initials. Yet with such difficulty is a false attribution disproved that a reputable critic has recently lamented the exclusion of these apocryphal verses from the Bonchurch Edition of Swinburne's works.

"time-worn turrets" of Windsor; troops line the way; at the monarch's feet offerings are laid; and the youthful poet beholds a vision of the Temple of Loyalty (*i.e.*, Eton) to which the great Queen comes. For nearly two hundred lines the "Triumph" continues in this fashion. As a literary curiosity it was worth preserving in privately printed form, but the editors of the Bonchurch Edition were well advised in excluding it. It offers no faintest promise of what was to come later from Swinburne's pen.

Of a stature too puny for any athletic sports save swimming, Swinburne nevertheless seems to have won at Eton the respect of his companions, inspiring affection in a few but in others a mingling of repulsion and fear. He was felt to be out of the common, a personality apart from ordinary people. Though nervous and irritable he seems to have been in general a courteous, quiet boy, solitary much of the time, without the arrogance which he was to assume in his middle years, friendly and gentle and somewhat aloof. That he was on the whole happy at Eton is proved by the affectionate regard in which he held the school always and which he expressed in one of the loveliest of his later poems. Nevertheless a restiveness manifested during his last years at Eton (concerning which we have no details) resulted in his being withdrawn when sixteen years of age.

The record of the next two and a half years is

almost a blank. He was tutored privately; and in the summer of 1855 went abroad for the first time, visiting Cologne, Wiesbaden, Nuremberg and a few other German cities. An ingenuous record of this excursion remains in letters to his family. On the return voyage from Ostend to Dover a storm occurred accompanied by unusually sensational meteorological phenomena. Swinburne never forgot this storm. Years later he wrote a magnificent description of it in prose, and he described it again and less successfully in "A Channel Passage", one of his latest poems. This was the one adventure aboard ship of the poet who associated himself preëminently with the sea but was never in his life out of sight of land. In comparison with this experience the shrine of the Three Kings, the wooded castles along the Rhine, and the home of Albrecht Dürer seem to have been unworthy of remembrance.

Swinburne's late, feeble and absurd play "The Sisters" is redeemed from utter worthlessness by the autobiographical allusions scattered through it and especially by the character of Redgie Clavering which is, as he himself admitted, a self-portrait. Clavering is fresh from Eton, eager for life as a soldier or sailor (careers which Swinburne contemplated for a while), ambitious and adventurous, glorying in Northumberland, luxuriating in the soft air of the Isle of Wight; and filled with the love of poetry, a student of Dodsley. The picture is a pleasant one and though idealized, probably not unfaithful in essentials to Swinburne's memories of his youth. But beyond his delight in riding and swimming and reading and writing it tells us nothing of these years between eighteen and twenty-one. There was desultory tutoring and probably a certain amount of verse-making, though his earliest serious poetry dates from a little later on. At length he came up to Oxford and entered Balliol in January, 1856.

It was the Oxford of the post-Tractarian generation. Loyal adherents of Pusey and Keble were there, and there was the tradition of Newman's eloquence and charm. With these associations Swinburne had at first some sympathy, for he had been reared in a milieu not untouched by these influences; and during his early months at Balliol he even passed through a phase of "High" Anglicanism. But the immediate disciples of Newman, like the great priest himself, had taken themselves elsewhere, and from the student-body as a whole the influence of the Catholic Revival was passing away. The center of interest had shifted. Opponents of the Tractarians — Maurice, Kingsley and the elder Arnold — had become the mentors of the more devout members of the younger generation of university men. Trust in dogma was yielding place to a consciousness of the ethical significance of Christianity. Along with this "muscular" Christianity and in part as a result of the Reform Bill and the

Chartist agitation, came legislation in favor of the amelioration of the social condition of the "lower orders"; factory acts, sanitation measures, child-labor laws and the like appeared in rapid succession. This new sense of social responsibility was reflected in the poetry of the period, which in "Locksley Hall", "The Song of the Shirt", "The Cry of the Children", the "Corn-Law Rhymes" and elsewhere "dealt boldly with substantial things." Beyond Church, the influence of Carlyle, which destroyed in many minds the old beliefs, could not compel the acceptance of the vague and austere substitutes which he offered.

The tide of the prestige of science was rising fast. Higher Criticism was delivering heavy blows upon the armor of orthodoxy, using as a chief weapon in its rationalistic assault upon the Scriptures the comparative method of research, in cult and ritual, in mythology, literature and philology. The new "uniformitarian" geology had forced the abandonment of a literal interpretation of the first chapters of Genesis, a victory which had far-reaching implications; and with its ally paleontology was extending the history of the earth and of organic life into "the dark backward and abysm of time." Astronomy was peering out beyond what had once been the flaming ramparts of the world. Evolutionists were on the eve of the publication of "The Origin of Species" and of the celebrated Oxford meeting of the British Association. This prestige of science was strengthened and popularized by Tennyson, while the writings of John Stuart Mill formed a more substantial foundation for the position assumed by the natural scientists. In a word, the solution of continuity effected by the Romantic Reaction was being bridged over and the more normal course of development in continuation of the rationalism of the Enlightenment was again becoming apparent.

All this prepared the way in many minds for the acceptance of, or at any rate sympathy with, the anti-metaphysical philosophy of Comte: Positivism, "the Religion of Humanity", which was presently to be imported into England by Frederick Harrison and his colleagues. This cult harmonized with the philanthropic tendencies of the age. The sense of social responsibility and a proud consciousness of the achievements of science made for a new confidence, strangely at variance with the evidence amassed by the scientists themselves, in the supremacy or at least the primacy of Man in the universe. England was entering upon the period which Lord Morley, in his "Recollections", has described as "an epoch of hearts uplifted with hope, and brains made active with sober and manly reason for the common good." More exultantly Swinburne was presently to exclaim, "Glory to Man in the highest, for Man is the master of things!"

Yet, despite all this, the eighteen-fifties was a melancholy and disillusioned decade, for many men viewed these changes with sadness and alarm. They saw themselves wandering between an old world that had gone down to destruction and a new world whose birth pangs they were witnessing. "We have seen," Professor Clifford, looking back upon these years, was to write somewhat later — "We have seen the spring sun shine out of an empty heaven, to light up a soulless earth; we have felt with utter loneliness that the Great Companion is dead." The song of triumph:

> Jesus lives! No longer now
> Can thy terrors, Death, appal us!

had fallen silent; and the words of Arnold found an echo in many hearts:

> Now He is dead; far hence He lies
>   In the lorn Syrian town,
> And on His grave, with shining eyes,
>   The Syrian stars look down.

Matthew Arnold is, indeed, so completely the type of the eighteen-fifties that, in order to "sense" the atmosphere into which Swinburne came at Oxford, it may be noted that Arnold's attitude towards belief vacillated in early life in obedience to the control exercised over him, now by the emotional and now by the intellectual side of his nature. Two souls dwelt within his breast. His aim was at open-mindedness; but in moods of blank despondency, as expressed for example in "Dover Beach", he is not far from the position later assumed by the author of "The City of Dreadful Night." At other times his agnosticism is hampered by a wistful clinging to old beliefs. Again, in certain moods he experienced what may come to all but the firmest sceptics: the acceptance of scepticism itself as a principle of faith, what Benn, the historian of English rationalism, has described as "the despairing return to faith from the manifold distractions of doubt." But never in Arnold's writings is there a suggestion of the advisability of sensual deadening of pain and fear. His view of life is in striking opposition to the ideas set forth in Fitzgerald's version of the "Rubâiyât" of Omar Khayyam, a poem which appeared while Swinburne was at Oxford but whose immense popular success, fostered by Rossetti's and Swinburne's enthusiasm, dates from a few years later. Not in the harsh repellent manner of Western pessimism, but voluptuous, slow-moving, melancholy and sadly smiling, clothed in gorgeous Eastern raiment, came forward the figure of the astronomer-poet of Persia. His words, issuing from the remote past and from the immemorial East, carried authority and were suggestive of the universal experience of humanity. In Fitzgerald's exquisite quatrains was heard a clear pronouncement of a view of life identical with the popular interpretation of that "New Cyrenaicism" which Pater was soon to be inculcating at Oxford. Yet beneath their promise of temporal pleasure was inscribed the epitaph which the traveler reads upon the archbishop's tomb at Toledo: *Hic jacet pulvis et cinis et nihil.*

Ah, make the most of what we yet may spend,
Before we too into the Dust descend;
  Dust into Dust, and under Dust, to lie,
Sans Wine, sans Song, sans Singer, and — sans End.

The alternative to this pessimistic hedonism was the elevation of morality to the supreme place once occupied by religion, the substitution of conduct for faith. "Has man no second life?" Arnold asks; and the answer is: "Pitch this one high!" This denial that the only moral sanction is one based upon the hope of reward and the fear of punishment in a future life is voiced at just this time not only by Arnold but by Rossetti, in "The Choice", by Huxley, in a noble and celebrated passage in his letters, and by Ruskin, in the beautiful and somber preface to "The Crown of Wild Olive."

It was into a society weighed down or exalted by ideas such as these that Swinburne entered when he took up his residence at Balliol early in 1856. It is not to be thought, however, that the impetuous young man was profoundly moved, either by memories of "lost causes and impossible loyalties" which drift like mist about the spires and cloisters and gardens of Oxford, or by the new ideas which filled the air. He seems to have kept for a while somewhat apart from his fellows; and thus isolated he reverted, as has already been remarked, to the

Anglo-Catholicism in which he had been reared, breathing no doubt the faint fragrance of Newmanism that still lingered near Saint Mary's church.[1] But his isolation was probably due less to any desire to be alone than to a certain unwillingness on the part of his fellow undergraduates to associate with him. His appearance at this time is recorded in several extant photographs and was evidently sufficiently abnormal to inspire uneasiness. There is little or no resemblance to the small fair boy who, in the painting by George Richmond in the National Gallery, sits quietly between his sisters and gazes thoughtfully into the distance. At the age of twenty-one the disproportion between the high forehead with its flaming crown of hair, above broad brows and fine eyes, and the sensual mouth and weak receding chin (features not yet hidden by a thin beard) was already marked. The large head was set upon a "slight light" body tightly buttoned into its little coat. The hands

[1] His studies at this time were chiefly in the fields of history and law. A manuscript volume of college essays survives in Mr. Wise's collection; it dates from the latter part of 1856 and the first months of 1857, but is probably indicative of studies begun some months earlier. Among the subjects of the essays are: "The Sources of Greek History", "The Origin of Moral Ideas", and (faintly significant) "The Constitutional Influence of Small Republics." A similar collection of somewhat later date contains among other things, papers on "The Crusaders", "Joinville" and "Hallam's 'Middle Ages' ", which are all suggestive of the current of Swinburne's interests in 1858. The initials "R. S." attached to some of these pieces are those of Robert Scott, Master of Balliol. Jowett, who in 1854 had stood for the Mastership and had been defeated by Scott, was but seldom seen in the common hall during the early period of Swinburne's residence, and it was not till somewhat later that he accepted the young poet as one of the most brilliant and promising of his protegés.

perpetually fluttered and vibrated with, as it were, an inner excitement. The voice, not unpleasing in periods of tranquillity, was wont, like Shelley's, to rise to shrillness when he was moved by any passionate conviction. Restless he was, and undisciplined, and ready to be led astray. Such letters as survive from this time show him to have been singularly idea-less. The early enthusiasms for love and liberty, wind and sea, Landor and Hugo, Shelley and the Elizabethans, remained unshaped and unfruitful. He was prepared to receive form from his surroundings and it was not long before a firm mold was at hand for his fluid spirit. The abler and more thoughtful undergraduates presently overcame their initial prejudice and received him as a member of the "Old Mortality" Society, where Swinburne found among his associates men destined to become famous in their several pursuits: James Bryce, A. V. Dicey, G. Birkbeck Hill, Thomas H. Green, and John Nichol.

The man who dominated the group was he who was to accomplish least in after life. The personality of John Nichol colored the opinions and the discussions of the "Old Mortality." "As a youngster," Swinburne wrote years afterwards, "I and others always, and justly, held in some awe as well as respect, his ultra-Scottish quality of strict critical judgment." Nichol was a republican in politics and an agnostic in religion. He came from the "advanced" intellectual circles of Glasgow. He was two years older than Swinburne, and in experience older still. He had already met Mill and Kossuth and Mazzini. Hard and dour, canny and cynical, he was now of first-rate intellectual energy and promise. He founded and edited a short-lived publication, the "organ" of the society, called *Undergraduate Papers*. Among his own contributions were, it is significant to note, essays on Louis Napoleon and on Mazzini. In this periodical appeared essays by Dicey, Green, Hill, and Swinburne himself.

In the heat of Nichol's opinions the mists of Anglo-Catholicism which had been drifting through Swinburne's mind evaporated and all the vague republicanism and free thought that had been fermenting there were precipitated into definite convictions. To his influence was doubtless due that Mazzini "cult" which the poet now practised with elaborate eccentricity, performing acts of homage before the portrait of the exiled patriot which hung in his room. Propaganda in England, directed by Mazzini and other exiles, had by now aroused a considerable body of opinion in favor of a free and united Italy. England's refusal to assist Italy in her struggle had roused Ruskin, Mrs. Browning and Rossetti, as later it was to arouse Morley and Meredith, to protest against the principle of non-intervention. These protests anticipate a dominant "note" in Swinburne's "Songs before Sunrise", though English liberal sentiment was divided over the monarchical as opposed to the republican solution of the Italian question. It is easy to picture the scene of discussions in Swinburne's or Nichol's rooms: the rugged young Scot, not easily moved but when moved utterly convinced, expounding the essentials of the political situation — the trickery of the French Emperor, the dangerous prestige of royalist Piedmont, the cautious realism of Cavour, the romanticism of Garibaldi, the idealism of Mazzini, the reactionary policy of the Vatican, the tyranny of Austria — to the voluble and gesticulating poet. As they talked the bottle passed from one to the other and back again, for while developing his republican principles Nichol encouraged Swinburne's taste for liquor. They experienced that bliss which comes in each generation to aspiring youth, to be alive in a new dawn; and they needed but brandy to imagine themselves "o'er all the ills of life victorious."

Thus prompted, Swinburne composed the first poem in which there are suggestions of the ideas, though not as yet of the poetic quality, of the work of his maturity. This is an "Ode to Mazzini", in which, along with echoes of Shelley and Landor, there are faint indications of the highly individual manner he was presently to master. It is an incoherent and inchoate production, awkward and unmelodious, and its chief interest to us is that it shows Swinburne already acquainted not only with the events of Mazzini's life but with the metaphysical basis of Mazzini's republicanism. To this extent Nichol's influence was in the main for good, and had it not been for the play of rival forces which turned Swinburne's thoughts and tastes into other channels, it might have produced in no long time those poems of republicanism which, as it was, were postponed for another decade. One cannot, however, regret an interruption that gave time for the poet's powers to mature.

But there was something sinister and not altogether wholesome in Nichol's hold upon his young friend.[1] The delights of whisky and brandy were not the only shady byways of experience along which the poet was now led or pursued his way unguided. It is noteworthy that in one of the dramas which he wrote about this time (of which something more will be said in a later chapter) there are evidences of abnormal eroticism, sadistic in tone. Swinburne's first long vacation was passed in part with Nichol in the Hebrides. It requires only a sufficiently scabrous imagination to reconstruct accurately enough a large portion of their conversation. The poet's curious taste for puerile indecencies, specimens of which survive in

[1] This fact Mr. Harold Nicolson has accurately divined, though he is apparently unaware that in the unpublished but extant correspondence between the two men there are letters which are quite unprintable but which prove beyond question the deleterious influence of Nichol. No description of these letters is necessary or possible, but one of their characteristics may be indicated by Swinburne's own remark, made in later years, that "the abuse of innocent foreign words or syllables by comparison with indecent native ones is a simple and schoolboy sort of jest." Shakespeare had set the example in "Henry the Fifth."

unpublished letters and other writings, seems to have developed about this time. Nichol encouraged it and contributed his share.

Yet he prepared the way for the reception of influences totally dissimilar from his own. It is a valid guess that he was primarily responsible for Swinburne's early disloyalty to Tennyson. We are accustomed to account for the "reaction" from Tennyson as a result of the idyllic poems of the Laureate's middle years, and it needs an effort to realize that in circles such as the "Old Mortality", where "advanced" young men congregated, this reaction had set in before the publication of the "Idylls of the King" and "Enoch Arden." For this the cloudy religiosity of "In Memoriam" may have been partly responsible, though it is unnecessary to seek for other explanation than that of youth's lack of sympathy with achieved success and its desire to champion new and less popular causes. Be that as it may, Swinburne's mind was swept and garnished, ready to receive new guests.

He experimented in various directions. Three dramas fashioned after Fletcher's model were begun and laid aside. In a brief series of sonnets he captured something of the Shakespearean cadence. Elsewhere we catch Shelleyan echoes and Arnoldian. He tried his hand at Landorian *pastiche*. He began to imitate the ballads of the Border country. He even made a version of the "Dies Irae." And then he came into touch with a new group of young men, his elders by several years, and was swept into the current of Pre-Raphaelitism.

While Swinburne was in Scotland with Nichol, William Morris, presently joined by Dante Rossetti and Edward Burne-Jones, was engaged in decorating the debating hall of the Oxford Union. In the autumn of 1857 Swinburne made the acquaintance of these three men. Rossetti for a while held aloof, but with Morris and Burne-Jones the acquaintance soon ripened into intimacy. A new world of poetry and romance, the world into which he had looked long since, when roving through the Ashburnham library, was opened to Swinburne. Morris read to him the poems that were soon to be published in "The Defence of Guenevere"; and in turn Swinburne read to Morris the first version of "Rosamond" (afterwards destroyed), in which, we may suspect that his own manner, albeit heavily encrusted with Pre-Raphaelitism, was breaking through the Jacobean mannerisms of his earlier experiments in dramatic form. Morris' influence, apparent in the earliest of the "Poems and Ballads", is still more obvious in other pieces that remained unpublished till after Swinburne's death: "Lancelot", for example, and "The Death of Rudel", and the ambitious narrative poem "Queen Yseult", planned as an epic in ten cantos but abandoned after the completion of the first six.[1]

Comment upon "Queen Yseult" is postponed to my chapter on Swinburne's Arthurian poems. The first canto was published in *Undergraduate Papers*, where during the university year of 1857–1858 he also published three prose pieces. The first of these, a paper on Marlowe and Webster, is of interest only as the earliest of a long series of studies of the Elizabethan and Jacobean dramatists. The second, an essay on "Church Imperialism", denounces the identification of the Catholic cause with imperial pretensions in France, proceeds to a bitter attack upon Napoleon III, and ends with a prophecy of the emperor's downfall. The third is a hoax purporting to be a review of a volume of poems by a member of the so-called "Spasmodic School." This is the earliest of Swinburne's *jeux d'esprit*.[2]

[1] Another poem on Rudel, called "Rudel in Paradise" and afterwards renamed "The Golden House", seems to be lost. It was apparently a piece of ambitious length. The story of the Troubador's passion for a far-off and unknown lady has appealed to many poets. Petrarch alludes to it in the "Trionfo d'Amore", a fact which may account for the celebrated stanzas in "The Triumph of Time" in which Swinburne returns to the theme. Warton's mention of it in the "History of English Poetry" attracted the attention of Burns. Leopardi based his "Consalvo" on the legend. It has also inspired ballads by Uhland and Heine. Swinburne of course knew Browning's "Rudel and the Lady of Tripoli" and was acquainted with the Provençal sources. The most popular modern treatment is Rostand's "La Princesse lointaine." Carducci made it the subject of a lecture and a poem.

[2] The term "Spasmodic" had been invented by Professor Aytoun to describe the poetry of Sydney Dobell and Alexander Smith, writers who are to-day little more than names but who in the eighteen-fifties were sufficiently popular to leave marks of their influence upon much of Mrs. Browning's verse and upon Tennyson's "Maud." Violent and sensational themes, set forth in strained hysterical language with an undercurrent of morbidity, were characteristics of

The year 1858, in which Swinburne attained his majority, witnessed a broadening of his horizon in various directions. From this time date the earliest of the poems published in the famous volume of 1866.[1] For a while he cherished the project of a complete translation of the "Decameron" into English verse; parts of his version of the Fourth Day survive in manuscript. A little later this plan was abandoned in favor of a "Triameron" of prose tales in the manner of Boccaccio. One of these stories, "Dead Love",[2] (more reminiscent of the

this school. Swinburne, before writing his burlesque, doubtless read Aytoun's clever parody of these poets, "Firmilian, a Spasmodic Tragedy, by T. Percy Jones." I have seen Swinburne's copy of the edition of 1854. The non-existent volume which he pretends to review is "The Monomaniac's Tragedy and Other Poems by Ernest Wheldrake, Author of Eve, a Mystery, London, 1858." The style mimics rather amusingly the primness of the typical mid-Victorian critique. It is enlivened by many samples of "Mr. Wheldrake's" verse, much of which is in praise of Napoleon III.

[1]The problem of the chronology of "Poems and Ballads" is a difficult one not yet completely settled. Mr. W. B. D. Henderson has studied it elaborately, but the conclusions which he reaches are not always acceptable, despite sound reasoning with regard to some poems and shrewd guesses with regard to others. "A Vigil", a short and very Pre-Raphaelitish version of "The Leper", survives in manuscript watermarked 1857. "The White Hind", an early draft of "The Two Dreams", was described by Swinburne in 1860 as "begun long ago" and may date from 1857–1858. To the latter year Sir Edmund Gosse hesitatingly assigns "Aholibah" and "Madonna Mia." In 1876 Swinburne conceived the design (never carried out) of publishing a volume of "Early Poems" which was to include, among other things, "The Leper", "Song in Time of Revolution", "Song in Time of Order", "Before Parting", "The Sundew", "At Eleusis", "August", "A Christmas Carol", "The Masque of Queen Bersabe", "The Two Dreams", "Aholibah", "After Death", and "The Year of Love." It is probable that all, or nearly all these pieces were written before he left Oxford, some so early as 1858.

[2]This is a slight and febrile tale of a woman who falls in love with the dead body of the man who has slain her lover. Through the intensity of her passion a ghastly mock life is instilled into the corpse. The delicately tinted prose reveals the disciple of Morris; but the theme suggests that Swinburne had been reading Italian *novelle*, and such Jacobean dramas as "The Duke of

Pre-Raphaelites than of Boccaccio) was published in 1862; some other parts, of which "The Chronicle of Queen Fredegond" (drawn from Gregory of Tours) is the longest, have been published posthumously. Another ambitious project was a narrative or dramatic poem (it is not certain which) on the theme of the Albigenses. Conscious of having insufficiently mastered his subject he put it by and never returned to it, though allusions in his volume on Blake show how long his interest in it continued. In February, 1858, he was working on an unnamed poem of unstated length which he characteristically described as —

a dramato-lyrico-phantasmagorico-spasmodic sermon on the grievous sin of flirtation. . . . It is of course meant for a picture of exceptional weakness; inaction of the man, impulsive irresolution of the woman; mutual ignorance of each other and themselves, with an extra dash of sensuous impulse; finally with no ostensible cause, rupture and spiflication.

The loss of this piece is not to be regretted. Some time during the same year he began the first version of "Chastelard." This he afterwards revised several times. How much of the original draft remains in the published text of 1865 it is impossible to say.

During the Easter recess of 1858 he made his first

Milan" and "The Second Maiden's Tragedy", and perhaps Gautier's "La Morte Amoureuse." Both this tale and "The Leper" exhibit a taste for the macabre which Swinburne contracted about this time from Rossetti and from Beddoes' "Death's Jest-Book", a taste which left scarcely a trace upon the work of his maturity.

visit to Paris, accompanying his parents; and there, according to the well-known anecdote, he evinced his hostility to Napoleon III in a bold and practical manner by refusing to raise his hat when, while driving in the Bois, the Swinburnes passed the imperial carriage. In the summer he made the acquaintance of Sir Walter Trevelyan and his charming and accomplished wife, Pauline, Lady Trevelyan, who, until her untimely death a few years later, was one of Swinburne's most valued friends, a mentor who exercised upon him a serene and tactful control.

In the winter of 1858–1859 Swinburne's turbulence increased markedly, rendering the authorities of the university uneasy and giving anxiety to Jowett who, it is said, feared lest Balliol, by expelling the poet, should repeat the mistake of New College in the case of Shelley. He worked intermittently upon dramatic, narrative and lyric poetry; wasted his ingenuity upon burlesque improprieties; and expended his spirit in riot. Meanwhile he was watching with intense interest the progress of events upon the continent. Napoleon's declaration of war upon Austria, followed by the victories of Magenta and Solferino, raised his excitement to a frantic pitch. At the Oxford Union he read a long tirade against Napoleon when the Peace of Villafranca dashed his hopes of immediate Italian independence and unity. Presently, acting upon Jowett's advice, he withdrew from Oxford; and in the summer of 1859 submitted himself to the tutorship of the Reverend William Stubbs (afterwards Bishop of Oxford and distinguished historian) at the little parish of Navestock in Essex. The burning of the first draft of "Rosamond", after Stubbs had protested against the amatory tone of parts of the play, took place during this sojourn. The stay with Stubbs was prolonged, with intermissions, during the following winter (1859–1860) and on the whole was both pleasant and profitable, though without any permanent effect upon the poet's temperament and way of life.

At Navestock he found his true voice.[1] In February, 1860, he read in the *Guardian* the announcement of a prize offered to any member of Oxford University for the best poem in rhymed verse on the subject of "The Life, the Character, and the Death of the heroic seaman Sir John Franklin, with special reference to the time, place and discovery of his death." The theme fired Swinburne's imagina-

[1] We have here to do with a question of date of by no means merely technical and academic interest. In the first edition of his "Life of Swinburne" Sir Edmund Gosse stated that "The Death of Sir John Franklin" was composed in 1858 and submitted in competition for the Newdigate Prize, the subject set being "The Discovery of the North-West Passage." Since neither in subject nor in meter (traditionally the heroic couplet) did Swinburne conform to the requirements, the examiners, according to Sir Edmund, could not be blamed for awarding the prize to another competitor. A controversy ensued during the summer of 1917 between Sir Edmund on the one hand and Mrs. Disney Leith and Mr. F. L. Latham on the other. Latham was the recipient of the Newdigate Prize in 1858. Mrs. Leith, the poet's cousin, had published letters of Swinburne's, tending to prove that "The Death of Sir John Franklin" was written in 1860. Gosse, however, resting his case upon the unreliability of Mrs. Leith's dating of the letters which she published, refused to be convinced; and his statement that Swinburne's poem was written in 1858 for the Newdi-

tion, for it offered an opportunity to develop three *motifs:* high courage in the midst of mortal danger; the greatness of England as exemplified by her heroic sons; and the mysterious grandeur of the northern ocean. He was, moreover, genuinely moved by the fate of the explorer and his gallant company. Choosing as his prosodic form *terza rima* (a meter rarely employed in English verse and even more rarely with success), he wrote "The Death of Sir John Franklin", a poem which is no mere academic exercise, no mere "copy of verses", but an authentic addition to the small body of English patriotic poetry of lasting worth. In it there are, appropriately, lines that echo the Shakespearean cadence and others that, not so appropriately, reveal the disciple of Morris and Rossetti; but in the main the accent is firmly individual, of a restraint and dignity worthy of the theme, yet here and there anticipating the style of the finest of the "Poems and Ballads." Yet it was rejected; and beyond

gate remains unaltered and even unqualified in the latest revision of his biography (volume xix of the Bonchurch Edition of Swinburne's works). Mr. Thomas J. Wise, in the revised edition of his "Bibliography" of Swinburne (Bonchurch, volume xx), brushes aside the claim that the poem is of 1860, not 1858. But Mr. Georges Lafourcade, in the *Literary Supplement* of the *London Times* for February 9, 1928, has proved beyond question that the later date is the correct date and that the poem was written for the special prize announced in the *Guardian,* not for the Newdigate. This special prize went to another competitor whose poem, judging from samples quoted by Mr. Lafourcade, was worthless. The judges in this special competition cannot, then, be relieved of the responsibility for rejecting Swinburne's noble poem, which both in form and theme conformed exactly to the requirements. Moreover, the rejection, coming as it did at the very close of the poet's career at Oxford, was a far more serious affront than it would have been had it happened in 1858, almost at the outset of Swinburne's university life.

doubt its rejection had much to do with his subsequent bitter feelings towards Oxford.

In October, 1860, he did, indeed, again take up his residence at Balliol, but he immediately resumed a career of drinking and license, and in the following November he withdrew permanently to escape the disgrace of being "sent down." In later years he used to return occasionally to visit Jowett, Pater and other friends, and there are records of riotous scenes in which he took part at Oxford about 1868; but though in protest against his treatment by the authorities he kept his name for twenty years on the register of Balliol as an undergraduate, he cherished no love and little respect for the "sweet city with her dreaming spires."

His anxious family took him off to Mentone, but he conceived an intense dislike for the Riviera and for "the tideless dolorous midland sea" and escaped presently into Italy. This first visit to the land to which so much of his love and his genius was later to be dedicated was of short duration and did not, as did the second visit in 1864, greatly enrich his experience. In December, 1860, he was again in England, settled in London chambers on an allowance granted him by his father.

Here he quickly renewed his intimacy with Morris and Burne-Jones, and at the latter's home often read aloud his poems. Rossetti was now drawn to him and while exercising a restraining influence upon Swinburne's exuberance was himself stimulated by the younger poet's learning and enthusiasm, which directed his own imagination and widened his culture. For several years Swinburne was now in contact with Ruskin, whom he met in Pre-Raphaelite circles. There is something piquant in the relationship between the author of "Unto This Last" and the author of "Dolores." "A demoniac youth," was Ruskin's comment. "Whether he will ever be clothed and in his right mind, heaven only knows"; but "he is infinitely above me in all knowledge and power." Swinburne submitted some of his poems to Ruskin and was surprised "by the enjoyment he seemed to derive from my work, and the frankness with which he accepted it", and testified that "it was impossible to have a fairer judge." Ruskin urged that there were redundancies to be pruned, but pleaded for the whole of "Faustine" which made him "all hot, like pies with the Devil's fingers in them." "It's glorious!" he exclaimed.

Another new friend was Richard M. Milnes (afterwards Lord Houghton), a man of taste and culture, influential in society, experienced in the world, and a valuable guide to the poet, who rewarded him with witty, facetious and occasionally improper letters. Milnes' appreciative reception of Swinburne's *facetiæ* encouraged the production of scabrous burlesques. Many of these things have perished but enough remain in manuscript or privately printed form to give an idea of the amount of misdirected energy that the poet devoted to the invention of unprintable jocosities. In 1870 we find Rossetti urging him to have a fair copy made of all his burlesques, including extracts from an imaginary newspaper called the *Bogshire Banner*. What is described as a "rollicking skit", dating from the early sixties, was a drama, now apparently lost, "La Sœur de la Reine", written in French and purporting to picture the early life of Victoria. Another French piece was "La Fille du Policeman", a parody of the vulgar French fiction of the period which dealt ignorantly with English life. George Meredith was delighted with the naughty wit of it. Probably of more moderate but not dissimilar tone was "The Diary of Mrs. Samuel Pepys" which Swinburne used to recite at the Burne-Joneses but which seems never to have been written down. These things were light and frothy enough; but there are more serious implications for the psychologist in "The Flogging Block: An Epic Poem in a Prologue and Twelve Eclogues" which Swinburne began in 1862 and which occupied his attention intermittently for nearly twenty years. It was illustrated with drawings by the brilliant and wayward Jewish artist, Simeon Solomon; the manuscript is, I believe, still in existence. Even more "curious" (in the booksellers' sense of the word) is a large and ornate volume which appeared in private form so late as 1888, more than a decade after Swinburne had taken up his residence with Theodore Watts-Dunton. Whether he was himself responsible for its appearance or whether the manuscript, written much earlier, had come into the hands of an unprincipled printer, I do not know. The reticent entry in Mr. Wise's "Bibliography" gives no further indication of its subject than that afforded by its title: "The Whippingham Papers." In it Swinburne gives free rein to his imagination to dwell upon a subject familiar to students of the psychopathology of sex: flagellation, a theme which inspired "Eton: Another Ode" and other unpublished pieces. Of his interest in the subject there are more than sufficient indications in some of his published work.[1]

These early London years were filled with plans, not all of them mischievous but many ill-directed. He worked from time to time on a novel, "Lesbia Brandon", the inception of which dates back to the last months of his Oxford residence.[2] The early

[1] Connected with these pieces in recklessness of tone are the blasphemous skits with which Swinburne used to amuse his friends, such as the outrageously profane but genuinely funny "Fragment of an Address from Saint Joseph to Saint Mary." A whole section of his correspondence remains unpublished because the letters are steeped in Rabelaisian humor of the broadest sort. Even in published letters a few ribald allusions to the Roman Catholic Church have escaped editorial censorship, and in the letters to Milnes there are numerous and significant allusions to the Marquis de Sade. Among William Hardman's vivid recollections of the early sixties was a dinner party at Rossetti's house when Swinburne shocked and disgusted the other guests by his vociferous praise of the "divine marquis" and his works.

[2] For a full account of the condition in which the text of "Lesbia Brandon" survives see Mr. Wise's "Bibliography." The history of its composition stretches over many years and had best be disposed of at this point. That in its earlier form it was — or at least parts of it were — harmless enough is indi-

sixties also saw the beginning of another novel, "A Year's Letters", which was finished in 1866, though not published till 1877.[1] Critics have praised the "pungent quality" of the social satire in this book, but I find it impossible to be pleased by the wit and humor it is supposed to contain or to take it very seriously. It is written in the form of letters, a compromise, as Swinburne says, between the dramatic and narrative form; but in a manner in which Richardson, Scott and Balzac have not achieved absolute success Swinburne does not evade dulness. A satire on English society and an attack on sentimentalism, it is faintly suggestive of the influence of George Meredith. The hero, a young poet who has been recently "ploughed" at Oxford and who is

cated by the fact that in 1864 Swinburne read aloud some chapters to his cousin Miss Gordon. But later his intentions changed, for in January, 1867, he writes to Sir Richard Burton: "I have in hand a scheme of mixed prose and verse . . . which I flatter myself will be more offensive and objectionable than anything I have yet done." Yet in this same year some chapters were set up in type and in 1868 Swinburne tried to find a publisher for it. Through the good offices of Henry Stoddard and Bayard Taylor the manuscript was submitted to Lippincott and was rejected by that firm. In 1877 it was again sent to the printers and reached the stage of proof sheets; and in 1878 it was submitted to Leslie Stephen for publication in *Cornhill*. Obviously the version which Swinburne allowed Stephen to read could not have been so naughty as that described to Burton. In the opinion of Sir Edmund Gosse and Mr. Wise the work should never be published. Of late, rumors have been current that the ban is to be lifted, but Mr. Wise assures me that these reports are false.

[1] The book appeared serially, under the pseudonym of "Mrs. Horace Manners", in the *Tatler*. Swinburne's characteristic reason for allowing it to appear in this obscure periodical was that he wished to requite the editor, Thomas Purnell, an old friend, for the service done him in introducing him to Karl Blind who introduced him to Mazzini. The novel was reissued with the title "Love's Cross-Currents" in 1905, when Swinburne acknowledged the authorship. For the original hoaxing and ironical introductory letter to "Mrs. Manners" there was then substituted a dedicatory epistle to Watts-Dunton.

devoted to France and to the cause of liberty, especially as expressed in the aspirations of Italy, is in love with a married cousin who, after some hesitation, refuses to leave her dull commonplace husband and elope with him. In his character there are evident autobiographical touches; and there are other Swinburnian elements in the book: the allusions to Hugo, the epithets bestowed upon the Pope, the enthusiasm for children, and the too frequent allusions to the subject of birching. Occasionally one finds passages of genuine wit, but on the whole it is thin and wearisome. For a realistic study of contemporary manners the poet was temperamentally not suited; and the experiment should have warned him against a second attempt which resulted in the flat failure of "The Sisters."

Far more appropriate to his genius are the translations from Villon which he now, probably encouraged by Rossetti, began to make. To 1861 belongs his version of the "Belle Heaulmière"; other ballads were translated from time to time during the next few years; and the group, with two exceptions, was published in 1878 in the second series of "Poems and Ballads."

Even more congenial to him was his work on the "Border Ballads." At Oxford he had begun an anthology of the finest genuine ballads, his aim being to provide an eclectic text with the restoration where necessary of the primitive diction which during the eighteenth century had been crowded out by inappropriate elegancies. There were to be notes explanatory and antiquarian. For this task he was admirably fitted; but the publication of Aytoun's "Ballads of Scotland" (1861) seems to have discouraged him and he put the scheme aside. It led, however, to the composition of his own remarkable series of ballads of the North country. These, though not published till much later,[1] belong to 1861–1863. Rossetti once said that Swinburne knew more about folk ballads than all the specialists; and the story goes that when Morris, many years afterwards, was planning an edition of the authentic ballads at the Kelmscott Press and Swinburne was suggested to him as editor, he said: "It would n't do at all. He would be forever writing in verses of his own that one could not tell from the original!" It is not accurate to judge Swinburne's work in this kind as mere *pastiche*, for the themes are ancient and several of the pieces are founded on original ballads that have survived in corrupt versions. There are, as Maurice Hewlett remarked, Pre-Raphaelite phrases and cadences which prevent an attentive reader from being deceived by them, and sometimes Swinburne's instinct for polish

[1] A few such pieces appeared in "Poems and Ballads, First Series" (1866); a larger group in "Poems and Ballads, Third Series" (1889). Eleven, among them several of the finest, were first published posthumously.

and regularity results in poems easily distinguishable from the genuine thing, the meters being too smooth, the rhymes too exact, the sense too clarified, the whole lacking the ruggedness characteristic of the type. But in other experiments he managed to curb this instinct for regularity and gained a close approximation to the manner of the old ballads, reproducing their sincerity and quaintness, their strength and uncouthness, their harshness mingled with poignant pathos. For the language and lilt of Northumberland were native to him; and the qualities of the folk ballad have added to his natural gifts others that do not often appear in the poetry by which he is more widely known: they have forced him to stand firm in human passion and human tragedy. The pathos of "A Jacobite's Exile" is hardly to be matched in his English verse; there is weird power in "The Witch-Mother"; and "The Tyneside Widow", the best of all these pieces, is not merely a scholar-poet's idea of grief; it is grief and loneliness rendered vocal.

But the posthumous group best illustrates Swinburne's ballad work as scholar and poet. "Lord Soulis" puts into ballad form the folk memories of an actual personage of the fourteenth century. Such an attempt had been made by John Leyden in a version that attracted the attention of Sir Walter Scott. Leyden gives the atrocious warlock but one paramour; Swinburne (with an eye to the effect gained by what the balladists call "incremental repetition") raises the number to three. But the legend of the wizard's death by boiling, after he had by devilish machinations escaped death in other forms, is old. "Lord Scales" reproduces to a puzzling degree the confusion of narrative and dialogue characteristic of the genre. In "The Earl of Mar's Daughter" the sophistications of the decadent form in which the lost original has survived are removed and the archaic simplicity is restored. It can hardly be considered an original work by Swinburne, for it is merely a scholarly and ingenious piece of text-establishment. "The Worm of Spindlestonheugh" supplies the place of a genuine ballad known to have been in existence so recently as the end of the eighteenth century, but since lost. The story (out of Maundeville) is that which Morris took as the subject of "The Lady of the Land" in "The Earthly Paradise." In Morris' version the youth who undertakes to rescue the bewitched damsel flees at the sight of the fearful dragon into which she has been transformed, leaving the charm unremoved; but Swinburne's more chivalrous hero kisses the "laidley mouth" not once but twice, to make sure, and thereby restores the lady to her own lovely shape. "Earl Robert" retells a tale of love and death that exists in Motherwell's "Minstrelsy" and several other versions. The tender and ingenuous "Duriesdyke" and the grim "Westland Well" both deserve mention.

The other pieces are of less interest except to the folk-lorist.

This digression upon the "Border Ballads" has taken us well beyond the point at which it began, and we must return to Swinburne's first years in London. It is possible that the flat failure of his first volume, "The Queen-Mother and Rosamond", published in 1860, was in part responsible for the sheer waste of so much time and talent during the next few years. Discussion of these two plays is postponed to my chapter on the Tragedies, and we have now to note that the year 1862 saw immense gains in the poet's development. Save for a visit to the Pyrenees in the spring, when he had the memorable experience of swimming in the cold dark waters of the Lac de Gaube, he passed most of this year with Rossetti and Meredith in Chelsea. Many anecdotes have been told about this singular *ménage* and it is needless to say more here than that, for all their admiration of one another, the temperaments of these three men of genius clashed and that after a time the arrangement proved unsatisfactory and was cancelled. The causes of Swinburne's later alienation from Rossetti can perhaps be traced back to the ill success of this domestic arrangement, but the two men remained for some years more on terms of cordial intimacy and Swinburne was of great service to Rossetti in 1869–1870 when the latter's poems, recovered from his wife's grave, were in preparation for the press.[1] There was something antipathetic in the natures of Swinburne and Meredith and though there was never any real quarrel the two men soon drifted apart.

Through Rossetti, Swinburne now became acquainted with Fitzgerald's version of the "Rubáiyát", and fired by enthusiasm he began his "Laus Veneris", written in a form adapted from the Omar-stanza. To this same year belongs the one romance of his life, his passion for the daughter of Sir John Simon which, according to Sir Edmund Gosse's narrative as told him by Swinburne, flamed up suddenly, inspired a declaration of love, and was met by the girl with laughter, caused probably by nervousness at her lover's violence rather than by unkindness. In grief and mortification Swinburne went up to Northumberland and there, when his anger had subsided, wrote the greatest of his poems based on personal experience of passion, the magnificent "Triumph of Time." This and "Laus Veneris" were more than sufficient to confirm his intimate friends (for as yet, since the stillborn plays

[1] The "Record of Friendship" which Swinburne started to write after Rossetti's death and which he left unfinished bears the ominous motto "*Nihil nisi verum.*" But it breaks off before any revelation of misunderstanding or disagreement. By 1877 the two poets seem to have completely separated, for we find Swinburne in a letter to Watts-Dunton contrasting to Rossetti's disadvantage his "way of loyalty and friendship" with Jowett's, Nichol's and Watts'. Undoubtedly the severance was largely due to the extreme suspiciousness of Rossetti in his later years which was a symptom of his abnormal mental condition.

of 1860 scarcely count, he had not sought the suffrages of a larger public) in their opinion of his genius. It was probably through the influence of Lord Houghton that he now received from Richard H. Hutton an invitation to contribute to the *Spectator*. Between April and September, 1862, he published seven poems and a number of reviews in that journal. The most significant thing about the appearance of the poems is that "Faustine", one of the pieces that gave greatest offense in 1866, caused no comment in 1862.[1] Of the reviews the longest, published in five installments, was of Hugo's "Les Misérables." The chief interest of this somewhat verbose critique lies in the evidence contained in it that Swinburne's admiration of Hugo had not yet blinded him to defects in the master's work. It contains praise a-plenty, but the critic takes issue with Hugo on his theories of reform and human perfectability; grudges the time spent by a great artist upon philanthropy and social schemes; and declares that the story is "clogged by superfluity of comment and remark."

[1] Four of these poems, all of minor interest, were reprinted without change in 1866. "The Sundew" was expanded from three stanzas to four. The other two present significant variations in the text. In 1862 "A Song in Time of Order" contained eleven stanzas instead of fourteen. I think it more likely that Hutton suppressed the other three than that they were afterwards added by Swinburne, for they contain allusions to the red flag of revolution, to the iniquities of the papacy, to "Buonaparte the bastard", to the scandals of the French political prison at Cayenne, and to Austrian tyranny — dubious topics to offer to Hutton's circle of Tory readers. "Faustine" was printed with the omission of stanza xxxiii which contains an allusion to abnormal eroticism. It seems that Hutton attempted to exercise a political and moral censorship.

He even asserts that "Les Misérables" exhibits "a curious confusion of scientific and artistic possibilities." Later in life Swinburne would never have written as he did here; that is probably the reason why he never reprinted or referred to this review.

In June Swinburne published, in reply to the *Spectator's* hostile review of Meredith's "Modern Love", a letter of importance in that here for the first time he enunciated those principles which were guiding him in the choice of subjects for poetic treatment. Signs of a deplorable tendency to rhetorical inflation of style and arrogant pomposity of manner are obvious in this letter, but it is the substance of a particular passage, not the style of the whole, that concerns us here. The passage is as follows:

There are pulpits enough for all preachers in prose; the business of verse-writing is hardly to express convictions; and if some poetry, not without merit in its kind, has at times dealt in dogmatic morality, it is all the worse and all the weaker for that. As to subject, it is too much to expect that all schools of poetry are to be forever subordinate to the one just now so much in request with us, whose scope of sight is bounded by the nursery walls; that all Muses are to bow down before her who babbles, with lips yet warm from their pristine pap, after the dangling delights of a child's coral; and jingles with flaccid fingers one knows not whether a jester's or a baby's bells.

Even more in the nature of a manifesto is the long review of Baudelaire's "Les Fleurs du Mal", published in September. That Hutton admitted it to his columns may be regarded as a sign of a change and broadening in English taste, but it is unlikely that he was deliberately leading his readers towards a more cosmopolitan point of view, and more probable that his acceptance of the review was due to an oversight or to a temporary suspension of judgment in the presence of Swinburne's genius. A few excerpts from this critique[1] will illustrate the prose style of which he was now a master and the theory of esthetics, derived from the French doctrine of *L'Art pour l'art*, which he had adopted. He declares:

The courage and sense of a man who at such a time ventures to profess and act on the conviction that the art of poetry has absolutely nothing to do with didactic matter at all are proof enough of the wise and serious manner in which he is likely to handle the materials of his art.

And later he goes on:

It may be worth while to say something about the moral and meaning of many among these poems. Certain critics . . . have discovered what they call a paganism on the spiritual side of this author's tone of thought. . . . There is not one poem of the

[1] It is not known when Swinburne first became acquainted with Baudelaire's verse; he seems to have known "Les Fleurs du Mal" first in the expurgated edition of 1861, not in the original prosecuted text of 1857, a copy of which did not come into his hands until 1864.

"Fleurs du Mal" which has not a distinct and vivid background of morality to it. Only this moral side of the book is not thrust forward in the foolish and repulsive manner of a half-taught artist. . . . If any reader could extract from any poem a positive spiritual medicine — if he could swallow a sonnet like a moral prescription — then clearly the poet supplying these intellectual drugs would be a bad artist. . . . But those who will look for them may find moralities in plenty behind every poem of M. Baudelaire's; such poems especially as "Une Martyre". Like the mediaeval preacher, when he has drawn the heathen love, he puts sin on its right hand and death on its left. It is not his or any artist's business to warn against evil; but certainly he does not exhort to it.

These passages adumbrate the esthetic creed which Swinburne was to reaffirm in defence of the "Poems and Ballads" four years later.[1]

The poet's connection with the *Spectator* was broken off as suddenly as it had begun. It would be amusing to recount in detail the characteristic cause of the break; but there is space for but the briefest indication. In one of the poems published in its

[1] It is probable that Swinburne contributed several other reviews to the *Spectator*. Sir Edmund Gosse "deprecates mere conjecture" and though he is "privately certain" that several are by Swinburne he refuses to name them. I do not share his reluctance and am willing to suggest that it is just possible that reviews of Henry Taylor's "St. Clement's Eve", of Christina Rossetti's "Goblin Market", and of Clough's work (two notices) are by him; that the earlier portions of a review of Richard Garnett's "Relics of Shelley" are so much in his manner as to make his authorship almost a certainty; and that beyond doubt he wrote the review of Mrs. Browning's "Last Poems" in the issue of March 29, 1862.

columns and again in the review of "Les Misérables" Swinburne referred to a certain French poet and critic, Félicien Cossu; in the same review he referred also to the "Études anglaises" of Ernest Clouet. Both these *littérateurs* existed only in Swinburne's imagination; and having prepared the way by these off-hand allusions, he sent to Hutton burlesque hoaxing reviews, with lavish excerpts from what purported to be the original French, of volumes by MM. Cossu and Clouet. The citations parody what may be described as the macabre-lascivious-pathological qualities in the poetry of Baudelaire's imitators. Actually (as Gosse has noted) there was no such school in France at that time nor did one appear till some twenty years later. Swinburne's foresight of the development of a school of poets in a foreign country is one of the curiosities of literary history. It was not because he was incapable of sustained seriousness but because he possessed a fund of mischievousness which was malicious rather than malignant that he set these traps for the respectable Mr. Hutton. His impishness was not deterred by any thought of obligation to the editor who had first provided him with a medium through which to reach a large public.

Hutton did not fall into the trap, however, but returned the burlesques to Swinburne and availed himself no longer of his inconvenient contributor's talent. Around the young man who played such malodorous tricks a legend was now growing up. He behaved riotously and boasted more riotously still. He proclaimed at a party that it was his ambition to build seven towers, in each of which in turn, on each several day of every week, it was his intention to enact one of the seven deadly sins. But the plain fact seems to be that his frail physique could not stand debauchery of any prolonged violence, and an amount of alcohol that would scarcely have flushed an ordinary man exalted him, as it exalted Poe, beyond reason. The circulation of his poems in manuscript in privileged coteries and his perfervid recitations to favored groups of people led to rumors of the rise of a new and unholy genius in English poetry. Sir Edmund Gosse has related in his inimitable manner how some febrile people at one such gathering listened in rapt ecstasy to Swinburne's chanting of "Dolores" and at the close of the recital fell on their knees before the poet. One may venture to believe that such manifestations of hysteria did not occur often, but even if this experience was unique it was obviously not the sort of thing to steady him. These days, filled with intellectual excitement, feverish composition, and still more feverish—though intermittent—dissipation, led to attacks of something like epilepsy, undermining Swinburne's health for years. Until the culminating attack in 1879 which nearly cost him his life and which led to his removal by Watts-Dunton to Putney, his creative and critical work was interrupted from time to time by spells of alarming illness which necessitated sojourns with friends or family at a distance from London, where, adapting himself to the normal life of an English gentleman, he invariably recovered his health and spirits with amazing rapidity. I shall not interrupt my narrative by records of these attacks, which have been chronicled in sufficient detail by Sir Edmund Gosse.

More serene and, apparently, less dissipated than 1862, the year 1863 was one of widening experiences and silent growth. In the spring Swinburne was in Paris where he met Manet, Fantin-Latour, and Whistler. The acquaintance with Whistler ripened into a friendship which survived a misunderstanding in 1866 but which was broken off many years later. On a visit to the Louvre he wrote the sonnets "Hermaphroditus" on a theme which attracted him strangely, as it had attracted Gautier. He passed many weeks of the summer at Tintagel in the company of John William Inchbold, the painter, whose influence upon him was altogether excellent. While Inchbold painted the poet swam and rode and began to work upon "Atalanta in Calydon." This summer on the Cornish coast never faded from Swinburne's memory, and when many years later he wrote his exquisite elegy on Inchbold he recorded in words and cadences whose sincerity is unmistakable his affection for the calm and gentle friend with whom he had visited "lone Camelford and Boscastle divine."

Work on "Atalanta" was continued in the autumn at East Dene where he stayed with relatives in the absence of his immediate family on the continent. There he saw much of his cousin Mary Gordon (afterwards Mrs. Disney Leith) and assisted her in the composition of a little romance, "The Children of the Chapel", which was published anonymously in 1864. The discovery of documents relating to Thomas Gyles, master of the Chapel Royal in the time of Elizabeth, suggested the theme to Miss Gordon. In the development of the narrative Swinburne had, I think, some share, and for this reason, as well as because little account has hitherto been taken of the book, it is worth glancing at it for a moment. The tale is of young Arthur Saville who is kidnapped by Gyles and borne off to London. There follows a long narrative of Arthur's life in the choir school; and into this account of Elizabethan education and discipline are introduced several episodes of birching, told with such zest as to betray the hand of Algernon Swinburne rather than of Mary Gordon. Rehearsals of a moral play by the boys are described in much detail; and the whole culminates in a performance of "The Pilgrimage of Pleasure" before the queen. This interlude, which has been reprinted separately but which is unfortunately not included in the Bonchurch Edition of Swinburne's works, was written by the poet. The lively narrative which interrupts the text in its original form imparts to the play a different flavor from that which it has when read apart from the context for which it was written. "The Pilgrimage of Pleasure", one of Swinburne's most interesting experiments in archaic form, is on the grand old theme of the *Pèlerinage de la Vie humaine*. Youth, despite the warnings of Life, Discretion and Sapience, follows Vain Delight, with Gluttony the Vice hanging on their train, in the pursuit of Pleasure. The quest is fruitless and in the end Death summons Youth away. Two motives of the genuine moralities — the conflict of Virtue and Vice for the possession of the Soul, and the Coming of Death — are thus combined. A typical passage, anticipating the mood of many of the "Poems and Ballads", is this:

> We have gone by many lands, and many grievous ways,
> And yet we have not found this Pleasure all these days.
> Sometimes a lightening all about her we have seen,
> A glimmering of her garments among the fieldës green;
> Sometimes the waving of her hair that is right sweet,
> A lifting of her eyelids, or a shining of her feet,
> Or either in sleeping or in waking have we heard
> A rustling of raiment or a whispering of a word,
> Or a noise of pleasant water running over a waste place,
> Yet have I not beheld her, nor known her very face.

At the close the morality, which is in the main merely a Pre-Raphaelite adaptation of an ancient traditional form, rises to genuine power in the somberly magnificent rendering of the theme of the

Trionfo della Morte. The piece cannot rightly be described as *pastiche*, for it would deceive no one familiar with the genuine interludes, but it is a highly accomplished *tour de force*.

In the spring of 1864 Swinburne paid his second visit to Italy. At Milan he saw the Ambrosian Library and the Brera, where he thought the "Sposalizio" of Raphael "moist and sugary" but was moved to enthusiasm by Carlo Crivelli, Gentile da Fabriano, Carpaccio, and Gentile Bellini. The taste for artists of the Quatrocento is noteworthy. At Brescia he was attracted by the calm and silvery-toned Moronis; and presently he crossed the Austrian border on his way to Verona, Padua, Vicenza and Venice. He then came to Florence where, with excursions to Pisa, Siena and San Gimignano, he remained for several months. At Siena he saw (and recollected vividly when he came to write his magnificent poem on that city) the house of Saint Catherine, Il Sodoma's grand pictures of Saint Catherine receiving the Stigmata and of Christ at the Column, and the Hellenistic group of the Three Graces which now stands inappropriately in the cathedral library. But "sweet San Gimignano" received then and afterwards the tribute of his warmest love. The "little laurelled town of towers" is an almost unspoiled relic of the Middle Ages; but this fact did not touch Swinburne's imagination so forcibly as the fact

From a photograph by Alinari

SAN GIMIGNANO

Thou too, O little laurelled town of towers,
Clothed with the flame of flowers.
A SONG OF ITALY

that it contained the "hall which saw Dante speaking" when he came to San Gimignano to plead for help for Florence. How often in later years did the poet recall to mind the tiny town, raising its many towers into the intensely blue Tuscan air! There is pathos in the fact that when in 1886, long immured with Watts-Dutton at Putney, he began an elegy in memory of Canonico Luigi Pecori, whom he had met when "the spring in heaven was golden" above the towers of San Gimignano, he broke off after writing but eight lines.

In Florence he enjoyed the company of Mrs. Gaskell with whom he visited the galleries, and of Seymour Kirkup who had known Blake and had been present at the funeral of Keats. Conversations with Kirkup influenced Swinburne to expand into an independent critical essay the review of Gilchrist's "Pictor Ignotus" upon which he was now engaged. In the Uffizi he obtained access to the collections of uncatalogued and unarranged drawings by various old masters. Of these he made a close study, assembling elaborate notes which formed the basis of his most remarkable effort in the field of art criticism, the "Notes on Designs of the Old Masters at Florence."

But the great event of this sojourn was the meeting with Landor. The story has been often told of how "the youngest singer that England bore" came with thoughts that half lingered in the past and half ran before into the future to pay homage to "the oldest singer." We need not retrace the familiar ground except to say that a first visit was woefully unsuccessful, for Swinburne had neglected to submit the letter of introduction provided by Lord Houghton and Landor was bewildered and irritated by his inexplicable young visitor. A second visit was, however, more formal and more successful. Landor graciously approved of Swinburne's purpose to dedicate "Atalanta in Calydon" to him, and with Olympian condescension laid his "most sacred hand" upon the poet's hair. Swinburne for his part was ready "to throw up all other things on earth and devote [himself] to playing valet to him for the rest of his days." But on his return to his hotel he received from the aged poet a letter informing him that he was too much exhausted ever to have the pleasure of seeing him again. It argues a lack of the sense of humor that forever after Swinburne was proud to exhibit this letter.

Shortly after his return to England in the autumn of 1864 he heard of Landor's death, and sang his threnody magnificently in Greek and English. He was himself now upon the threshold of fame.

CHAPTER TWO

Beauty and Revolt

The first tentative efforts of the new school of poets — Morris' "Defence of Guenevere", Swinburne's "Queen-Mother and Rosamond", and Dante Rossetti's "Early Italian Poets" — failed to win any wide public recognition; but the modest success won by Christina Rossetti's "Goblin Market" made smooth the path for Atalanta's swift feet. On Swinburne's return from Italy his father, prompted by the desire to draw his son out from the deleterious atmosphere of coterie admiration, offered to pay the costs of producing any book the poet chose to publish, whether his Greek tragedy or a volume of miscellaneous poems or his prose work on Blake. The publisher who was willing to issue "Atalanta", Bertram Payne of Moxon and Company, does not seem to have called upon Admiral Swinburne for financial assistance, but so sceptical was he as to the success of the play that he printed a very small edition and fortunately insisted upon distinguished beauty of appearance as the best means of attracting attention. As publisher of the enormously successful "Enoch Arden" in the previous year Payne was doubtless blind to the evidence in "advanced" circles of restiveness under the long domination of Tennyson. Moreover he had not reckoned upon the support of Swinburne's influential friends, such as Lord Houghton, who were determined that the failure of 1860 should not be repeated. These friends spread the report of the new poem's supreme beauty and prepared the way for the welcome which greeted the slim, tall, cream-colored, gold-ornamented volume that appeared towards the end of April, 1865. "Atalanta" did not sell widely, but critics were practically unanimous in praise. "He has more of the right thing than Browning and Co.," wrote Fitzgerald, "but a fiery, unquiet spirit." To Swinburne Burne-Jones wrote: "The thought in it is momentous, and the rhythm goes on with such a rush that it's enough to carry the world away." Tennyson congratulated the poet magnanimously: "It is many a long day since I have read anything so fine; for it is not only carefully written, but it has both strength and splendour, and shows that you have a fine metrical invention which I envy you."

What led Swinburne to the legend of Atalanta? Neither his extant letters nor reports of his conversation supply an answer to the question. Mr. Nicolson has suggested that an allusion to Atalanta in "As You Like It" may have prompted him to turn to a classical dictionary which in turn would have directed him to Ovid. There is better foundation for Mr. Henderson's surmise that two allusions to the myth in Landor's writings may have sown the seeds of the tragedy in Swinburne's mind. But speculation need not take us this far afield. He must have known the versions of the story in Homer and Ovid. The tale of the Calydonian boar, the curse of Artemis, as told in the ninth book of the "Iliad", contains no mention of Atalanta; Meleagros is already married to Kleopatra. In the eighth book of the "Metamorphoses" the theme is elaborated and clarified. Guided by Jowett or by his own industry Swinburne could easily have found other versions of the tale and allusions to it in Apollodorus, Hyginus, Suetonius and elsewhere. Since we know that in "Erechtheus" he later made use of a fragment of Euripides, there is no reason to suppose that he did not know the Euripidean fragment on Meleager. But though in tone and style his tragedy is far removed from the courtliness and superficiality of Ovid, he follows in main outline the Ovidian narrative, omitting of course the final transformation into birds (which, essential to Ovid's plan, would have been absurd in a tragedy) and by introducing Althæa at the opening, whereas Ovid brings her into the narrative only after the slaying of the brothers, emphasizing her position at the center of the tragedy, the instrument and victim of the gods.

Under the hypnotic spell of the swift bright choruses and surging blank verse some readers have confessed their inability to follow the course of the story; the late Edward Thomas went so far as to surmise that to most people the story is revealed only by the poet's prefatory argument in archaic prose. It is impossible to refute a statement of individual experience; but there are other readers to testify that the cloudy luminosity of the diction never obscures the remorseless progress of the tragedy. From the opening invocation to Artemis by the master-huntsman who looks out over the wide, dawn-illumined Calydonian plain, and the colloquy of Althæa with her maidens, through the assembling of the huntsmen, the warning of the Queen to Meleager against the perils of love, the coming of Atalanta, and the rude words addressed to her by Toxeus and Plexippus, the tragedy is charged with bodeful anticipations. With the departure of the huntsmen in pursuit of the boar a second "movement" commences, in which the chief episodes are the report of the herald of the slaying of the boar; the second herald's announcement of the dire consequences of the quarrel over the spoils; the rage and vengeance of Althæa for the death of her brothers; the slow entrance of the woeful company bearing the dying Meleager; and the matchless and most moving final scene of the hero's death amid the wailing of the chorus. Mr. Nicolson, whose chapter on "Atalanta" is the most satisfying part of his study of Swinburne, has summarized in technical fashion the plan of the drama, accompanying his analysis with a detailed account of the action with many quotations from the text. It is needless to do again what he has so admirably accomplished; but it must be urged that though it exhibits a confident awareness of Greek technique "Atalanta" does not conform so closely to the model as does "Erechtheus."[1] More fundamental is the divergence in tone from Hellenic tragedy. "Atalanta" is a work such as could have been written only in an age of romanticism. The exuberance of its form and the angry fatalism of its contents are alike un-Greek.

This fact, which has been advanced as an objection to the play, is in reality one of its chief merits. Swinburne was not content to compose a mere imitation, mere *pastiche* like Arnold's "Merope." Into the old wineskins of Greek form he poured the new wine of modern thought. The Hellenism does but lend an exotic flavor to the poem and a sense of detachment from the issues of the mid-nineteenth century. The wrath and woes of the Calydonians, their sense of the futility and helplessness yet of the essential nobility of man in the presence of a blind or malignant fate, reverberate through the long centuries that separate us from legendary Greece, and the voice of age-long

[1] In one place no less than six actors with speaking parts are admitted upon the stage at one time. The choruses are often on grandiose generalized themes and do not fulfill the requirement, as do the choruses in "Erechtheus", that they be connected in some way with outlying portions of the myth. In this latter respect, as in tone, "Atalanta" is nearer to Euripidean tragedy than to Sophoclean.

experience is heard by modern ears. In this respect the effect produced by the tragedy is not unlike that produced by Fitzgerald's "Rubáiyát", a poem with which, in fact, the drama has more than a little in common. In the mouths of his virginal chorus the poet puts words of terrific denunciation of God:

Who turns the large limbs to a little flame
And binds the great sea with a little sand;
Who makes desire, and slays desire with shame;
Who shakes the heaven as ashes in his hand;
Who, seeing the light and shadow for the same,
Bids day waste night as fire devours a brand,
Smites without sword, and scourges without rod;
The supreme evil, God. . . .
Lo, with hearts rent and knees made tremulous,
Lo, with ephemeral lips and casual breath,
At least we witness of thee ere we die
That these things are not otherwise, but thus;
That each man in his heart sigheth, and saith,
That all men, even as I,
All we are against thee, against thee, O God most high.

No Greek, not even Euripides, would have dared this extremity of defiance; and even were this not so, it is obvious that the arraignment of the divinity is no mere literary archaism but a direct challenge to the religious ideals of Victorian England. It is important to observe the agreement of this celebrated passage with the sentiments of other poets of the period. The original draft of Fitzgerald's poem contained a stanza which he deleted before publication:

Nay, but, for terror of his wrathful Face,
I swear I will not call Injustice Grace;
Not one Good Fellow of the Tavern but
Would kick so poor a Coward from the place.

A few years later James Thomson put into the mouth of the "demonist" in "The City of Dreadful Night" these terrible words:

Who is most wretched in this dolorous place?
I think myself; yet I would rather be
My miserable self than He, than He
Who formed such creatures to His own disgrace.

The vilest thing must be less vile than Thou
From whom it had its being, God and Lord!
Creator of all woe and sin! abhorred,
Malignant and implacable! I vow

That not for all Thy power furled and unfurled,
Not for the temples to Thy glory built,
Would I assume the ignominious guilt
Of having made such men in such a world.

In "Atalanta" wrath and woe and death are the offspring of love. Atalanta, "the blast of the envy of God", is the devotee of the goddess who has sent the curse upon Calydon. The hint that Meleager's fate crashes down upon him because he dares love a virgin dedicated to Artemis strengthens the sense of the irrational arbitrariness of the divine decree against pitiable men. Althæa warns her son:

Abstain thy feet from following, and thine hands
From amorous touch; nor set towards her thine heart,
Son, lest hate bear no deadlier fruit than love.

The ensuing chorus begins as a hymn of praise: "We have seen thee, O Love, thou art fair"; but modulates quickly into reproach and denunciation:

For bitter thou wast from thy birth,
Aphrodite, a mother of strife;
Before thee some rest was on earth,
A little respite from tears,
A little pleasure of life. . . .
What hadst thou to do among these,
Thou, clothed with a burning fire,
Thou, girt with sorrow of heart, . . .
For division of soul and disease,
For a dart and a sting and a thorn?
What ailed thee then to be born?

This philosophy of despair was first enunciated in the celebrated second chorus of the tragedy ("Before the beginning of years"); it recurs again and again. But the solemn vague abstractions in which it was couched veiled the import of the words. The opening chorus in celebration of the returning spring seemed to echo in later scenes long after the mood which inspired it had changed, and thus threw a warm glow of loveliness over the chill despair of the thought. The shimmering beauty of the music, the sun-drenched landscape through which the fair strong figures of the drama moved, and the sense of remoteness from modernity — all combined to obscure from many contemporaries the implications of "Atalanta." Between his readers and himself Swinburne had established an entire sympathy which no uneasiness as to the "philosophy" of the tragedy could overthrow. Often in short poems but never again throughout the course of a poem of ambitious length was he to effect this complete intellectual and emotional accord between poet and poem, poem and reader.

Later in 1865 Swinburne published "Chastelard." This first part of his trilogy on Mary Stuart will be discussed in my chapter on the Tragedies, but here it behooves us to note that the direct and outspoken passion of the piece initiated those "low growlings of British prudery" against which Meredith presently cautioned Swinburne. The fact is that Swinburne could not but shock the admirers of Tennyson and Patmore and encourage those who hoped to see the range of modern poetry escape from the restrictions imposed upon it by the most popular poets. The portrayal in "Chastelard" of a code and manner of love altogether different from that presented in "Dora" and "The Angel in the House" was a breath of perfumed air in the musty corridors and prim drawing-rooms of the period. No part of Swinburne's verse has lasted less securely or "dates" more definitely than the poems of passion which we now recognize as belated manifestations of adolescent lustfulness. But they showed themselves differently to his contemporaries. They were a wind of liberation, destroying and invigorating. Patmore's "married lover" who must woo his lady all his life because, as he says:

though free of the outer court
I am, this Temple keeps its shrine
Sacred to Heaven; because in short,
She's not and never can be mine;

and Tennyson's Guinevere who sees in the "blameless king" "the highest and most human too", dwell in another world from the brave, passionate, preposterous French poet who knows Queen Mary's

ways of loving, all of them:
A sweet soft way the first is; afterwards
It burns and bites like fire; the end of that
Charred dust, and eyelids bitten through with smoke.

To argue the historical accuracy of this conception of the courtier of Medicean France, the companion of Brantôme, would have been useless. Tennyson supplied and confirmed the popular demand for domestic love. Over against Swinburne's portrait of Mary Stuart — "No maid . . . but one to live and die for" — rose up the queens of romance fashioned by the Laureate into Victorian gentlewomen. So much had to be said at once of "Chastelard", for the hue and cry against Swinburne which was raised on the publication of "Poems and Ballads" found voice, though as yet but a murmur, in the preceding year.

Not without some trepidation Swinburne's friends now encouraged him to assemble and publish the best parts of the large mass of lyric verse which he had written during the past eight years. In making arrangements with a publisher the poet availed himself of the advice and assistance of Charles Augustus Howell, who now became not only his man of business but also the partner of his amusements and the recipient of his confidences.[1] The poems were submitted to John Murray who declined to publish them, and then to Bertram Payne (Moxon and Company) who agreed to issue the volume. Some years earlier the firm of Moxon had been prosecuted and fined for republishing Shelley's

[1]Howell was the son of a Lisbon schoolmaster. In Oporto he had been convicted of card-sharping and was forced to seek his fortunes elsewhere. After many adventures he came to London and by steps that need not be traced here moved into the inner circles of literary society. In the eighteen-sixties he was on intimate terms with Ruskin, Rossetti, Whistler and other prominent people. His charm and address fascinated them, and his experiences lost nothing in his telling of them. F. M. Brown called him "the Munchausen of the Pre-Raphaelite circle." He conducted negotiations with clients for the purchase of Rossetti's pictures, and on the side a smart little business in faked Old Masters. He robbed and swindled Rossetti and Whistler. He sponged on most of his acquaintance. When asked why he kept Howell so long in his employ, Ruskin replied, "I can't give him a character and I can't let him and his family starve." It is not apparent that he involved Swinburne in any direct pecuniary losses but he got the poet's finances into a great muddle (as he did those of Rossetti), and it was from him that Watts-Dunton rescued both poets when he took over the management of their affairs. His personal influence on Swinburne was deplorable, but for a while so strong that it has seemed necessary to give this much information about him. It may be added (so that we shall not need to refer to him again) that the burlesque and indecent letters which Swinburne wrote to Howell came about 1885–1886 into the possession of one George Redway, an obscure publisher, who under threat of publishing them extorted from Swinburne the copyright of one of his poems. The affair alarmed and distressed the poet greatly. Howell in later years harmed Swinburne's reputation by malicious or at any rate ill-considered gossip. He died in sordid circumstances in 1890. He appears as De Castro in Watts-Dunton's romance, "Aylwin."

"Queen Mab"; the recollection of that unpleasant experience probably had something to do with Payne's timidity when the storm of adverse criticism broke around "Poems and Ballads."

In May, 1866, while Swinburne was busy with his proofs, the annual dinner of the Royal Literary Fund took place. Lord Houghton and other friends persuaded Swinburne to reply to the toast, "The Historical and Imaginative Literature of England." Their object was obviously to make the new genius known to a wider circle of influential people. Sir Edmund Gosse has described this occasion entertainingly and has quoted the chairman's speech introducing Swinburne as testimony to the interest not unmingled with alarm with which the young poet was watched by his elder contemporaries. But he has not quoted Charles Kingsley's sly remarks on Swinburne nor the most significant passages in Swinburne's address. Kingsley, after paying his compliments to the female writers of the day and enlarging on the significance of the entrance of women into the profession of literature, continued:

It is both creditable to the ladies and creditable to literature that the change has taken place. As long as literature was the coarse, fierce, and often vain thing that it was two hundred or one hundred years ago, ladies dared not deal with it. . . . Till Mr. Swinburne arose . . . I was ready to say, Who will write for us such poetry as that of Miss

Rossetti, that of Miss Jean Ingelow, or that of that exquisite spirit, lost to earth but not to heaven, Miss Adelaide Procter?

The picture of Swinburne as the successor of Adelaide Procter and Jean Ingelow is amusing; was Kingsley disingenuous or had Swinburne's reputation not reached him?

In his speech Swinburne voiced his admiration of Hugo and Baudelaire; but what gives it significance is that he seized the opportunity to enunciate the artistic creed which England then needed to learn, the creed of literary cosmopolitanism.

Take the last few years only, and you will see the son of the greatest French poet attempt and accomplish the best translation possible of the greatest English poet; you will see the father of that son dedicate to the memory of Shakespeare, inscribe to the people of England, such a book as no Englishman could have written since the death of Shakespeare himself. . . . He who has best praised Shakespeare is hitherto the sole successor of Shakespeare — Victor Hugo. This is one point of contact, and one worth notice; another is this: that M. Charles Baudelaire, one of the most exquisite, most delicate, most perfect poets of the century — perfect in sound, in colour, in taste of metre, and in tone of emotion — has devoted half his time to the translation of English writers among the French — not without fruit and not without cost. In England I will take but one instance; French influence is no less visible than Grecian in one of the most admirable among poets, one of the most brilliant and subtle among essayists now alive; whose claim to either crown is not less recognized in France than in England. For the higher literature of either country I can imagine no fairer augury than such omens as these afford.

It does not need this concluding tribute to Arnold to show how much he and Swinburne had in common. In French literature they culled flowers from very different fields, but they worked together for a broader and more cosmopolitan culture, breaking down the parochial barriers of English taste.[1]

It had been Swinburne's intention to publish his book about the middle of May, but errors and delays on the part of the printer held it up and it did not appear till the end of July. The date is not insignificant, for the journalists were entering upon what they called the "silly season" and were, as usual, in need of a sensation. In "the brabble and the roar" which instantly arose the *Saturday Review* took the lead with a trenchant and bitter article (August 4, 1866). This diatribe, qualified by recognition of the "forceful and vigorous imagination" displayed in some pieces, is directed against the poet's lasciviousness and perversity and against his nihilistic philosophy.

[1] This banquet was the only occasion on which Swinburne ever spoke in public. He did not publish this address, but portions of it, taken either from stenographic notes or more probably from his manuscript, were printed in the "Report of the Seventy-seventh Anniversary Dinner of the Royal Literary Fund" (1866).

The bottomless pit encompasses us on one side, and stews and bagnios on the other. He is either the vindictive and scornful apostle of a crushing and iron-shod despair, or else he is the libidinous laureate of a pack of satyrs.

Sir Edmund Gosse has lately revealed the fact that this article was by John Morley, who was then winning his way to the forefront of English journalists. Setting aside the uncharacteristic insobriety of tone which Morley permitted himself to employ, the modern reader is likely to find himself in sympathy with many of the strictures passed upon the "Poems and Ballads", for it is in a measure true that Swinburne "riots in the profusion of color of the most garish and heated kind" and that he is "like a composer who should fill his orchestra with trumpets." To say that throughout the book "we are in the midst of fire and serpents, wine and ashes, blood and foam, and a hundred lurid horrors" was, however, to rival Swinburne's own brassy orchestration.

Morley's article started the pack of reviewers in full cry. The press was practically unanimous in condemnation, some critics uttering warnings against this danger to public morals, others declaring that flippant uncleanliness could do no hurt. Nearly half a century later Thomas Hardy, in his beautiful elegy on Swinburne, thus described the sensation produced by "Poems and Ballads":

It was as though a garland of red roses
Had fallen about the hood of some smug nun
When irresponsibly dropped as from the sun,
In fulth of numbers freaked with musical closes,
Upon Victoria's formal middle time
His leaves of rhythm and rhyme.

The storm did not soon die down;[1] but while older people were denouncing publicly the book they were reading secretly, the younger generation received it with enthusiasm. Especially at the two universities were there eager neophytes. Professor Saintsbury has told of the band of students, of whom he was one, who marched in lock step around the courts and cloisters of Oxford, chanting "Dolores." No undergraduate of to-day would chant that poem; "that time is past with all its dizzy raptures." But properly to understand Swinburne's prestige and influence from 1866 till about 1880 we must call into service that same historic sense which is necessary if we would understand the power of "Byronism" a generation earlier. In Swinburne's case we must forget not only the later movements, esthetic and "decadent", which staled his by no means infinite variety but also the long slow decline after his own flaming zenith; and we must put ourselves in the place of his young contemporaries to whom his name was, as Mr. Nicolson

[1] In November *Punch*, which faithfully reflected public sentiment, printed this facetious proclamation: "Having read Mr. Swinburne's defence of his prurient poetics, *Punch* hereby gives him his royal license to change his name to what is evidently its true form — SWINEBORN." At a much later date we shall find F. J. Furnivall referring to Swinburne with gross vulgarity as "Pigsbrook."

says, "a flaming symbol of emancipation, the very wine of freedom, the zest of heresy, the whole music of passion."

At a rumor that the *Times* was preparing to discharge a thunderbolt against the book, Bertram Payne took fright and withdrew it from circulation. Swinburne was determined not to yield to public clamor, but where was he to find a new publisher? The old respectable houses would certainly have nothing to do with his poems. At this juncture the man who had the courage to offer himself as a publisher was John Camden Hotten. The poet's connection with this energetic person of by no means savory reputation[1] undoubtedly enhanced his own disrepute. Acting on the advice of Lord Lytton, with whom he was

[1] Hotten, according to H. S. Ashbee, was "almost the only respectable English publisher of tabooed literature and in this he took great delight. His private library of erotic literature was extensive." Under the innocuous general title of "A Library Illustrative of Social Progress" he published such things as "The History of the Rod" and "The Rodiad." He re-issued Payne Knight's "Worship of Priapus" and may have been the publisher who in this same year 1866 reprinted surreptitiously the notorious pseudo-Byronic "Don Leon" about which I have given some information in my "Byron in England." — To have done at once with the matter of Swinburne's relations with Hotten: this publisher cheated the poet by reprinting "Poems and Ballads" without informing him, so as not to have to pay royalties on the new copies. He also mulcted him of royalties on other books. Affairs gradually became more and more entangled and about 1868 Swinburne looked about for another publisher. He arranged with F. S. Ellis to issue "Songs before Sunrise", and its appearance was long delayed by Hotten's claim that he had a verbal agreement with Swinburne to publish all his books. A little later Watts-Dunton suggested that Swinburne turn to Chapman and Hall, but that idea came to nothing, for Hotten died in 1873, his business was taken over by Chatto and Windus, and under the new management all irregularities ceased. For further details see Mr. Wise's "Bibliography."

now staying, Swinburne arranged to have not only the sheets of "Poems and Ballads" but the unsold copies of his other books, including the unpublished "Blake", transferred from Moxon to Hotten. Payne desired to retain the other works but Swinburne insisted upon a complete transfer, which was promptly effected.[1] The Hotten reissue of "Poems and Ballads" appeared at once.

The first sign of a reaction in the poet's favor, with a disposition to consider dispassionately the

[1] From Lord Lytton's residence Swinburne wrote the following letter (undated but of about the end of August), now first published from the original in my possession, which sheds light upon these transactions. —

Knebworth,
Stevenage,
Herts.

Sir

Before leaving London I asked my friend Mr. Howell to let you know that I accepted your offer of £200 for 1000 copies of my Poems, made through Mr. Knight.

My agreement with Moxon is cancelled by his own act. Having undertaken to sell the edition in hand, he now of his own act has withdrawn it & intends to sell the copies as waste paper. This in your interest as in mine must not be allowed. They must either be bought directly by you, or as waste paper by me acting thru' a third party. This is the advice of my friend Lord Lytton with whom I have talked over this whole affair. It should be done at once that there may be no delay in the reappearance of the book. Moxon has no further claim than on these copies, & of the profit on these his nonfulfilment of contract has robbed me. It is the same with the copies of Atalanta & The Queen Mother he has on hand, and with the proofs of my forthcoming prose work. These I am free to call in & resell, having received nothing for them & desiring no further dealings with Moxon. He has paid for 1000 copies only of Chastelard. I am willing to treat with you separately for these, & shd. of course be glad to see all my books issued by the same publisher. You will let me know your offers for these (at the rate of 1000 copies of each, not deducting whatever you may to Moxon for his copies) & I will at once let you hear from me in answer as soon as I have consulted the eminent men of letters, by whose advice I have hitherto been guided.

Yours truly,

A. C. Swinburne.

Knebworth
Stevenage
Herts

Sir

Before leaving London I asked my friend Mr. Howell to let you know that I accepted your offer of £200 for 1000 copies of my Poems, made through Mr. Knight.

My agreement with Moxon is cancelled by his own act. Having undertaken to sell the edition in hand, he now of his own act has withdrawn it

LETTER FROM SWINBURNE TO J. C. HOTTEN:
FIRST PAGE

2

once let you hear from me in answer, as soon as I have consulted the eminent man of letters by whose advice I have hitherto been guided.

Yrs truly

A C Swinburne

LETTER FROM SWINBURNE TO J. C. HOTTEN: LAST PAGE

vexed question of the morality of the poems, was an article in the *Examiner*, September 22, 1866, (probably by Henry Morley) in which it was contended that in his treatment of lascivious subjects the poet subordinated the "animalism" of the theme to an emphasis upon the nemesis which pursues those who submit themselves to lust. A defence along these lines must meet the objection that the poet indisputably did intend (like Baudelaire) deliberately to shock and scandalize; but it is equally indisputable that in such poems as "Laus Veneris" and "Dolores" (as in many of "Les Fleurs du Mal") there is discoverable, implicit if not explicit, Dante's lesson:

Intesi, ch' a così fatto tormento
eran dannati i peccator carnali,
che la ragion sommettono al talento.

Hotten now published by way of self-exculpation a little brochure by William Michael Rossetti, moderate in tone and not without value for forming a correct estimate of the meaning and worth of the poems.[1] It was followed by Swinburne's own defence, "Notes on Poems and Reviews", undertaken, as he says, for his publisher's sake, not his

[1] Desiring to know whether Swinburne had solicited aid from this quarter, I wrote to Mr. Rossetti shortly before his death for information regarding the circumstances in which his "Poems and Ballads: A Criticism" appeared; and he replied: "When I spontaneously undertook to write that Criticism I informed Swinburne, who cordially approved; but he did not hear or see any of what I wrote until he read it in the published form. He was much gratified, though there were two or three things he did not relish. Both before and after the date of the Criticism he and I were firm and affectionate friends up to the last."

own, and forming a manifesto in which the Victorian conception of the function of poetry is definitely repudiated. The tone is unpleasantly arrogant and shrilly defiant, but the interpretation of various poems is interesting and the passages dealing with general principles are of lasting importance. Three passages must be quoted:

It would seem indeed as though to publish a book were equivalent to thrusting it with violence into the hands of every mother and nurse in the kingdom as fit and necessary food for female infancy. Happily there is no fear that the supply of milk for babes will fall short of the demand for some time yet. There are moral milkmen enough, in all conscience, crying their wares about the streets and byways. . . . We, meanwhile, who profess to deal neither in poison nor in pap, may not unwillingly stand aside. Let those read who will, and let those who will abstain from reading. *Caveat emptor.* No one wishes to force men's food down the throats of babes and sucklings. . . .

Literature, to be worthy of men, must be large, liberal, sincere; and cannot be chaste if it be prudish. Purity and prudery cannot keep house together. Where free speech and fair play are interdicted, foul hints and evil suggestions are hatched into fetid life. And if literature indeed is not to deal with the full life of man and the whole nature of things, let it be cast aside with the rods and rattles of childhood. Whether it affect to teach or to amuse, it is equally trivial and contemptible to us; only less so than the charge of immorality. . . . It is good to be praised by those whom all men should praise;

it is better to be reviled by those whom all men should scorn. . . .

When England has again such a school of poetry, so headed and so followed, as she has had at least twice before, or as France has now; when all higher forms of the various art are included within the larger limits of a stronger race; then, if such a day should ever rise or return upon us, it will be once more remembered that the office of adult art is not that of the cloister or the harem; that all things are good in its sight, out of which good work may be produced. Then the press will be as impotent as the pulpit to dictate the laws and remove the landmarks of art; and those will be laughed at who demand from one thing the qualities of another — who seek for sermons in sonnets and morality in music. . . . No one will then need to assert, in defence of work done for the work's sake, the simple laws of his art which no one will then be permitted to impugn.

Turning now to the celebrated volume which caused all this commotion, we have first to determine what share actual experiences had in the making of these poems. Rumor had it that the poet practised sins of unimaginable voluptuousness, and the learned were wont to couple with his name such "daughters of dreams and of stories" as Semiramis, Pasiphaë, Phædra and Mirrha. But unprejudiced *quellenstudien* have confirmed the suspicion of less ingenuous people, like William Morris, that the "inspiration" of "Poems and Ballads" was almost wholly literary and derivative. From books

Swinburne derived a response as sharp and bracing as other poets have won from immediate contact with life. Very few of the poems are based upon personal experience in the usual sense of the term, and those few were, with one possible exception, inspired by the unsuccessful love affair of 1862. Of these the greatest is "The Triumph of Time." It is significant, since Swinburne arranged the order of his poems with great care, that that magnificent lyric of passion is immediately followed by two others which were undoubtedly suggested by the same experience. "Les Noyades" tells how

> When France was glorious and blood-red, fair
> With dust of battle and death of kings,

Carrier came down to Touraine and slew many Royalists, men and women, by hurling them in pairs, bound together, into the Loire. A rough workman had for long loved a noble lady hopelessly. Now, "naked and wed", they were to die together; and the man rejoiced. The poet turns sharply to a personal application:

> O sweet one love, O my life's delight,
> Dear, though the days have divided us,
> Lost beyond hope, taken far out of sight,
> Not twice in the world shall the gods do thus.

The very cadences are transmuted into those of "The Triumph of Time" and we recall that in that poem there is told the tale of how Rudel died with the kisses of his lady on his lips; and there, too, the personal application is made:

Brother, the gods were good to you. . . .
Rest, and be glad of the gods; but I,
How shall I praise them, or how take rest?

The third poem in this group is "A Leave-Taking" in which, as in "The Triumph of Time", the poet turns to the sea for healing and consolation:

Let us rise up and part; she will not know;
Let us go seaward as the great winds go.

Here the mood is mournful, contemplative, elegiac; in the greater poem it rises to heights of lyric ecstasy; but undoubtedly the occasion of each is the same. Nearly forty years later, in the Dedicatory Epistle to his Collected Works (1904),[1] Swinburne remarked that in "Poems and Ballads" "there are photographs from life and there are sketches from imagination." These three poems are indisputably the authentic "photographs from life."

It is likely that there is a faint glimmering of autobiography in "Dolores." The tawdrily picturesque actress, Adah Isaacs Menken, who is the only woman to whom Swinburne is known to have referred as his mistress, often called herself "Dolores", and in a copy of her little volume of poems, "Infelicia", Swinburne wrote the line from his

[1] This Dedicatory Epistle to Theodore Watts-Dunton is unaccountably and most unfortunately omitted from the Bonchurch Edition of the Collected Works. It is of first importance as the poet's own formal survey and estimate of his life-work in poetry and drama, and I shall have occasion to allude to it several times in the course of this book.

poem: "Lo, this is she that was the world's delight." It is possible that she may have inspired the poem which Swinburne described as a reverie upon "the transmigrations of a single soul . . . clad always in the same type of fleshly beauty."[1]

No success has attended the efforts of the critics who have attempted a formal classification of the various poems: Classical, Medieval, Pre-Raphaelite, and so forth; for there is much overlapping between these categories. Poems written under Pre-Raphaelite influence include most of the earliest pieces in the collection and are on the whole nearly negligible. A special aspect of that influence is, however, seen in the poems inspired by works of art, such as "Hermaphroditus", "A Cameo", "Before the Mirror" (in honor of Whistler's "The

[1] She was married five times, her second husband being Isaac Menken whose religion she embraced. In early life she was a ballet dancer, actress, entertainer, sculptor and contributor of verses to newspapers, all in the United States. She had little success in any line of endeavor save matrimony till she created the once famous rôle of Mazeppa in the spectacle of that name at Astley's Theatre, London, in 1864. Bound to a horse she galloped around the stage, her good figure having more to do with her success than any histrionic talent. In 1867 she was again in London and on friendly terms with various literary celebrities, including Dickens and Rossetti. On a wager with the latter it is said that she went to Swinburne's lodgings and announced that she had come to pass the night with him. The story goes that in the morning she began to talk about poetry, and Swinburne said, "Darling, a woman who has such beautiful legs need not discuss poetry." The poet allowed himself to be photographed with her. In this picture he looks pathetically diminutive and innocuous, but it came into the hands of relatives who were not intended to see it and, as Swinburne recorded, "kicked up a great row." The old rumor that Swinburne helped to compose the poems in "Infelicia" is baseless; but for her he wrote the French lines entitled "Dolorida" whose authorship he afterwards repudiated. She died in Paris in August, 1868. Swinburne's only elegy was the comment: "The death of my poor, dear Menken . . . was a great shock to me and a real grief. She was most lovable as a friend as well as a mistress."

From the painting in the National Gallery

WHISTLER'S "THE LITTLE WHITE GIRL"

Deep in the gleaming glass
She sees all past things pass.
BEFORE THE MIRROR

Little White Girl''), and ''Erotion'' (in honor of a drawing by Simeon Solomon). Yet in ''Dolores'', which is entirely un-Pre-Raphaelite in manner and mood, it is also possible to discern the influence of the art of painting, for several stanzas are close transcripts of pictures by Gérôme of Imperial Rome: ''The Gladiators'', ''Christian Martyrs'', and ''Nero's Torches.'' The two ''Ballads'' with which the collection opens, though deriving ultimately from the *canzoni* of Dante and Cavalcanti, spring immediately from Rossetti's ''Early Italian Poets.''

Of the poems on classical subjects ''Phædra'' and ''At Eleusis'' are mere experiments in the style of ''Atalanta.'' ''Itylus'', technically very wonderful and one of Swinburne's most celebrated poems, is a rhapsody upon the song of the nightingale as heard one evening at Fiesole. The same motive of the bird's song caught and rendered into words was to reappear in ''On the Cliffs'', a poem of much later date. Another piece that anticipates ''On the Cliffs'' is ''Anactoria.'' Here Swinburne attempts to suggest the passion of Sappho; but the loose violence and volubility of his style are totally dissimilar from the tense and terse concision of the Lesbian. The sadistic note in ''Anactoria'' is modern and personal rather than Sapphic and derivative. Of lasting interest are two passages only: that in which Sappho foretells the immortality of her fame, and that (of later date than the context into which it was inserted) in which ''the gods" are denounced in the manner of "Atalanta." The quantitative "Sapphics", metrically a *tour de force* unmatched in English verse, tell how the poet beheld the song of Sappho soaring as a bird soars:

> Newly fledged, her visible song, a marvel,
> Made of perfect sound and exceeding passion,
> Sweetly shapen, terrible, full of thunders,
> Clothed with the wind's wings.

The modern French influence is felt throughout the book but is not directly evident in many poems. The macabre tone of some pieces and the tendency to relate together pleasure and pain, love and death, are suggestive of Baudelaire, but it is remarkable that neither here nor elsewhere in Swinburne is heard any echo of the "Satanic" *motif* which Baudelaire employs and which is heard once in the poetry of Carducci; nor does Swinburne share Baudelaire's taste for artificiality. The hard gold-encrusted gorgeousness of a few pieces ("The Masque of Queen Bersabe" and parts of "Dolores") is faintly reminiscent of "Salammbô." One or two things owe something to Gautier. "Fragoletta" was suggested by the novel of the same name by George Sand's friend Latouche, a book for which Swinburne had an inexplicable predilection. There are echoes of older French writers, for Swinburne's scholarship led him to remote sources of inspiration. Thus, from Lacour's "Trésor des pièces rares ou inédites" he obtained the *motif* of "April"; and "A Match", which quickly became one of his most popular poems, is an adaptation of an Old French wooing-song, "Les Transformations":

> *Si tu te mets en dame dans un couvent,*
> *Je me mettrai en pretre, gaillard chantant,*
> *Confesserai les dames de ton couvent —*

and so forth. Another piece that quickly became popular is "In the Orchard", with its celebrated rendering of the Provençal refrain, "*Oi deus, oi deus, de l'alba! tan tost ve!*" "Ah God, ah God, that day should be so soon!" To compare Swinburne's version of this *aubade* with the original (or with the wonderful rendering into English in George Moore's "Héloïse and Abélard") is to note the loss of power and passion that are due to Swinburne's excessive wordiness.[1] Several poems are inspired by the vogue of medievalism inherited from Keats and the Pre-Raphaelites. The very impressive "Ballad of Burdens" stands apart from all the rest, epitomizing that sense of the vanity of pleasure which accompanies the very glorification of pleasure.

The republican sentiment of Swinburne's Oxford years is expressed forcibly, though with an ingenuousness that is indicative of immaturity, in "A Song in Time of Order: 1852" and "A Song in Time of Revolution: 1860." In the former year

[1] Another *aubade* is "Before Dawn." French influence is visible here and there in other pieces. It has been lately shown, for example, that "The Garden of Proserpine" owes something to Casimir Delavigne's "Les Limbes."

Italy was in the midst of reaction, throughout Europe the fires of revolutionary enthusiasm were low, and republicans everywhere were nearly despairing. Nevertheless, as W. K. Clifford was afterwards to write, "So long as two or three are gathered together, freedom is there in the midst of them"; and Swinburne pictures such men leaving Europe to seek liberty elsewhere:

> While three men hold together,
> The kingdoms are less by three.

Rejoicing in the bright glad ocean, they push out across the breakers:

> We have done with the kisses that sting,
> The thief's mouth red from the feast,
> The blood on the hands of the king,
> And the lie at the lips of the priest.

The rollicking meter and the crude thought are alike boyish, yet here, as in the companion "Song in Time of Revolution", there is a faint promise of "Songs before Sunrise."[1]

The same revolutionary sentiment sounds in the ode "To Victor Hugo"; but while the fatalism of this poem connects its thought with "Atalanta" there is also an assertion of the independence of the human spirit which points forward to "Songs before Sunrise":

[1] In "A Song in Time of Order" there is an allusion to the scandals of the French policital penal settlement at Cayenne. At Oxford Swinburne read François Attibert's "Quatre Ans à Cayenne" (Brussels, 1859), an exposure of these scandals. His autographed and much thumbed copy of this book, dated October 27, 1859, is now in my library.

Yea, one thing more than this,
We know that one thing is,
The splendour of a spirit without blame,
That not the labouring years
Blind-born, nor any fears,
Nor men nor any gods can tire or tame;
But purer power with fiery breath
Fills and exalts above the gulfs of death.

Accompanying the fatalism of many of the poems is a denial of immortality. In "Atalanta" death had been regarded as a baffling mystery,

the empty weary house,
Where no flesh is nor beauty nor swift eyes
Nor sound of mouth nor might of hands and feet.

But in "Poems and Ballads" death is often looked to for relief "from too much love of living"; and in some of his most celebrated lines the poet thanks "whatever gods may be" that "no life lives forever" and that in Proserpina's domain there shall be "a sleep eternal in an eternal night." In so far as these sentiments are sincere they are a symptom of that satiety which is the sequel to the eroticism of the poems; the suspicion that they are not sincere but imitative and derivative is the reason why many of these poems impress the modern reader as meretricious.

Swinburne's hostility to Christianity takes the form of the accusation that Christianity is hostile to the principle of Beauty: "Thou hast conquered, O pale Galilean; the world has grown grey with thy breath." But the sense of the vanity of the world which so poignantly accompanies this loyalty to Beauty is itself Christian, and below the defiant and strident "paganism" even of "Dolores" there is a recognition of the phenomenon of remorse that is part of Christian ethics. Mr. Chesterton has contrasted the picture of Hellenic Beauty as celebrated in "Poems and Ballads" with that other picture of Hellenism that is drawn in "Atalanta in Calydon." "When Swinburne went forth," says Mr. Chesterton, "as the champion of pagan change and pleasure, he heard uplifted the grand choruses of his own 'Atalanta', in his rear, refusing hope."

The positive *motif* of the poems is Hedonism. Most audible is the note of eroticism which first found voice in "Chastelard" and is clangorous in "Poems and Ballads." The sensuality which some apologists have glossed over with the more comfortable term "sensuousness" is not only blatant and extravagant but wearisome and absurd. The erotic poems shade off from suggestions of actual experience (as in "Before Parting") through a group in which dreams and fancies embroider the stuff of actuality, to poems that have sprung wholly from Swinburne's imagination. Even in 1866 there were people who knew Swinburne well enough to realize that the poems of passion did not spring from the inmost sources of his temperament. They were inspired, says William Michael Rossetti, by "one of the less genuine constituents of the author's mind." Thus it has come about that whereas contemporaries were shocked by them we are merely bored. Lithe limbs are doubtless as attractive as ever, but Swinburne's celebration of them has ceased to move us. Despite the shimmering or glittering beauty of the prosody, the bright swift imagery alternating with somber reveries, the flaunted and audacious hymns to physical loveliness, these poems do not fascinate us as they fascinated men and women sixty years ago. Our attention drowses as under the hands of a hypnotist and our judgment, struggling to assert itself, protests that this is not the voice of real passion. Eroticism was not one of the fundamental qualities of Swinburne's character; otherwise its extreme manifestations would not have disappeared so soon. But even in the poems of his maturity his conception of love is wholly physical and has in it nothing of the spiritual exaltation of Rossetti and of Donne. Donne's profoundly passionate nature was ready to admit that

> Love's mysteries in souls do grow,
> But yet the body is his book;

but he rebukes those "dull sublunary lovers" "whose soul is sense."

> We by a love so much refined,
> That ourselves know not what it is,
> Inter-assured of the mind,
> Care less, eyes, lips and hands to miss.

Swinburne seems never to have conceived the idea

of a relationship between men and women who are "inter-assured of the mind."

Yet it is injudicious to go to the extreme of dismissing "Poems and Ballads" almost in entirety as immature, meretricious and insincere. This is to be intellectually as priggish as the shocked admiration of our ancestors was morally priggish. Some of the erotic poems are of lasting appeal, and it is significant that of these not the least excellent but the best are those of purely "literary" inspiration. Of such the greatest is "Laus Veneris." Since there is more of what Rossetti called "fundamental brain-work" in this poem than in the other poems of passion and since it is much more firmly wrought, it is proper to examine it in some detail.

Tieck's "Erzählung" of Tannhäuser gave a new popularity to the old legend among the Romanticists, and Swinburne was acquainted from many sources with the theme of a mortal held in captivity by an amorous goddess. Wagner's music-drama he had had no opportunity to see, nor did he read Baudelaire's pamphlet "Wagner et Tannhäuser à Paris" until after he had written his poem.[1] I

[1] The connection between Swinburne's poem and Wagner's music-drama is part of the history of English appreciation of the great composer. Still misunderstood, derided or ignored by the public, Wagner had, by the later eighteen-sixties, been accepted by the younger generation of Romanticists in Paris as an exemplar and master. Franz Hueffer and Swinburne's friend George Powell were influential in initiating the vogue of his music-dramas in England. The ringing dedicatory stanzas of John Payne's "Songs of Life and Death" and the note attached to this dedication are milestones in the progress of Wagnerian appreciation in England.

think it likely that he may have derived a first impulse to recreate the story from reading a now forgotten poem by "Owen Meredith" and a collaborator, "Tannhäuser; or the Battle of the Bards" (1861). Moreover, the general theme of the fallen Olympians, "grown diabolic among ages that would not accept them as divine", was in the air; Heine had written his "Gods in Exile", Mérimée his "Vénus d'Ille"; and a little later the subject was to exercise a morbid attraction upon the imagination of Walter Pater.

To some minds the final salvation of Tannhäuser through the mercy of Christ and the intercessions of the holy Elizabeth seems a sentimentalization of the theme, just as such minds will prefer Marlowe's interpretation of the Faust legend to Goethe's, holding that when Faust is led by the Pœnitentium to the feet of the Divine Mother, Mephistopheles is unjustly cheated out of the wager he had won. Swinburne, who did not believe that

Das Ewig-Weibliche
Zieht uns hinan,

retained the traditional ending of the legend of Tannhäuser: the blossoming of the Pope's staff, sign of God's pardon, came too late. The poet's own exposition of "Laus Veneris" in the "Notes on Poems and Reviews" is so admirable and so magnificent an example of his prose style at its best that it may be quoted entire:

To me it seemed that the tragedy began with the knight's return to Venus — began at the point where hitherto it had seemed to leave off. The immortal agony of a man lost after all repentance — cast down from fearful hope into fearless despair — believing in Christ and bound to Venus — desirous of penitential pain, and damned to joyless pleasure — this, in my eyes, was the kernel and nucleus of a myth comparable only to that of the foolish virgins and bearing the same burden. The tragic touch of the story is this: that the knight who has renounced Christ believes in him; the lover who has embraced Venus disbelieves in her. Vainly and in despair he would make the best of that which is the worst — vainly remonstrate with God, and argue on the side he would fain desert. Once accept or admit the least admixture of pagan worship, or of modern thought, and the whole story collapses into froth and smoke. It was not till my poem was completed that I received from the hands of its author the admirable pamphlet of Charles Baudelaire on Wagner's "Tannhäuser." If anyone desires to see, expressed in better words than I can command, the conception of the mediaeval Venus which it was my aim to put into verse, let him turn to the magnificent passage in which M. Baudelaire describes the fallen goddess, grown diabolic among ages that would not accept her as divine. In another point, as I then found, I concur with the great musician and his great panegyrist. I have made Venus the one love of her knight's whole life, as Mary Stuart of Chastelard's; I have sent him, poet and soldier, fresh to her fierce embrace. Thus only both legend and symbol appear to me noble and significant. Light loves and harmless errors must not touch the elect of heaven or of hell. The queen of evil, the lady of lust, will endure no rival but God; and when the vicar of God rejects him, to her only can he return to abide the day of his judgment in weariness and sorrow and fear.

Three other celebrated poems — "Dolores", "The Garden of Proserpine", and "Hesperia" — are to be read as contrasted movements in a symphonic suite, if Swinburne's own exegesis be accepted. Hypnotized by the coiling and uncoiling stanzas of "Dolores" which moving in gyrations seem never to get anywhere, the reader of to-day is not likely to be attracted by this reverie upon the sensualities of a man foiled in love and weary of loving who "decorates with the name of goddess, crowns anew as the mystical Cotytto, some woman, real or ideal, in whom the pride of life with its companion lusts is incarnate."

In "Hesperia" the "worship of desire" has ceased and the spirit "dreams now of truth discovered and repose attained." Between these two poems is set the meditation upon Proserpina's garden wherein the soul is freed from "too much love of living" and where the boon of endless sleep is wrested from the jealous gods.

Metrically these three poems are among Swinburne's greatest achievements. To-day, with our ears attuned to a more delicate music of fluctuating, hovering, hesitating rhythms, their technical mastery does not appeal as it did to Swinburne's contemporaries. But all three illustrate Swinburne's amazing gift for adapting old rhythms and stanzaic forms to new uses by some cunning change which resolves the commonplace into enchantment. "Hesperia" is written in anapæstic equivalents for dactylic hexameters. "The Garden of Proserpine" stanza can be traced back through Keats' song "In a drear-nighted December" to Dryden's song "Farewell, ungrateful traitor" in "The Spanish Friar." Keats eliminated Dryden's vulgarity but altered and marred the rhyme-scheme. Swinburne retained Dryden's rhyme-scheme and softened and enriched Keats' cadences. The history of the "Dolores" stanza, which is popularly more closely associated with Swinburne than any other that he employed, is complicated and can be barely indicated here. Gay used the eight-line anapæstic trimeter for comic effect in "The Beggar's Opera"; Byron turned it to serious purpose in the "Stanzas to Augusta" and gave it greater weight by employing double rhymes in alternate lines. The stroke of inspiration by which Swinburne turned this jog-trot stanza into a thing of beauty was the truncation of the last line. When, with this shortened eighth line, consonantal and vocalic harmonies are employed, Gay's old jingle becomes dignified and majestical, as in this description of the Roman amphitheater:

On sands by the storm never shaken,
Nor wet with the washing of tides;

Nor by foam of the waves overtaken,
Nor winds that the thunder bestrides;
But red from the print of thy paces,
Made smooth for the world and its lords,
Ringed round with a flame of fair faces,
And splendid with swords.

Here, as in many other stanzas, Swinburne plays upon the open and closed, front and back, vowels as upon an instrument.[1]

"Poems and Ballads" is closely related to Pater's "Renaissance." Its particular appeal was to the younger generation of men of culture among whom Pater's influence was soon to be felt. Like Pater, Swinburne celebrates "the principle of Beauty in all things." Both men were extraordinarily, morbidly sensitive, though Pater's sensibility was more exquisitely refined. Like the Child in the House, Swinburne "experiences a passionateness in his relation to fair outward objects"; and like Gaston de Latour he tends towards "a new religion, or at least a new worship, maintaining and visibly setting forth a single overpowering apprehension."

[1] Of the thousands of people who have chanted Swinburne's perverse litany to his Lady of Pain probably but few have paused to note his use of scales of vowels to gain his effect. A single stanza will illustrate this:

O g*a*rment not g*o*lden but g*i*lded,
O g*a*rden where *a*ll men may dw*e*ll,
O t*o*wer not of *i*vory but b*ui*lded
By h*a*nds that reach h*ea*ven from h*e*ll;
O m*y*stical r*o*se of the m*i*re,
O h*ou*se not of g*o*ld but of g*ai*n,
O h*ou*se of unq*ue*nchable f*i*re,
Our L*a*dy of P*ai*n.

With this keen sensuousness (and again the analogy to Pater is close) Swinburne combined an acute consciousness of the brevity of life. Here the poet is at one with a main movement of emotion in the later nineteenth century. In "Marius the Epicurean" Pater describes Cyrenaicism as "the characteristic philosophy of youth." The remark is a commentary upon "Poems and Ballads." With these two attributes, the delight of the eyes and the sense of the fleetingness of mortality, combined, the appeal of Cyrenaicism was strong in Swinburne. "What is secure in our existence," said Pater in the most celebrated passage in his writings, "is but the sharp apex of the present moment between two hypothetical eternities"; and the problem is "How such actual moments as they pass may be made to yield their utmost, by the dexterous training of capacity." To young men Swinburne became the great exemplar of Pater's doctrine that "to burn always with this hard gem-like flame, to maintain this ecstasy, is success in life." Art and Song fill best and to the fullest the brief interval that is allowed us. The Heraclitean doctrine that all things are in flux and that nothing remains, upon which Pater based his Cyrenaicism, is at the foundation of such philosophy as is discoverable in "Poems and Ballads"; and it is best set forth in the dramatic monologue of the "Hymn to Proserpine", sung by an Epicurean after the proclamation of Christianity at Rome. Proserpina is the goddess of Change; she has overcome Olympus; in the end she will conquer Christianity.

Ye are Gods, and behold, ye shall die, and the waves be upon
you at last.
In the darkness of time, in the deeps of the years, in the changes
of things,
Ye shall sleep as a slain man sleeps, and the world shall forget
you for kings. . . .
Thou art more than the Gods who number the days of our
temporal breath;
For these give labour and slumber; but thou, Proserpina, death.

The thought is in line with much of the poetry of the later century. Meredith accepts this philosophy of Change joyfully as an augury of life; Francis Thompson as boldly rejects it ("The angels keep their ancient places!"); but Swinburne hymns it with solemn exultation as though he were the hierophant of the destroying goddess.

CHAPTER THREE

The Risorgimento and the Ideal Republic

"A Song of Italy" and "Songs before Sunrise" form together the culmination of the long series of "English Songs of Italian Freedom." Italy, "that pleasant country", has always[1] won the love of the English poets. The beauty of her landscapes, the splendor of her art, the romance of her ruins and the unique quality of her cities have made in each generation an unrivalled appeal to wanderers from the northern island of mist and rain. In the Romantic Period a wider range of vision and a more profound intensity of feeling enter into English poetry dedicated to the praise of Italy than ever before. From Napoleon she had gained more reforms and less oppression than came to any other country within the range of his conquests; but Waterloo retarded the progress of democracy, restored old tyrannies — Papal, Austrian, Bourbon, and what not — and ushered in an era of reaction and dynastic oppression. She was forced again into

[1]The love of Italy by our poets can be traced from the time of Chaucer and more fully from the Elizabethan age. Among the poets who have sung the praises of Italy are Spenser, Drummond, Drayton, Milton, Dryden, Addison, Thomson, Akenside, and Goldsmith. The full story of the influence of Italy on our poetry has never been completely told.

the spiritual lethargy from which she had almost escaped. This was the era of Leopardi who addresses *questa terra fatal:*

> *O patria mia, vedo le mura e gli archi*
> *E le colonne e i simulacri e l'erme*
> *Torri degli avi nostri,*
> *Ma la gloria non vedo,*
> *Non vedo il lauro e il ferro ond' eran carchi*
> *I nostri padri antichi.*

This was the appeal to English poets, and Byron and Shelley made England aware of that appeal. When Byron took up his residence in Italy his unrivalled fame caused English eyes to turn hither with an attention which, for all her loveliness and all her sorrows, she had never won before. From Byron Englishmen learned to contrast Italy's past glory and her present desolation; the debt of all the world to her; the duty of England, traditional fount of freedom, to give aid and comfort to a people aspiring towards liberty; above all, the beauty, "the fatal gift of beauty", of the land — the crumbling palaces and silent lagoons of Venice, sunset on the Brenta, the twilight hour in the pine forest at Ravenna, the murmuring Arno and the "holy precincts" of Santa Croce, and the innumerable wonders and storied associations of Rome. He made familiar to Englishmen the thought of a free and united Italy. He voiced the aspirations of a people. Shelley sings of the Italian ideal, the Italian dream. He was far less closely in touch with political affairs in Italy than was Byron; but no other poet has caught so much of the haunting mysterious beauty of "the Paradise of exiles."

> Beneath is spread like a green sea
> The waveless plain of Lombardy,
> Bounded by the vaporous air,
> Islanded by cities fair. . . .
> Lo, the sun floats up the sky,
> Like thought-wingéd Liberty,
> Till the universal light
> Seems to level plain and height;
> From the sea a mist has spread,
> And the beams of light lie dead
> On the towers of Venice now,
> Like her glory long ago.

With the exception of one magnificent sonnet, Wordsworth's many poems on Italian subjects are unimportant. Rogers' "Italy" with Turner's illustrations increased English familiarity with Italian scenes. Landor, though he resided for years in Italy and though there are exquisite descriptions of Italian landscape scattered through his poems, was not so much moved to the expression of sympathy as might have been expected.[1] Mrs. Hemans, Edward Reade, and other minor bards we must leave aside. Nor can we attempt to trace the multitudinous strands of Italian associations in the poetry of Robert Browning. While his interests lay in Italian history and art and letters and character and he stood aside from modern affairs, Mrs.

[1] The "Ode to Sicily" and the lines "To the Nobles of Venice on the Reception of the Austrian" certainly influenced Swinburne.

Browning's concern with Italy was primarily political. "Casa Guidi Windows" is a record of her observations of the events of 1848 and 1851. In the preface to "Poems before Congress" and in some notable passages in "Aurora Leigh" she formulated a noble statement of the cosmopolitanism inherent in true patriotism. She is the immediate predecessor of Swinburne as the laureate of Italian freedom and independence.

Enthusiasm for Italy had, then, been part of the endowment of nearly all later English poets: her romantic past and present desolation, her glorious aspirations and noble struggle, her splendid literature and consummate art — these combined with her natural loveliness to form an appeal of unequalled force. How any critic, mindful of this inheritance, can express wonder, as does Sir Edmund Gosse, at Swinburne's devotion to Italy, I do not understand. It is true that he visited Italy but twice, but even had he never set foot within her borders his love, inherited from Shelley and Landor, might have been as ardent. His strong sense of tradition would have inspired devotion to the land which is, with Greece, the *fons et origo* of Western culture. He wrote to a friend: "At an early age . . . I became convinced of the truth and justice of the republican principle, and I have always looked to the land of Dante and Mazzini — *magna parens* — to take the lead in realising that idea in Europe."

In all modern history there is no more moving theme than that of the making of Italy. Swinburne passed his youth in the years of struggle, defeat, and renewed struggle; and the events of the *Risorgimento* sank deep into his memory, became part of himself. Pre-Raphaelitism and other influences turned him for a decade after leaving Eton into other courses, but in 1867 the old enthusiasms reasserted themselves.[1] In that year Jowett had his famous interview with Mazzini and Karl Blind to decide how the currents of Swinburne's genius and energy, which had been falling through dangerous cataracts, might be turned into safer channels. Mazzini consented to see the poet, who was introduced to him by Blind and was told by Mazzini, as Sir Edmund Gosse has narrated, that "there must be no more of this love-frenzy; you must dedicate your glorious powers to the service of the Republic." His powers were already dedicated to that service, for Swinburne's reply was to recite

[1]To that year belongs the "Ode on the Insurrection in Candia", written at the request of certain sympathizers with the Candians, strained in tone, but containing the germs of ideas later elaborated in "Songs before Sunrise." In November, 1867, the condemnation of three Fenians, found guilty of murdering a constable, excited much interest in England; and on the day before their execution Swinburne published in the *Morning Star* "An Appeal to England against the Execution of the Condemned Fenians." This was widely copied in the press, circulated as a broadside, and posted on hoardings in Manchester. The poet does not explicitly defend the murderers but appeals to mercy. A hint at the possibility of erecting an Irish Republic returned to vex Swinburne twenty years later when he opposed the first Home Rule Bill. The "Appeal" had no effect; and the only result was that the Reform League suggested to Swinburne that he stand for Parliament, an idea which, after taking counsel with Mazzini, he wisely put by.

"A Song of Italy", sitting the while at Mazzini's feet. Facetious critics have done what they can to mar the inherent nobility of this episode.

The wavelike rise and fall of these unresting, unhurrying lines is, for all their monotony, a metrical marvel.[1] The allegorical opening is a stumbling-block that must be passed over before the greatness of the "Song" is apparent. This opening is a vision of two women, the one resembling Love, the other lying prone upon the ground. They are Freedom and Italy. Freedom summons Italy to rise: "I were not Freedom if thou wert not free."

A second *motif* is then introduced: the Italian tricolor as the symbol of life and hope spread abroad through all nature. A suggestion for this came from Mrs. Browning who had declaimed:

> Red, for the patriot's blood,
> Green, for the martyr's crown,
> White, for the dew and the rime,
> When the morning of God comes down.[2]

[1] Of Jonson's use of this meter Swinburne later remarked that "this metre, though very liable to the danger of monotony, is to my ear very pleasant." In his handling of it it rises to heights far beyond Jonson's reach.

[2] They are the colors worn by the three Christian Virtues in the Triumph of the Church in the "Purgatorio." In the "Song of the Standard" Swinburne uses Dante's symbolism:

Green as our hope in it, white as our faith in it, red as our love.

— So rare and tenuous are the links between Swinburne and Carducci that the following passage from the Italian poet's address "Per il Tricolore", delivered at Reggio where the tricolor was first unfurled, must be quoted. The parallel to Swinburne is very close:

Reggio fu degna che da queste mura si elevasse e prima sventolasse in questa piazza segnacolo dell' unico stato e della innovata libertà, la bella la pura la santa bandiera dei tre colori. Sii benedetta! benedetta nell' immacolata origine, benedetta nella via di

But Swinburne turns the banner into music:

Fly, O our flag, through deep Italian air,
  Above the flags that were. . . .
Fly, green as summer and red as dawn and white
  As the live heart of light. . . .
From Alpine white, from Tuscan green, and where
  Vesuvius reddens air. . . .
Red hills of flame, white Alps, green Apennines,
  Banners of blowing pines,
Standards of stormy snows, flags of light leaves,
  Three wherewith Freedom weaves
One ensign that once woven and once unfurled
  Makes day of all the world.

In contrast to the tricolor is the Austrian imperial banner, yellow and black, the symbol of autumnal decay and of death. George Meredith in "Vittoria" had already succinctly phrased the antithesis: "Black and yellow drop to the earth; green, white and red mount to heaven."

Various heroic events of the *Risorgimento* are then passed in review, with particular allusion to episodes in Mazzini's life; and this historico-biographical portion of the "Song" leads to the great climax in which all Italy, all nature, is summoned to praise and glorify the Chief. Viewed through the

prove e di sventure per cui immacolata ancora procedesti, benedetta nella battaglia e nella vittoria, ora e sempre, nei secoli! Non rampare di aquile e leoni, non sormontare di belve rapaci, nel santo vessillo; ma i colori della nostra primavera e del nostro paese, dal Cenisio all' Etna; le nevi delle alpi, l'aprile delle valli, le fiamme dei vulcani. E subito, quei colori parlarono alle anime generose e gentili, con le ispirazioni e gli effetti delle virtù onde la patria sta e si augusta: il bianco, la fede serena alle idee che fanno divina l'anima nella costanza dei savi; il verde, la perpetua rifioritura della speranza a frutto di bene nella gioventù de' poeti; il rosso, la passione ed il sangue dei martiri e degli eroi. E subito il popolo cantò alla sua bandiera ch' ella era la più bella di tutte e che sempre voleva lei e con lei la libertà. . . .

From a photograph by Brogi

FLORENCE

Fiesole's embracing arms enclose
The immeasurable rose.
A SONG OF ITALY

matter-of-fact spectacles of cynical critics these lines have sometimes seemed absurd in their high-wrought emotionality; they have been called "windy"; but the wind that blows through them is that which blows in "Childe Harold" and upon it streams the banner of Freedom, "torn but flying":

> Praise him, O winds that move the molten air,
>   O light of days that were,
> And light of days that shall be; land and sea,
>   And heaven and Italy:
> Praise him, O storm and summer, shore and wave,
>   O skies and every grave;
> O weeping hopes, O memories beyond tears,
>   O many and murmuring years.

And so on, through the tempestuous roll call of the Italian cities: Brescia, Verona, Milan, Mantua, Padua, Venice, Genoa, Florence, San Gimignano, Siena, Naples, and at length Rome — all summoned to magnify the liberator. *Benedicite, omnia opera Domini!*

Then Italy is bidden to look upon her fallen foe, Austria, beaten to her knees (by Prussia):

> Because they spared not, do thou the rather spare:
>   Be not one thing they were. . . .
> Because they had no pity, have thou pity.

The "Song" ends with a prophecy that the liberation of Rome is at hand and that she will be the crown of the republic.

It is obvious that Swinburne is out of touch and tune with the political situation in Italy in 1867.

Mazzini's hope of founding a republic had long since become impossible; and in the years between Cavour's death and the entry of Victor Emmanuel into Rome the disciples of the great Piedmontese Premier were engaged in a loyal though often bungling attempt to carry out his program. Not for many years (if ever) had the idea of a republic been within the sphere of practical politics. Mazzini was an extreme example of the pure idealist, prepared to die for his ideals. It is well to set over against Swinburne's adoration of him the opinion of a modern historian who is anti-Mazzinian in sympathies and point of view. In his recent biography of Cavour, M. Maurice Paléologue says of Mazzini:

> He displayed all the symptoms that inspire great fanatics, great redressors of wrong, great lovers of justice: belief in a supernatural calling, immeasurable pride, irritability of temper, gloomy spirits, enduring passion, arrogant talk upon one unending topic, dogmatism in argument, and an absolute indifference to facts.

The historian does something less than justice to Mazzini. His part in the *Risorgimento* was one which probably no other man could have taken. Swinburne called him the "Prophet"; we might call him the Propagandist — it amounts to much the same thing. The patient, practical genius of Cavour, while knowing how to turn to political account the sentiment roused by Mazzini, knew also that his fanaticism, impracticality and unreason were enormous dangers to ultimate Italian success. Cavour was responsible for Mazzini's exile. This Swinburne could not forgive. Cavour's own program was the union of an independent Italy under the House of Savoy. He had, moreover, trafficked with Napoleon III, trading Nice and Savoy for the emperor's support. That support culminated in the premature Peace of Villafranca which Swinburne never ceased to regard as the betrayal of the Italian cause. This ineffectual conclusion of the French incursion into Lombardy in 1859 is the chief count in the poet's indictment of the emperor. Swinburne ignores the fact that the threat of Prussia upon the Rhine frontier forced Napoleon to make peace. As for the emperor's support of the temporal claims of the Papacy as the price paid for the support of his own Catholic subjects, Swinburne regarded this as ignoble truckling which made Napoleon the more contemptible.

From the facts thus briefly summarized it will be seen that "A Song of Italy" and the "Songs before Sunrise", in so far as they reflect Italian politics and not eternal ideals, belong not to 1868 but to 1848. Swinburne is at once twenty years behind the times and generations before them. Thus it happens that Mr. Chesterton, an unsympathetic critic, can say that "Songs before Sunrise" are of "a sunrise that never came up." The sympathetic reader feels that just because they are not "of an age" they are all the more "of all time."

"Songs before Sunrise" appeared in 1871.[1] The tide of English liberalism was then at the flood. The Irish Land Bill, the Education Bill, the foundation of the Birmingham League, the extension of the Civil Service, and the reforms in the army are among the achievements of the period that are products of something of the same spirit that inspired the "Songs." Charles Bradlaugh, the radical atheist, was then notorious. The Royal Family was at its nadir of unpopularity, and republican sentiment was vocal in the land. This radicalism is part of the background of Swinburne's poems. But they were directly inspired by events in Italy; and it is uncritical to minimize the Italian influence, as some commentators on Swinburne have done.

The famous Manifesto which Giuseppe Mazzini addressed to "Young Italy" from his exile (1831) and which roused countless thousands of Italians from the lethargic indifference[2] which it was the

[1] The date gives a false idea of the position of the volume in Swinburne's development. Actually the majority of the poems belong to 1867–1868 and the manuscript, unrevised and unenlarged, was in the hands of F. S. Ellis the publisher in the autumn of 1868. The long delay before the book's appearance was due to the already mentioned dispute with Hotten. It is noteworthy that two poems had already appeared in the *Fortnightly Review*, for under Morley's editorship this periodical was becoming the organ of "advanced" opinion, political, social and philosophical.

[2] Compare, from "Mater Dolorosa":

> But their children, by kings made quiet, by priests made wise,
> Love better the heat of their hearth than the light of her eyes.

(The light in the eyes of Freedom.) The simplification of social problems into a general accusation of "kings" and "priests" is of almost Shelleyan ingenuousness, though not so completely incorrect as a diagnosis of the ills of Italy as some critics have asserted.

policy of Austria to encourage, forms a recurrent *motif* in the "Songs." Swinburne sings of this proclamation in "Super Flumina Babylonis":

By the rivers of Italy, by the sacred streams,
By town, by tower,
There was feasting with revelling, there was sleep with dreams,
Until thine hour.

By the rivers of Italy, by the dry streams' beds,
When thy time came,
There was casting of crowns from them, from their young men's heads,
The crowns of shame.

The Mazzinian ideal which accomplished this moral revival is stated in the same poem in words of lofty eloquence and ethical intensity:

Unto each man his handiwork, unto each his crown,
The just Fate gives;
Whoso takes the world's life on him and his own lays down,
He, dying so, lives.

Whoso bears the whole heaviness of the wronged world's weight
And puts it by,
It is well with him suffering, though he face man's fate;
How should he die?

Seeing death hath no part in him any more, no power
Upon his head;
He hath bought his eternity with a little hour,
And is not dead.

"The Pilgrims", a great and too little known poem in which Swinburne achieves as austere a moral utterance as any of the century, is inspired by the same thought. It is a colloquy between *l'homme sensuel moyen*, mindful of his own cares and pleasures, and the Pilgrims, devotees of their Lady of Liberty, leaving all things for her sake and content to wait and watch and work. Men think them mad:

> But ye that might be clothed with all things pleasant,
> Ye are foolish that put off the fair soft present,
> That clothe yourselves with the cold future air.

They are indeed weary, but "the inexorable desire" keeps them in their path.

> — And these men shall forget you. — Yea, but we
> Shall be a part of the earth and the ancient sea,
> And heaven-high air august, and awful fire,
> And all things good.

A few months before Swinburne wrote "Super Flumina Babylonis" George Meredith in "Vittoria" had paid splendid tribute to Mazzini:

He cried out to Italians to wait for no inspiration but their own; that they should never subdue their minds to follow any alien example; nor let a foreign city of fire be their beacon. Watching over his Italy; her wrist in his meditative clasp year by year; he stood like a mystic leech by the couch of a fair and hopeless frame, pledged to revive it by the inspired assurance, shared by none, that life had not forsaken it. A body given over to death and vultures — he stood by it in the desert . . . Arise, he said, even in what appeared most fatal hours of darkness. The slack limbs moved; the body rose and fell. The cost of the effort was the breaking out of innumerable wounds, old and new; the gain was the display of the miracle that Italy lived. She tasted her own blood, and herself knew that she lived.

The same idea, clothed in a parable, appears in Swinburne's "Tiresias", in which the prophet meditates beside the tomb of Antigone:

> Antigone, men say not thou didst ill,
> For love's sake and the reverence of his awe
> Divinely dying, slain by mortal law.

Through her sacrifice her brother has won a place of honor in the land of shadows. Is she indeed dead? Is it not rather the man-made laws of tyranny that must die? At the close the parable is briefly interpreted. Three prophets, Dante, Michelangelo and Mazzini, watch over the tomb of Italy, slain by tyranny; and they echo the question of Tiresias:

> Are these dead or art thou dead, Italy?

Another poem inspired by the Mazzinian vision is "Siena", which stands with "Ave atque Vale" and the "Prelude" to "Tristram of Lyonesse" at the summit of Swinburne's lyrical verse. "Siena" is fashioned out of memories of the poet's visit to the city of Saint Catherine. He tells of the saint's work among the plague-stricken, of her widening influence in public affairs, of her journey to Avignon during the great schism to persuade Pope

Urban V to return to Rome, and of how afterwards she

> fed her faith with silent things
> And lived her life with curbed white wings,
> And mixed herself with heaven and died:
> And now on the sheer city-side
> Smiles like a bride.

Her story calls to mind Il Sodoma's frescoes; and they in turn suggest the "Christ at the Column"; and contemplating that austere picture the poet says:

> In vain on all these sins and years
> Falls the sad blood, fall the slow tears;
> In vain poured forth as watersprings,
> Priests, on your altars, and ye, kings,
> About your seats of sanguine gold;
> Still your God, spat upon and sold,
> Bleeds at your hands; but now is gone
> All his flock from him, saving one;
> Judas alone.

Close by is the group of the "Three Graces", the battered memorial of a fairer time, which suggests the question, "What do ye here?"—for the land is war-worn and desolate; Italy is another Pia pleading for remembrance. To her cause the poet has been consecrated from his youth, and now at length "those red roads thy footprints trod" are passed over and the day is at hand.

> Let there be light, O Italy!
> For our feet falter in the night.
> O lamp of living years to be,
> O light of God, let there be light!

From a photograph by Alinari

IL SODOMA'S "CHRIST AT THE COLUMN"

In vain on all these sins and years
Falls the sad blood, fall the slow tears.

SIENA

With fervent love he foresees the day when the Soul and Freedom and Nature shall be one, and Time shall make manifest the divine Republic.[1]

The stanza on the *Cristo alla Colonna* in "Siena" contains in little the theme of the celebrated poem "Before a Crucifix." This gave widespread offence. A parallel to the contemporary misunderstanding of Swinburne's intention is the misunderstanding of Voltaire's famous phrase *Ecrasez l'infâme* which was popularly interpreted in England to refer to Christ himself but which does, in fact, refer to the persecuting and privileged orthodoxy against which Voltaire fought. Swinburne, too, denounces not the Author of Christianity nor the Christian ideal but the church's ministers,

> Because of whom we dare not love thee;
> Though hearts reach back and memories ache,
> We cannot praise thee for their sake.[2]

Just as in "The Modern Prometheus" Herbert Trench has interpreted the legend of the Titan upon the Caucasian crag in terms of the condition

[1] The poems passed in review form the group permeated with the Mazzinian ideal. A second group, suggested by actual events in the Italian struggle, is "occasional" in character and ephemeral in interest. Almost as entirely "topical", though here a broader horizon gives ampler room for the poet's imagination, are three poems — "The Eve of Revolution", "A Watch in the Night", "The Litany of Nations" — in which he looks out over all Europe. "Quia Multum Amavit" stands apart from the majority of the "Songs" in that it is inspired by French, not Italian, history.

[2] This is in precisely the spirit of Voltaire's epigram "Sur un Christ habillé en Jésuite."

> *Il vous ont habillé comme eux,*
> *Mon Dieu, de peur qu'on ne vous aime.*

in which modern humanity finds itself, so in "Before a Crucifix" it is humanity that now hangs upon its cross. The people's hands and feet are pierced; the people has nowhere to lay its head; there is no angel to roll away the stone:

> O sacred head, O desecrate,
> O labour-wounded feet and hands,
> O blood poured forth in pledge to fate
> Of nameless lives in divers lands,
> O slain and spent and sacrificed
> People, the grey-grown speechless Christ.

Meanwhile altars are blood-blackened and the cross of Christ "shadows the sheltered head of kings" — the old Shelleyan simplification of the social quandary, but perhaps justifiable at a time when pope and emperor were in league to thwart the purposes of the liberators of Italy. If the Crucified be the God of such men, He should come down from the cross and hide Himself.

The "Hymn of Man", to be sung during the sessions of the Vatican Council, was designed as a companion piece to the "Hymn to Proserpine." But what in the earlier poem had been interpreted as purposeless Change is now seen to be the beneficent indwelling and all-pervading Force which works for progress. To that Immanence is dedicated the magnificent trilogy of "Genesis", "Hertha", and "Mater Triumphalis" — a solemn prelude, a weighty central movement, and a brilliant postlude. In "Genesis" the poet's conception is of the dawn of life upon "the sad shapeless horror increate" of inorganic matter, that life which "of itself begets, bears, rears, and slays" and of which the human spirit, abiding forever though the individual passes, is the crowning evidence. This is the central thought of "Hertha", a poem into which many threads of thought are woven: the Scandinavian myth of the tree Yggdrasil whose blossoms are human lives; Hindu pantheism through the medium of Emerson; hints and suggestions from Blake and Whitman; echoes of *Job*.[1] Hertha, the old Teutonic earth goddess, the counterpart of Demeter, here represents three ideas: to the religious-minded, God; to the scientist, Force; to the philosopher, the Unknown Reality. Emerson had written in "The Oversoul":

> And this deep power in which we exist . . . is not only self-sufficing every hour, but the act of seeing and the thing seen, the seer and the spectacle, the subject and the object are one.

And Swinburne chants:

> I the mark that is missed
> And the arrows that miss,

[1]The words of the Lord to Job were: "Who is this that darkeneth counsel by words without knowledge? Where wast thou when I laid the foundations of the earth?" Hertha, addressing man who presumes to question her, demands:

> Who hath given, who hath sold it thee,
> Knowledge of me?
> Hath the wilderness told it thee?
> Hast thou learnt of the sea?
> Hast thou communed in spirit with night? have the winds taken counsel with thee?

I the mouth that is kissed
  And the breath in the kiss,
The search and the sought and the seeker, the soul and the body
  that is. . . .

I the grain and the furrow,
  The plough-cloven clod
And the ploughshare drawn thorough,
  The germ and the sod,
The deed and the doer, the seed and the sower, the dust which
  is God.

The faith of man is fashioned according to the needs of the stages in his advance; when he trod the path of night "the shadow called God" was set in the heavens to guide him on his way; but now the morning is risen and the soul stands revealed.

A creed is a rod,
  And a crown is of night;
But this thing is God,
  To be man with thy might,
To grow straight in the strength of thy spirit, and live out thy
  life as the light.

I am in thee to save thee,
  As my soul in thee saith;
Give thou as I gave thee,
  Thy life-blood and breath,
Green leaves of thy labour, white flowers of thy thought, and
  red fruits of thy death.[1]

The twilight of God has come; "Love, the beloved Republic" reigns; and Hertha is identified with the human spirit:

[1] Note in this use of the *motif* of the tricolor the affirmation of the universal applicability of the principle of the Republic of which the Italian patriots were the living exemplars.

One birth of my bosom;
  One beam of mine eye;
One topmost blossom
  That scales the sky;
Man, equal and one with me, man that is made of me, man that is I.[1]

The final movement of this trilogy is "Mater Triumphalis", which hymns with resplendent fervor that spirit of Liberty of which the poet is the herald and the trumpet.[2] The Triumphant Mother is the Life Force, as in "Hertha", working in each organism secretly and bringing each, through internal processes, from a lower to a higher plane. Such processes are the result of no external compulsion but are the result of free action in each individual. Hence Freedom is necessary to every organism to bring it to perfection; and not alone within the individual soul but in the social order as well. The social organism cannot progress except through the exertion of conscience and reason, and it is this action, thus working, that Swinburne has in mind when he hails the coming Republic. Hertha, the Unknown Reality, the Life Force,

1 "Hertha" has been compared to Meredith's "Earth and Man", which is, however, as Paul de Reul notes, very different in spirit, naturalist and evolutionist, inculcating the doctrine of man's solidarity with nature but not exalting the human spirit as the only God. Compare also Sir William Watson's magnificent "Ode in May", which is nearer to Meredith's poem than to Swinburne's.

2 Metrically this poem is one of Swinburne's signal successes. For the meter Swinburne is probably indebted to Frederick Myers' "Saint Paul" (1867). John Payne, also, had used the meter about the time that Swinburne's poem was written.

Mater Triumphalis, God — called by whatever high august name — is

> . . . the resurrection and redemption,
> The godhead and the manhood and the life.

How this Living Force works out the destiny of all things remains a mystery, suggested in the consummate final stanza of "To Walt Whitman in America"

> Freedom we call it, for holier
> Name of the soul there is none;
> Surelier it labours, if slowlier,
> Than the metres of star or of sun;
> Slowlier than life into breath,
> Surelier than time into death,
> It moves till its labour be done.

This conception is summarized in Swinburne's succinct account of the religion of Emily Brontë:

> Her goddess mother was in both senses the same who gave birth to the divine martyr of Æschylean legend: Earth under one aspect and one name, but under the other Righteousness. And therefore was the first and last word uttered out of the depth of her nature a cry for that one thing needful without which all virtue is as worthless as all pleasure is vile, all hope is shameful as all faith is abject — a cry for Liberty.

But how comes the poet by this intuitive knowledge of the secret meaning of life? This question, which must arise in every reader's mind, Swinburne answers in "On the Downs", a poem curiously anticipatory of Meredith's "A Faith on Trial." It opens with a description of a wind-worn heath whence the poet sees the sad serenity of plain and flat sea line; and his mood taking color from the scene, he hears the murmur of Fate's "old imperious semitones" and the Unknowable encompasses him. Is there no God? he asks; No end to these things? No reason in it all? No power to strengthen the weak and raise the fallen? — And his soul is conscious of the "wise word of the secret earth":

> There is no God, O son,
> If thou be none.

There falls upon him that serene and blessed mood in which the burden of the mystery is lightened, and he sees into the life of things, conscious in dust and flower and sea, and in his own soul, of the presence of the Divine, "one forceful nature increate." It bides its time, waiting for all men to urge them to sublimest effort. His gloom vanishes:

> And the sun smote the clouds and slew,
> And from the sun the sea's breath blew,
> And white waves laughed and turned and fled
> The long green heaving sea-field through,
> And on them overhead
> The sky burnt red.

Here the *motif* of the tricolor attains its highest interpretation.

The "Prelude" to the "Songs" is probably one of the latest in date of the collection. In it, putting aside the hedonism if not as yet the excesses of former years, the poet assumes the responsibilities and ideals of mature manhood. Youth harkens to the truths taught him by Time and casts from him fear of change and fate; he refuses to build a cenotaph for his soul or to sell his freedom for gold, and to those who cry "What profit save in love and song?"[1] he replies:

> Play then and sing; we too have played,
> We likewise in that subtle shade.
> We too have twisted through our hair
> Such tendrils as the wild Loves wear. . . .
> We too have tracked by star-proof trees
> The tempest of the Thyiades; —

but pleasure and passion pass, and action and suffering remain to control life and death. Man can depend upon no guidance external to himself; "save his own soul he has no star." In the lofty disillusionment yet serene independence of this "Prelude" one may read, if one will, the acknowledgment that the Republic is but a dream, too fair for the real world. But life remains to be passed abjectly or nobly, in service or disservice.

At Étretât in 1870 Swinburne composed the "Epilogue"; and it was from his experiences as a

[1] "Youth" is of course Swinburne himself; by "Time" Landor is probably intended. The builder of a cenotaph (an empty sepulcher) for his own soul is the poet who writes of spiritual despondency and doubt, such as Arnold. The allusion to the selling of freedom for gold is perhaps to be applied to Tennyson. The question "What profit save in love and song?" perhaps alludes to the "New Cyrenaicism" which was becoming fashionable at Oxford, with a side glance at William Morris, "the idle singer of an empty day", whose "Earthly Paradise", which had lately appeared, seemed so remote from modern needs, so empty of significance.

swimmer there that he derived the superb simile with which the "Songs" close. As a swimmer heads due eastward before the dawn and sees the coming sun turn all the waves gradually to fluent gold, so the soul strikes out boldly; and as the swimmer could not sustain himself in the darkness save for trust in the coming day, so it were better for the soul, if hope be ill-founded, to sink forthwith and leave the sun alone upon a worldless sea.

"My other books are books; 'Songs before Sunrise' is myself," said Swinburne to a visitor. The unique quality of these noble poems witnesses to the sincerity of the remark. It is not the less sincere because literary influences, as well as personal and political, helped to make them what they are.

Swinburne was proud of the epithet "our younger Shelley" bestowed upon him by some of his admirers.[1] Nowhere is the influence of Shelley so apparent as in the "Songs." The devotion to Italy, the aspirations towards intellectual and political freedom, the hatred of priests and kings, the emphasis upon reason as the highest intellectual expression of the human spirit and upon love as the highest emotional expression of the same, the thought of love as the moving spirit of the universe, the mystical tinge imparted to the ideas — all these motives are Shelleyan; and it is appropriate that

[1] "In the Bay" contains a striking autobiographical allusion in which Swinburne himself affirms this kinship.

the sonnet "Cor Cordium", in honor of Shelley, is inserted among the "Songs." The influence of Blake is also apparent, for though Blake's doctrine of self-expression and fullness of life as opposed to repression, sacrifice and asceticism, is out of accord with the Mazzinian ideal, his other doctrine of the Man-God, the One-ness of the human and divine, reappears in the "Songs"; and the spirit of Blake has something in common with the humanitarianism voiced again and again by Swinburne.

> For Mercy has a human heart,
> Pity a human face,
> And Love the human form divine,
> And Peace the human dress.

From Mrs. Browning Swinburne derived not only the *motif* of the tricolor but various other themes. She recurs constantly to the theme of the dawn of democracy upon the world; she speaks out boldly against England's selfish isolation and against the insularity that refused to recognize the greatness of France. Her love of Italy was as ardent as Swinburne's and far more intimate; and her knowledge of the events of the *Risorgimento*, based as it was upon personal experience, more direct than his.[1]

Despite the presence among the "Songs" of a

[1] In "Casa Guidi Windows" (I, iii) Mrs. Browning just misses the idea expressed in Swinburne's sonnet, "In San Lorenzo." This piece was, however, directly suggested by Michelangelo's celebrated quatrain upon his figure of "Night" in the chapel of the Medici, itself a reply to a quatrain by Giovanni Strozzi. Translations of both these quatrains appear in Swinburne's "Poems and Ballads, Third Series."

poem addressed to Walt Whitman, critics have overlooked Swinburne's debt to "Leaves of Grass," especially in the section called "Songs of Insurrection." Parallels are many and obvious; two may be cited as examples. First, this from "To a Foil'd European Revolutionaire":

What we believe in waits latent forever, through all the continents, and all the islands and archipelagos of the sea;
What we believe in invites no one, promises nothing, sits in calmness and light, is positive and composed, knows no discouragement,
Waiting patiently, waiting its time.

And then this, from "Europe":

Meanwhile corpses lie in new-made graves — bloody corpses of young men. . . .
Those martyrs that hang from the gibbets — those hearts pierc'd by the grey lead,
Cold and motionless as they seem, live elsewhere with unslaughter'd vitality.

They live in other young men, O kings!
They live in brothers, again ready to defy you!
They were purified by death — taught and exalted.

Not a grave of the murder'd for freedom but grows seed for freedom, in its turn to bear seed,
Which the winds carry afar and re-sow, and the rains and the snows nourish.

But of all previous political poetry "Les Châtiments" most closely influenced Swinburne. Hugo was himself part of what he wrote; his poems are based on direct personal experience. Swinburne's, totally disinterested, are pitched in a loftier tone and are without the rancor and personal animus of Hugo. It is not in the denunciatory pieces in "Les Châtiments", however, but in others, less numerous but nobler and filled with idealism, that resemblances to the "Songs before Sunrise" are most apparent. "Carte d'Europe" is just such a survey of the several European States as Swinburne makes several times in his book. "Á un Martyr" attacks the priests who have sold Christ for gain as does Swinburne in "Before a Crucifix." The glad sufferings of the martyrs for freedom are chanted in the "Hymne des Transportés" and elsewhere. "Á un qui veut se détacher" contains parallels of astonishing closeness to Swinburne's style as well as to his thought.[1] The incomparable poem "Lux" with which "Les Châtiments" closes is a Song at Sunrise:

Au fond des cieux un point scintelle,
Regardez, il grandit, il brille,
Il approche, énorme et vermeil.
O République universelle,
Tu n'es encore que l'étincelle,
Demain tu seras le soleil.

[1] With "A Song of Italy" compare:

Quand l'Italie en deuil dressa, du Tibre au Pô,
Son drapeau magnifique,
Quand ce grand peuple, après s'être couché troupeau,
Se leva république,

C'est toi, quand Rome aux fers jeta le cri d'espoir,
Toi qui crisas son aile,
Toi qui fis retomber l'affreux capuchon noir
Sur sa face éternelle.

This parallel and the general indebtedness of Swinburne to Hugo's volume were first carefully noted by Sir Edmund Gosse.

The same poem ends in the very mood of "The Pilgrims":

Et nous qui serons morts, morts dans l'exil peut-être,
Martyrs saignants, pendant que les hommes, sans maître,
Vivront, plus fiers, plus beaux. . . .

When Swinburne died the journals of Rome expressed belated gratitude for his devotion to Italy. The *Tribuna*, as reported in the London *Times*, said:

His love was neither exclusive nor selfish; he caught the voice of a people who yearned for freedom, and in his "Songs before Sunrise" their desire for life and liberty becomes an augury for the future of the whole human race.

And George Meredith, in his famous letter to the *Times* (April 15, 1909), wrote:

Had Italy been native to him he would have borne the renown of a poet fired on the instant to deliver himself orally. And had he been Italian, the glow of a people's adoration would have clad him during life.

"Songs of Two Nations" (1875) takes its title from "A Song of Italy" and the "Ode on the Proclamation of the French Republic" here reprinted together.[1] With them was included a series of

[1] The "Ode", composed at Étretât in 1870, is a hasty, windy production of no permanent worth, memorable only for the fine clangorous opening lines which soon degenerate into bombast.

sonnets with the ominous title "Dirae." The ex-emperor of the French had died on January 9, 1873. During the following spring Swinburne contributed twenty political sonnets to the *Examiner*, which with four earlier sonnets originally published in the *Fortnightly*, were now brought together in one sequence. These excoriating pieces were written in the mood of the invocation at the close of "Nox" in "Les Châtiments":

> *Toi qu'aimait Juvénal gonflé de lave ardente,*
> *Toi dont la clarté luit dans l'oeil fixe de Dante,*
> *Muse Indignation, viens, dressons maintenant,*
> *Dressons sur cet empire heureux et rayonnant,*
> *Et sur cette victoire au tonnerre échappée,*
> *Assez de piloris pour faire une épopée.*

Later, in "Les Quatres Vents de l'Esprit", Hugo was to declare: "*Parfois c'est un devoir de féconder l'horreur.*" In the "Apologia" which closes his sequence Swinburne offers his own defence: as all qualities are known by their contraries, heat by chill, desire by fear, so the flame of hate makes plain "the exuberant light and burning bloom of love." The "Dirae" present the reverse of the picture in "Songs before Sunrise"; as the latter poems idealize fellowship, selflessness, freedom, republicanism, humanitarianism, so here is the idealization of all that Swinburne opposed. The ethical and esthetic justification of the sonnets is this: that only a man who possessed the capacity of hatred of hateful things to the degree here exhibited could carry conviction of his sincerity when elsewhere he expresses a fervor of devotion equally unbounded. The sonnets are directed against Ferdinand of Naples, Napoleon III, Pius IX, the Austrian government, and the Roman Catholic Church. The generous reader may be inclined to exclaim of the sonnets on Napoleon, with old Thomas Nashe: "Out upon thee! Strike a man when he is dead!" But chronology must be reckoned with. The most terrible of the sonnets, the four called "Intercession", were published in the *Fortnightly* before the overthrow of the Empire, when Morley, as Swinburne afterwards remarked, "took not a little credit for moral courage in printing them." The two sonnets directly inspired by the news of Napoleon's death form a sequel required by what has gone before. Napoleon was in Swinburne's eyes something other than and something more than a fallen monarch who might be suffered to die in peace; he was the symbol of the forces of reaction and despotism. "The Descent into Hell" not of the forlorn soul of a Bonaparte but of the idea which he had embodied is what mattered to the poet. In Paris, in 1869, Swinburne had expressed the hope to live to say "The Dog is dead." Now he wrote:

What shapes are these and shadows without end
That fill the night full as a storm of rain
With myriads of dead men and women slain,
Old with young, child with mother, friend with friend,
That on the deep mid wintering air impend,

Pale yet with mortal wrath and human pain,
Who died that this man dead now too might reign,
Towards whom their hands point and their faces bend?
The ruining flood would redden earth and air
If for each soul whose guiltless blood was shed
There fell but one drop on this one man's head
Whose soul tonight stands bodiless and bare,
For whom our hearts give thanks who put up prayer,
That we have lived to say, The Dog is dead.

The literature of defamation is never of the highest type; but if we must have curses, Swinburne in these sonnets and in later sonnets directed against the Czar, provides them both loud and deep. To object that Napoleon's sensitiveness to the horrors of Solferino was one of the causes of the Peace of Villafranca; that that peace probably avoided another war (with Prussia); that the need to placate his Catholic subjects forced the emperor to support the Papacy against Piedmont; and that Prussia, not France (though Swinburne could not know this) forced the issue in 1870 — to raise these and other well-founded objections is to take from this terrible sonnet and the others in like mood their value as symbols and to reduce them to mere political diatribes. Even as symbols they constitute one horn of the dilemma upon which the poet impales himself; for the difficulty of any philosophy approaching pantheism is to account for the existence of evil; and Swinburne, execrating the evil, admits its existence. The "holy spirit of man" brought forth strange fruit in the Bonapartes. The poet's loneliness, irritability, intemperance and violence during the middle-seventies account in part for these repellent outbursts.

Yet is was in the autumn of 1875 that he wrote "Erechtheus." This second drama on the Greek model is often compared with "Atalanta"; but the resemblance is formal only; in spirit "Erechtheus" belongs with "Songs before Sunrise." The metrical resourcefulness of the earlier tragedy reappears unabated though not quite so fresh; but the primary impression is no longer made by the wealth of rhythms. "Erechtheus" is severe, allusive, aloof, restrained, austere. Like the best of the "Songs" it displays a peculiar combination of surging energy with solidity of thought not often visible elsewhere in Swinburne's verse. The closely knit organization and symmetrical unity of the play (the result of a thorough study of Æschylus undertaken under Jowett's direction) are in surprising contrast to the but partially assimilated confusion of material in "Bothwell" which Swinburne had completed two years earlier.

The tragedy is based on the outline of Euripides' lost play on Erechtheus which is preserved by Lycurgus the orator.[1] Poseidon had borne enmity

[1] A fragment of Euripides (quoted by Lycurgus) in which Praxithea tells her daughter that she must be sacrificed for the city's sake is introduced by Swinburne in his tragedy in the lines beginning

Turn from me, turn thine eyes
A little from me.

against Athens since the citizens had preferred Athena's gift of the olive to his gift of the horse; and in the reign of Erechtheus, Eumolpus, the son of Poseidon, led the Thracians against the city. The king sent to Delphi to learn of the oracle how the attack might be repulsed and the city saved. The response was that the Athenians would prevail if Chthonia, daughter of the king, were sacrificed before the battle. Erechtheus reveals to his wife, Praxithea, the message of the oracle; and her reply is a thanksgiving to the gods that

> No eye but mine
> Weep of all women's in this broad land born
> Who see their land's deliverance; but much more,
> But most for this I thank them most of all,
> That this their edge of doom is chosen to pierce
> My heart and not my country's.[1]

Chthonia enters and her fate is revealed to her by her mother. There follows the splendid Oreithyia chorus:

> Out of the north wind grief came forth,
> And a shining of a sword out of the sea.[2]

[1] Swinburne evidently intended that Praxithea's noble words should recall by contrast the words of revolt expressed by Clytemnestra at the sacrifice of Iphigenia. Chthonia resembles Iphigenia; but Swinburne seems to have remembered Aristotle's criticism that Iphigenia, as portrayed by Euripides, exhibited at Aulis a weakness at first that is inconsistent with her subsequent courage. The criticism is shallow but it may have influenced Swinburne to portray Chthonia as courageous from the first moment of hearing the words of the oracle.

[2] This theme is introduced in strict accord with the principles of the Greek chorus, since the rape of Oreithyia, another daughter of Erechtheus, is an outlying portion of the myth.

Then enters the Herald of Eumolpus, challenging the Athenians and met by the king's defiance. The chorus gives expression to dread of the coming sacrifice; what man shall not fear to take so stainless a life? The parting of Chthonia and Praxithea leads to the central chorus, voicing the main mood of the tragedy, a lyrical utterance of the exalted enthusiasm that supports the queen and her daughter in their ordeal, together with a hymn to the Earth Mother to whom Chthonia is about to offer her life. The women depart; a messenger brings word of Chthonia's death; a second messenger, following hard upon the first, tells of the self-immolation of the two other daughters of Erechtheus, who have sacrificed themselves to seal their country's safety; the chorus chants the onrush of battle, its terrors and hopes for Athens, and ends with a prayer to the sun whose shining forth from the clouds is taken as a sign of coming victory. Then enters a Herald to proclaim that victory, but with the triumph marred by the king's death, stricken by the thunderbolt of Jove, wrathful for the defeat of his brother's son.[1] "What wilt thou say now of this weal and woe?" the Herald asks the queen. Praxithea's first words are: "I praise the gods for Athens!" But she has borne overmuch and her prayer is:

[1] Subsidiary details, such as the death of the two other daughters and the death of Erechtheus, Swinburne obtained from Apollodorus, Pausanias, Ovid or elsewhere. To introduce these additional deaths by violence was to risk the charge of exaggeration, even of melodrama, and though Swinburne employs them to justify the appearance of Athena, these sacrifices strike a false note.

Give me too
Death, and the sight of eyes that meet not mine. . . .
Be thou
Dear God and gracious to all souls alive,
Good to thine own seed also; let me sleep,
Father, my sleepless darkling day is done.

Athena appears[1] to give her blessing to the queen and to the citizens, and to prophesy the greatness of their city:

Thine shall be
The crown of all songs sung, of all deeds done
Thine the full flower for all time; in thine hand
Shall time be as a garland; not one leaf
Shall change or winter cast from out thy crown
Till all flowers wither in the world; thine eyes
Shall first in man's flash lightning liberty,
Thy tongue shall first say freedom.

A larger joy, a joy in the life of her people, surges through Praxithea's breast, and her last words are:

[1] The introduction of the goddess, a Euripidean *dea ex machina*, has seemed to some critics to strike another false note, perhaps because the incident is an almost solitary instance of the supernatural in all Swinburne's poetry. (For the brand in "Atalanta" is symbolic of purposeless fate; the supernatural in some of the "Border Ballads" is part of the literary *pastiche;* and in the Arthurian poems the supernatural is reduced almost to the vanishing point.) The objection is worth considering briefly. Horace, elaborating Aristotle's conception of the "machine", enunciated in the "Ars Poetica" the doctrine that a god should not be introduced into the action of a play unless a complication has arisen to justify it. Swinburne's introduction of Athena might be defended on the ground that the root of the conflict was in the rivalry of Athena and Poseidon. But he does not employ the device to bring about his dénouement, which is by definition the function of the *deus ex machina*. As in several of Euripides' tragedies, the divinity is introduced, not to "resolve" the action, but to further and emphasize that purging of the emotions which, according to Aristotle, is the function of tragedy. The divine epiphany at the close of "Erechtheus" instills the "peace and consolation" and "calm of mind" which come when all passion is spent.

> There is no grief
> Great as the joy to be made one in will
> With him that is the heart and rule of life
> And thee, God born of God; thy name is ours,
> And thy large grace more strong than our desire.

The drama closes with the rolling anapæsts of the chorus welcoming the friendship of the sea, no longer their enemy but the sharer in their fame.

Swinburne concentrates attention upon the lofty spirit of Praxithea and Chthonia. Mother and daughter show no cold stoicism; self-sacrifice does not quench maternal and filial love but rather renders each more ardent. The other characters are more slightly drawn, even Erechtheus himself being upon a lower plane of interest. The play is Æschylean in its admission of but two actors at one time upon the stage and in its introduction of the powers of earth and sea. The designedly archaistic language and style indicate Swinburne's close study of his model; and in tone, too, the play is Æschylean rather than Euripidean. For in contrast to the dark rebellious fatalism which sounds through the grace and glitter of "Atalanta", "Erechtheus" contains no abuse of the gods. To our minds the tragedy may seem to evolve from the petty and directionless cruelty of the old divinities; but the actors therein know otherwise:

> The soul runs reinless on sheer death,
> Whose grief or joy takes part against the gods.
> For what they will is more than our desire,
> And their desire is more than what we will.

Thus is put into a form harmonious with Hellenic tragedy a thought that runs beneath the surface of "Songs before Sunrise." The play is, as a recent critic has admirably phrased it, "a picture of the unhesitating sacrifices which idealised human nature should make to the conception of corporate freedom." Man lives under "the perfect law of liberty"; but that law requires the subordination of the individual to the general good. A decade later Swinburne was to return to the same theme in "Marino Faliero." The Doge who joins in a conspiracy against the State of which he is titular head and who before his death gains a vision large enough to realize that the cause for which he had striven is the cause of humanity is, like the little group in far-off legendary Athens, among the "Pilgrims" who march side by side with Mazzini, "life being so little and death so good to give." The antiphonal lamentation for Chthonia is the fine flower of the seed planted by Mazzini in Swinburne's imagination:

Children shalt thou bear to memory that to man shall bring forth none;
Yea, the lordliest that lift eyes and hearts and songs to meet the sun,
Names to fire men's ears like music till the round world's race be run.

We have now to recapitulate the several interrelated ideas which are at the foundation of Swinburne's poetry during the period dealt with in this chapter. From his youthful opinions there has been some departure but it has been in the main a matter of development rather than of change. The febrile temperament expressed in the early eroticism (itself a gesture on behalf of freedom) is now turned to noble account and remains as an enthusiasm which for all its exaggeration is wholly sincere. The poet has well-nigh outlived negation; his purely negative and destructive poetry is but a clearing of the ground in preparation for his poetry of affirmation. The repeated attacks upon the diety — God, who is but "the shade cast by the soul of man"; God, against whom sentence has gone forth; God, the conception of whom is evolved from human fear — are a consistent and essential part of his thought. But the emphasis is no longer on negation and revolt.

A passage in Meredith's "France, 1870" summarizes the philosophy discoverable sometimes as scattered fragments and again as well-reasoned entities in Swinburne's poetry:

> Lo, Strength is of the plain root-Virtues born;
> Strength shall ye gain by service. . . .
> It is the offspring of the modest years,
> The gift of sire to son, through those firm laws
> Which we name Gods; which are the righteous cause,
> The cause of man, and manhood's ministers.

These lines are precisely contemporaneous with "Songs before Sunrise." Both poets advocate a philosophy of serene acceptance of what *is*. Yet

Swinburne sees more than the blind purposelessness that was all that confronted the searching gaze of James Thomson, whose meditations at the very period when Swinburne was writing the "Songs" took this shape:

I find no hint throughout the Universe
Of good or ill, of blessing or of curse;
  I find alone Necessity Supreme;
With infinite Mystery, abysmal, dark,
Unlighted ever by the faintest spark
  For us the flitting shadows of a dream.

But of his "Pilgrims" Swinburne sang:

One thought they have, even love; one light,
Truth, that keeps clear the sun by night;
One chord, of faith as of a lyre;
One heat, of hope as of a fire;
One heart, one music, and one might,
One flame, one altar, and one choir.

Confronting life, he bears witness to the Trinity: Nature, Man, and Liberty. From contemplation of these three supreme facts come the three great motives of this poetry. Already in his youthful verse there had been a sense of the goodness of Earth which might have developed into pure pantheism. Traces of pantheism remain, but no more than traces, for on the one hand there is the recognition of evil and on the other the glorification of the "holy spirit of man" whereby he singles out one element in the universe in lieu of worshipping the All. The human soul is the highest manifestation of the spirit in Nature. The life of man is seen to have a continuity apart from the individual life. This Oversoul is the only true God —

Not each man of all men is God, but God is the fruit of the whole.

The only immortality vouchsafed to the individual is that of influence; and this present life is not a period of probation for a life-to-come but a rounded whole, complete in itself, to be passed in service or disservice. *Im Gatzen, Guten, Schönen resolut zu leben* is to vibrate with the glory of life and hence to share in that immortality which is in the Life Force. Freedom is the essential complement of the human soul, the essence of life, the symbol of power and beauty, faith and courage, as illimitable as the sea, as dazzling as the sun, fair and immortal, the Triumphant Mother who demands sacrifice in her service. With an intensity of devotion unmatched elsewhere in English verse, save in occasional passages in Blake and Shelley, Swinburne dedicated himself to Liberty:

I that have love and no more
Give you but love of you, sweet:
  He that hath more, let him give;
He that hath wings, let him soar:
Mine is the heart at your feet
  Here, that must love you to live.

Liberty is the appointed destiny of mankind, prompting the complete extension of personality. But it is not an unconditioned gift; it carries with it obligations. The ideal is expressed in Meredith's noble words: "A soul made strong for divinity of service."

CHAPTER FOUR

Old Thoughts in New Moods

The poetry inspired by the republican ideal has now been passed in review without the interruption or digression of biography; and it is time to resume briefly the outward events of Swinburne's troubled middle years from the time of "Poems and Ballads" to the beginning of his life at Putney.

The scandal and notoriety occasioned by the volume of 1866 demoralized Swinburne and his dissipation increased. The first symptoms of ill health manifested themselves. The years 1867 and 1868 marked the high tide of republican fervor, but by 1869 there were signs of dejection and languor. In 1868, during a sojourn at Étretât, he was nearly drowned (an experience afterwards memorialized in "Ex-Voto"); and in 1869 he passed a happy time at Vichy with Sir Frederick Leighton, Sir Richard Burton and Adelaide Kemble (Mrs. Sartoris). During these years he saw much of the Burtons whenever they were in England; association with the robust, gallant and audacious adventurer led to a way of life for which the poet's frail physique was not suited. He drank brandy, sometimes in company, more often in the solitude of his chambers. He began to assume that arrogance of deportment which marked his middle years, affronting old friends and sometimes verging upon insult to casual acquaintances.[1] "I knew Swinburne intimately," writes Julian Field of these years. "He came down to Oxford many times when I was at Merton (1869–1873), and how drunk he used to get!" There is a vivid picture of him in the "Life of Sir Charles Dilke" which may be quoted in lieu of a more extended account of this unhappy period:

A wreck of glasses attested the presence of Swinburne. He compared himself with Shelley and Dante; repeatedly named himself with Shelley and Dante to the exclusion of all other poets; assured me that he was a great man only because he had been properly flogged at Eton, the last time for reading "The Scarlet Letter" when he should have been reading Greek; confessed to never having read Helvétius though he talked of Diderot and Rousseau, and finally informed me that two glasses of green Chartreuse were a perfect antidote to one of yellow, or two of yellow to one of green. It was immediately after this that Watts-Dunton took charge of him and reduced him to absolute respectability.

Sir Edmund Gosse, who became intimate with Swinburne in the early seventies, has exhaustively and inimitably portrayed him as he was during these years. To his "Life", supplemented by the extremely entertaining chapter in "Portraits and

[1]The first alarming instance of such behavior occurred in 1865 when at a second meeting with Tennyson, Swinburne's conduct was so boisterous and braggart as to invite admonition and reproof from Lord Houghton.

Sketches", the reader should turn for a great variety of illuminating anecdotes of the poet. To repeat them here would be simply to do again and less well what Sir Edmund has done perfectly and once for all. We must therefore pass over such incidents as the poet's enthusiastic organization of a celebration, long overdue, of the centenary of Landor's birth, a similar celebration in honor of Lamb, his reading of "Bothwell" into the small hours of the night, his excitement over the Balkan Question, over a visit to the Channel Islands, over the dramas of Chapman, over his controversies with Buchanan and Furnivall. Many of Swinburne's old friends had fallen away from him, and for a while his way of life often cut him off almost completely from his family, though in so far as it was possible they continued to take anxious care of him. Jowett remained a loyal friend, entertaining him in Scotland, reading with him, and at Oxford guarding him from the deleterious influence, as Jowett thought it, of Walter Pater. Despite intermissions caused by fast living and ill health, he accomplished in these years a surprising amount of poetical, dramatic and critical work. In the background, watching over him, was the benign, patient and increasingly influential figure of Walter Theodore Watts.[1]

We have now to pass in review the poetical work

[1]Watts did not assume the hyphenated name Watts-Dunton till late in life; but by that name he is remembered and it is more convenient to use it, as I have done, throughout this book.

of this period other than that inspired by Mazzini. This review will take us somewhat beyond the beginning of the "Putney Period", but the narrative of Watts-Dunton's "rescue" of the poet, together with an estimate of the "rescuer", is postponed to our final chapter.

The early years of mutiny faded gradually into the long later period of acquiescence, the two phases overlapping at points. Sometimes Swinburne's poetic mind outruns, as it were, his actual daily life, and he is found composing lyrics or meditative pieces of serene, detached and mellow melancholy in intervals of the riot and license which he continued to practise at an age when men of discretion have put such ways of life behind them. At other times echoes of the old amorousness are still heard in his music. He had remained in the adolescent stage for a longer period than most men; and now, as has often been remarked, he, the symbol of flaming and rebellious youth, was becoming prematurely middle-aged. That he was himself conscious of this change many poems suggest, as also that he was aware of his detachment from ordinary men. Throughout his poetry there is heard during these middle years a note, ever and anon, of frustration, of loneliness, and of futility. The tide of republican sentiment quickly passed its full, the accomplished fact of the Italian monarchy and the rivalries and intrigues of the Third French Republic alienating his sympathies from the political causes to which he had once dedicated his genius. In "Poems and Ballads, Second Series" (1878) all this is apparent.[1]

The prevalent mood is one of withdrawal from life around him into the intimate world of meditations and memories and into the ever-expanding world of books. The atmosphere is personal, reminiscent, elegiac, literary. Old thoughts are called again to mind in a mood of wistful serenity.

> Out of the world of the unapparent dead
> Where the lost Aprils are and the lost Mays,

the poet summons up memories of his own lost youth, "the lovely April of his prime." The new mood is perfectly reflected in the changing character of Swinburne's prosody. The tambourines, cymbals, kettledrums, timbrels and taborets of 1866 are heard no longer, nor the trumpet tones of "Songs

[1] This volume must not be judged as the work of the time immediately before the beginning of the life at Putney. It is a gathering together of the miscellaneous poetry of a decade or more. Though its arrangement and publication were accomplished just before the complete breakdown that led to Watts-Dunton's intervention, the best poems had all been written some time earlier. "Ave atque Vale", the poem which gives weight and tone to the entire collection, was written in 1867; "At a Month's End" is of 1871; the "Memorial Verses" on Gautier, of 1872; the exquisite song "Love laid his sleepless head", of 1874; "A Vision of Spring in Winter", of 1875; "The Last Oracle" and "A Forsaken Garden", of 1876; and only "Ex-Voto" and some of the translations from Villon of so late a date as 1877.

before Sunrise"; but in their place there sounds a new music, as of a flute, not less melodious but tenderer.[1]

Even in "At a Month's End", that superb lyric of personal amorous experience upon which may be detected "the print and perfume of old passion", the mood is reminiscent:

For the unlit shrine is hardly lonely
As one the old fire forgets to touch.

Technically this poem is one of Swinburne's supreme achievements, a marvel and delight forever. The metrical foundation of this brilliant example of how varied a combination of rhythms he could produce on one basic pattern is iambic, but there is a liberal use of anapæstic "equivalents", and the "throw-back" accomplished by the double rhymes in each first and third line gives an effect of trochees eddying up and mingling with the main iambic stream of the music. Rigid unimaginative scansion destroys the intricate melody. The poem opens:

The night last night was strange and shaken:
More strange the change in you and me.
Once more for the old love's love forsaken,
We went out once more toward the sea.

[1] This change was noted at once by John Payne, who in a "Villanelle (with a copy of Swinburne's 'Poems and Ballads, Second Series') " wrote:

The thrush's singing days are fled, . . .
The nightingale shall sing instead.

For the old love's love-sake dead and buried,
One last time, one more and no more,
We watched the waves set in, the serried
Spears of the tide storming the shore.

In this second stanza trochaic beats are heard in the first two lines; the third is a succession of severe iambs; and there is a wonderful "resolved stress" in the fourth. These are phenomena characteristic of the entire poem. The theme is scarcely sturdy enough to carry the weight of a technique so gorgeous. It is a study in the psychology of satiety: the poet (a "sea-mew" as in several other poems) must leave his mistress (a "sleek black pantheress"). Sky and wind and waters serve as the setting for a passing passion.

This celebrated piece is the outstanding example of the "overlapping" of the poet's first period upon his second. More characteristic of the volume of 1878 is, however, the poem with which the collection opens: "The Last Oracle." The legend of the death of the Emperor Julian appealed to Swinburne's imagination. There is historical as well as symbolic significance in Swinburne's praise of Apollo, for Julian, as Gibbon tells us, was a special devotee of the Sun God. He made a last attempt to save Hellenism from the wreck effected by Christianity, and died acknowledging his failure and recognizing "the drift of the wild world's tide." Formerly it had seemed to Swinburne that amid the flux of all things the law of Change was alone lasting: "Nought may endure save Mutability." Later in the development of his thought the human spirit seems stable amid Change. And now, refining upon that idea, he discovers steadfastness in one aspect of human achievement: in Art and Song. His affirmation of the immortality of Apollo is the sign of his confidence in the eternity of Art:

> For thy kingdom is past not away,
> Nor thy power from the place thereof hurled;
> Out of heaven they shall cast not the day,
> They shall cast not out song from the world.

He is not so ready as once he was to deny the possibility of personal immortality; there are puzzling fluctuations and vacillations in his reveries upon that problem; but of the immortality of Art he is assured. This idea connects "The Last Oracle" with the numerous elegies in "Poems and Ballads, Second Series."

"In the Bay", the first fruit in verse of Swinburne's devotion to the Elizabethan dramatists, stands next: a glorification of the spirit of Marlowe with tributes to Webster, Ford and "the twin-souled brethren of the single wreath", and with the assumption of the benign overlordship of Shakespeare. A description of sunset across a bay leads on to a meditation upon the possibility of a land beyond the sunset, where are gathered together those mighty spirits whose stars rise not and set not, because their day is eternal.

"Ave atque Vale" is generally and rightly regarded as the greatest of Swinburne's shorter poems. It has so often been compared to the other three greatest elegies in English that not much need be said on this point. It has not the organ music, the depth of scorn, and the Christian assurance of "Lycidas"; nor the piercing indignation and soaring mysticism of "Adonais"; nor the intimate tenderness and wistful modernity of "Thyrsis." In one respect, however, it makes a more profound impression than these other three, an impression peculiarly appropriate to the theme of death. This is difficult to analyze; some critics have been content with the word "macabre"; but it is more than that. It is a sense of profound penetration into the mystery of death, of straining with "foiled earnest ear" and with "eluded eyes" after the departed spirit. Pater, in his essay on Michelangelo, attempts to express the same "range of sentiment" which Swinburne is groping after in this elegy:

> Dumb inquiry over the relapse after death into the formlessness which preceded life, the change, the revolt from that change, then the correcting, hallowing, consoling rush of pity; at last, far off, thin and vague, yet not more vague than the most definite thoughts men have had through three centuries on a matter that has been so near their hearts, the new body — a passing light, a mere intangible, external effect, over those too rigid or too formless faces; a dream that lingers a moment,

retreating in the dawn, incomplete, aimless, helpless; a thing with faint hearing, faint memory, faint power of touch; a breath, a flame in the doorway, a feather in the wind.

The poet, upon the same quest of a vision of "the new body", follows the footprints of that "sweet strange elder singer", Charles Baudelaire, venturing *nell'aura che trema . . . ove non è luca, per luogo eterno*, where straining his eyes to behold *gli antichi spiriti dolenti*, he is conscious only of

Some dim derision of mysterious laughter
  From the blind tongueless warders of the dead,
  Some gainless glimpse of Proserpine's veiled head,
Some little sound or unregarded tears.

The elegy is more heavily charged with imagery than is usual in Swinburne's verse, and that imagery is drawn largely and appropriately from "Les Fleurs du Mal." A passage in the critique on Baudelaire published in the *Spectator* in 1862 anticipates the main movement of the thought of the poem:

Throughout the chief part of this book, he has chosen to dwell mainly upon sad and strange things — the weariness of pain and the bitterness of pleasure — the perverse happiness and wayward sorrows of exceptional people. It has the languid lurid beauty of close and threatening weather — a heavy heated temperature, with dangerous hothouse scents in it; thick shadows of cloud about it, and fire of molten light.

These "fervid languid glories" of tropical skies bring to bloom the flowers of evil —

> Half-faded fiery blossoms, pale with heat
> And full of bitter summer —

fitter offerings upon the dead poet's tomb than "the gleanings of a northern shore."[1] They call to mind "*le pays parfumé que le soleil caresse*" whose landscapes, seen once in youth, haunted Baudelaire's imagination. The thought then wanders from the "heavier suns in mightier skies" to the sea that sobs around Lesbos, not knowing that beneath the Leucadian promontory Sappho, "the supreme head of song", sleeps.[2] In similar fashion image and allusion succeed each other as the elegy progresses in slow and solemn measure. Vague speculation upon the world of the departed suggests the question:

> Hast thou found place at the great knees and feet
> Of some pale Titan-woman like a lover,
> Such as thy vision here solicited?—

that vision which Baudelaire had described in

[1]This contrast between south and north is, as I have remarked, very typical of Swinburne. By the "white wandering waste of sea far north" he heard of Landor's death at Florence. From within the "northern summer's fold" he sent his thoughts southward to Siena. The little poem called "Relics" in this same collection, inspired by tender recollections of San Gimignano, was originally called "North and South."

[2] The association of ideas is here not obvious and has puzzled some commentators (Edward Thomas, for example); but we have only to remember "Anactoria" and the splendid "Sapphics" and the later poem "On the Cliffs"; and then couple these recollections with Baudelaire's "Lesbos" (remembering meanwhile that the original rejected title of "Les Fleurs du Mal" was "Les Lesbiennes") and the links in the chain of associations become clear.

"La Géante." Still in pursuit of the departed spirit, the poet ventures onward into the "low lands where the sun and moon are mute" (*dove il sol tace*); but the "thin flame", the "wind and air", of the dead elude him and his hand grasps but the shadow of the swift spirit, "the shut scroll" of his song. These memories and melodies he salutes while through his ears rolls the sound of many mourners, among whom he stands, doing reverence to the gods of the dead and laying across the tomb of his master "a curl of severed hair", as did Orestes across the tomb of Agamemnon — "a tress for his upbringing and one for his mourning." The thought of the tears that fall "down the opening leaves of holy poets' pages" (the beginning of the "Choëphoræ") suggests that no Orestes or Electra is left to mourn for this dead poet; but "the most high Muses" weep and "our God's heart yearns." Then come, as in "Lycidas" and "Adonais", the mourners for the dead. Not "Camus, reverend sire" nor Saint Peter; not the "wingéd Persuasions and veiled Destinies" of Shelley; but Apollo and Aphrodite. The lord of light and music will, by the immortality vouchsafed to great verse, save this dust "from blame and from forgetting"; and with him in the paths of Lethe weeps "that obscure Venus of the hollow hill", the "bitter and luxurious god" who had compelled Baudelaire, a sad and second Tannhäuser, into the Horselberg.

No choral salutation, as in the music-drama which Baudelaire had interpreted so magnificently, will lure to light this spirit; and whither he has gone

> Shall death not bring us all as thee one day
> Among the days departed?

The note of hopefulness upon which the English elegy traditionally closes is absent from this poem which ends in austere contemplation of the inevitability of death:

> For thee, O now a silent soul, my brother,
> Take at my hand this garland, and farewell.
> Thin is the leaf, and chill the wintry smell,
> And chill the solemn earth, a fatal mother,
> With sadder than the Niobean womb,
> And in the hollow of her breasts a tomb.
> Content thee, howsoe'er, whose days are done;
> There lies not any troublous thing before,
> Nor sight nor sound to war against thee more,
> For whom all winds are quiet as the sun,
> All waters as the shore.

Swinburne never fashioned elsewhere a more fitting medium for his thought and mood than the stanza of "Ave atque Vale." Its principal elements are two quatrains, rhyming *a-b-b-a*, separated by a couplet. The effect of this intermediate couplet is to bring the music to a pause, after which it mournfully renews itself. The second quatrain is followed by a truncated concluding line, echoing the interior rhymes of that quatrain and firmly molding the entire stanza.

To turn from this elegy to the "Memorial Verses" on Théophile Gautier is to fall to a lower level of poetry. The lines seem done to order,[1] as though the poet (who at Ford Madox Brown's house and elsewhere in London associated with a group of devotees of Gautier) felt compelled to pay homage to the dead master and to act his part in the cult. The theme reaches back to "The Last Oracle": the immortality of the creations of the imagination. With light touch, more satisfying than the diffuse allegory with which the poem opens, Swinburne suggests rather than describes Gautier's chief writings, thus furnishing a first example of a genre he was from now on to work in frequently: the "critical elegy", as Sir Edmund Gosse has called it, in which in lieu of conventional tributes there is offered an imaginative and laudatory summary of the subject's achievements.[2]

There are other elegies in this collection, notably

[1] They were originally published with several other poems by Swinburne (in English, French, Latin and Greek) in Alphonse Lemerre's memorial anthology "Le Tombeau de Théophile Gautier."

[2] The metrical scheme is interesting: a novel combination of the Omar stanza (*a-a-b-a*) and the Italian *terza rima;* that is, the third line of each stanza (which in Fitzgerald's Omar is rhymeless) rhymes with the first, second and fourth of the next stanza, and so on: *a-a-b-a*, *b-b-c-b*, *c-c-d-c*, and so on. This new meter Swinburne called *quarta rima*. Obviously there are dangers lurking in it; and Swinburne was well aware of them, for he wrote to Morley: "The metrical scheme is, I think, not bad, but the danger of such meters is diffuseness and flaccidity. I perceive this one to have a tendency to the dulcet and luscious form of verbosity which has to be guarded against, lest the poem lose its foothold and be swept off its legs, sense and all, down a flood of effeminate and monotonous music, or be lost and spilt in a maze of draggle-tailed melody."

"Inferiae" in memory of his father, Admiral Swinburne, and the lovely lines in memory of "Barry Cornwall". But these we must pass over to come to the tributes to the living. First among these is the "Dedication" to Sir Richard Burton, reminiscent of the days in France in 1869.[1] "A Birth-Song" for one of the Rossetti children marks the first appearance in Swinburne's poetry of a theme that was to be wearisomely repeated: the praise of children and of babyhood. Two sonnets are addressed to Victor Hugo, and another much more notable pair to Cardinal Newman and Thomas Carlyle, "Two Leaders", one "the last flower of Catholic love", the other "the storm-god of the northern foam":

> Honour not hate we give you, love not fear,
>   Last prophets of past kind, who fill the dome
> Of great dead Gods with wrath and wail, nor hear
>   Time's word and man's: "Go honoured hence, go home,
> Night's childless children; here your hour is done;
> Pass with the stars, and leave us with the sun.

In two sonnets in honor of Giordano Bruno there reverberate echoes of "Songs before Sunrise";

[1] In volume iii of the Bonchurch Edition, which includes the second and third series of "Poems and Ballads", the "Songs of the Springtides", and the "Border Ballads", the "Dedication" of the second series to Burton is removed from its proper place and seems to embrace the entire volume. The "Dedication" of the third series to W. B. Scott is omitted altogether, and the "Epilogue" to the third series is misplaced, following the "Songs of the Springtides." This deplorable confusion is rendered worse by the omission from the table of contents of the individual titles of these three volumes of verse.

and in two others, on "The White Czar", the invective of "Dirae" has become contaminated with jingoism.[1]

Elsewhere the spirit of serene reminiscence is undisturbed. There are evocations of the past that are almost Proustian in their sense that the world of memory contains all that abides amid the transitoriness of life. This thought receives most exquisite expression in the Keatsian harmonies of "A Vision of Spring in Winter", where the poet, watching for the returning spring, looks back upon other springs now gone forever. He asks for no return of youth and hope and morning, for "no flower thought once too fair for death", for "no leaf once plucked or once fulfilled desire." A sense of oncoming age shadows this beautiful poem; and the *Memento Mori* is the theme of the solemn stanzas "Ex-Voto"; while in "A Forsaken Garden" the encroaching sea along the English coast is the type of Time that devours years and flowers and love and lovers. Out of hearing of the cataract of greedy Acheron he retires into the substantial world of books, whence, for the remainder of his life, he was to draw the themes of a large proportion of his poems.

A spirited "Ballad of François Villon" is an

[1] The attacks on Russia and the accompanying sonnets on Poland and on the patriot Kossuth should be read along with the prose "Note of an English Republican on the Muscovite Crusade" (1876). Together these four sonnets make up the only group of political poems in the collection and are out of harmony with all the rest.

appropriate introduction to the group of translations from Villon included in this collection.[1] In this same year (1878) John Payne's complete "Villon" was published. The compact strength of the French is reproduced more accurately in Payne's rendering, but in Swinburne's there is more of the original melody left undisturbed.[2] With the Villon translations may be associated "The Complaint of Lisa", another example of Swinburne's reworking of old material. Founded on the story in the "Decameron" (X, vii) of how Lisa loved the king, its chief interest is technical, for in form it is a double sestina. On the difficult art of sestina-writing there is no room to expatiate here, but it may be said that to write a double sestina far more than doubles the difficulty of the problem.

"Poems and Ballads, Second Series" is, then, Swinburne's farewell to his youth, a farewell, too, to the world from the threshold, as it were, of Watts-Dunton's home at Putney. Hither he retired in 1879; but the three volumes of verse

[1] The vogue of verses in "Old French Form" was at its height in the later eighteen-seventies. It had been started in France by Banville and Richepin and brought into England by Calverley, Dobson, Lang and Gosse. Parallel to and partly in consequence of this fashion went the vogue of Villon versions, begun long since by Rossetti, continued, though privately, by Swinburne in the early sixties, imitated by Lang in some of his "Ballads and Lyrics of Old France" (1872), and reaching its climax in Payne's complete rendering of Villon. The researches of Auguste Vitu and Auguste Longnon in the eighteen-seventies did much to stimulate interest in Villon.

[2] Swinburne withheld his version of the "Ballade de la Belle Heaulmière aux Filles de joie", which was first published in the "Posthumous Poems" of 1917. His forceful rendering of the "Ballade de Villon et de la Grosse Margot" is accessible only in a privately printed pamphlet.

published in 1880 may be included within the limits of this chapter. To them we now turn.

"The Heptalogia, or the Seven against Sense. A Cap with Seven Bells"[1] was published anonymously and not acknowledged until its inclusion in the Collected Edition of 1904. These parodies were written at widely separated intervals, that on Patmore dating from 1859. "The Person in the House" is so excellent as scarcely to be distinguished from Patmore at his most namby-pamby. "The Poet and the Woodlouse" reproduces while it exaggerates eccentricities of Mrs. Browning's thought and style without caricaturing any one poem. "John Jones's Wife" is a more direct take-off on Browning. In "The Higher Pantheism in a Nutshell" Swinburne ridicules the vague and insubstantial metaphysics of Tennyson's "Higher Pantheism." The "Sonnet for a Picture" makes good fun of Rossetti's mannerisms; and in the much-praised but to my taste tedious "Nephelida" Swinburne parodies his own excessive redundancy and alliteration. The "Last Words of a Seventh-Rate Poet" stands apart from the other six pieces. An attack on the second Lord Lytton ("Owen Meredith"), it is the only parody that displays malice in its composition. Various reasons have been

[1] By an unfortunate blunder the title of this collection is given in the Bonchurch Edition merely as "The Heptalogia, etc.", an editorial memorandum indicating the position of the book in the edition being reproduced *verbatim*.

suggested for his violent prejudice against the son of a man who had befriended him when he needed friendship. The most reasonable explanation is that Watts-Dunton, who had been snubbed by Lytton, encouraged the attack. This really astonishing *tour de force* requires for its appreciation more knowledge of Lytton's poetry than most people possess now-a-days; and it suffers from the fate of all satire directed against ephemeralities: to be appreciated by contemporaries and in a later age to be kept above the waters of oblivion only by the bladders of commentary.[1]

The two volumes of serious poetry published in the same year are characterized by a lack of restraint, a growing verbosity, an incoherence, and a flatulence and feebleness that alienated from

[1] I relegate the requisite commentary to this footnote. Swinburne seizes upon the two least defensible characteristics of Lytton's verse: its incredible, never-ending fluency and its plagiarisms from other poets. The parody is modelled on Lytton's "Last Words." Swinburne has studied Lytton's writings with cruel care, for his mannerisms, his *penchant* (as he would himself have said) for French phrases, his glimpses of "high life" and the *demimonde*, and his conveyings from other poets are mercilessly exposed. To understand such lines as:

'Tis a dark-purple sort of a moonlighted kind of a midnight, I know;
You remember those verses I wrote on Irene, from Edgar A. Poe?

one needs to know that Lytton's "Count Rinaldo Rinaldi" begins:

'Tis a dark-purple moonlighted midnight,

that his heroine is named Irene, and that the cadences of the piece are lifted straight from Poe's "Ulalume." Swinburne's poem ends with a "Specimen of the Speaker's [*i.e.*, Lytton's] Original Compositions", a stanza imitating grotesquely Tennyson's "Come into the Garden, Maud." So difficult is it to understand outmoded parody that even Mr. Wise misunderstands the point of this concluding stanza and in his "Bibliography" describes it as a parody of Tennyson. It is, of course, another thrust at Lytton's habit of plagiarizing other poets.

Swinburne many admirers of his earlier verse. It is likely that these traits are due in part to the poet's slow recovery from illness. The two books were unfortunate in the time of their appearance which coincided approximately not only with Rossetti's "Ballads and Sonnets" but with "Ballads and Other Poems", that wonderful rebirth of Tennyson's genius, and with Browning's "Dramatic Idyls, Second Series." The two greatest poets of the age were now emerging from the partial obscurity which had shadowed them for the past decade and were assuming the preëminence which they were not again to lose till death. Swinburne's new volumes served to make conspicuous the gulf fixed between those two poets and himself.

"Thalassius", of which I have spoken at the beginning of this book, is the first of the "Songs of the Springtides." Apart from its value as autobiography the poem has great beauties but they are apparent only to the reader who is already familiar with Swinburne's life, character and poetry. The form, an ode in irregular stanzas with irregular rhyme-arrangement (two dangerous experiments that opened the door wider for the fatal fluency), conceals rather than reveals the autobiographical interest. "On the Cliffs", which follows, contains passages of rhetorical vigor and some wonderful renderings of the fragments of Sappho; but these are overwhelmed in the tide of verbiage upon which the tenuous idea is tossed about. "The Garden of

Cymodoce", a memorial of a visit to Sark in 1876, is an irregular ode interrupted several times by sequences of strophes and antistrophes. Few readers probably have persevered to the close of this spilth of words. After a long description of the island (into which is introduced the notion, reminiscent of "Erechtheus", that it was to Sark that Boreas carried his bride Oreithyia), comes the inevitable thought that it was to the Channel Islands that Hugo came as an exile; and we have a passage of repulsive invective against the memory of Napoleon III, shockingly out of place in this poem of nature's loveliness, and then a return to Hugo with a simile of Prometheus on his rock which we would willingly spare. Even yet we have not done with Hugo, for the volume closes with the quite intolerable "Birthday Ode" for the master's seventy-eighth anniversary. Here Swinburne attempts the feat of suggesting, without actually naming, all Hugo's works; the notes supply the titles of some forty-six volumes. "Periphrase", says Martin Scriblerus, "is another great aid to Prolixity; being a confused circumlocutory manner of expressing a known idea, which should be so mysteriously couched as to give the reader the pleasure of guessing what it is the author can possibly mean."

In "Studies in Song" a like tribute is paid to Landor, for in the "Song" for his centenary Swinburne manages in fifty sixteen-line stanzas to refer to all Landor's most noteworthy works without naming any of them. Much misdirected enthusiasm was wasted upon this most unsingable of songs.

If "the noble pleasure of praising" is here gratified to the utmost, the capacity for vituperation is at the full in three sonnets on "The Launch of the Livadia" (the Czar's pleasure yacht). This short sequence is the most powerful of all Swinburne's poems of hate, for the passion is held within bounds by a fine idea finely expressed. The decks, the cordage and the sails, the gulfs that are to receive the ship and the winds that are to waft her are alike filled with awful fate:

> Hope be far
> And fear at hand for pilot oversea
> With death for compass and despair for star,
> And the white foam a shroud for the White Czar.

The remainder of "Studies in Song" is made up mainly of poems of nature-description, a genre of which there are but few examples in Swinburne's earlier work but in which he was now to work constantly under the not very wise influence of Watts-Dunton. "Off Shore" and "Evening on the Broads" are rhapsodic studies of marine subjects, the latter of some importance to the student of prosody and containing some lovely word pictures of twilight atmosphere on sea and seacoast. But when Swinburne elected to sing the praises of the sea, as he did with increasing frequency from now on, he relinquished gladly the unnecessary function of thought and yielded himself to the rhythmic undulations and eddies of the verse that seems to take color and motion from its theme. The finest of these nature-pieces is "By the North Sea." The description of a coast where are

> Miles and miles and miles of desolation,
> Leagues on leagues on leagues without a change

cannot be continued through more than five hundred lines without becoming monotonous; yet a variety, not merely metrical, is introduced into this poem in which Swinburne celebrates the mysterious appeal of the Suffolk coast near Dunwich, "the sterile glitter and desolate fascination of the salt marshes, their minute splendours and barren beauties and multitudinous monotony of measureless expanse", as he was to describe the scene in his Dedicatory Epistle. In parts of this poem the effect suggested is that of a land which does not belong to humanity but touches the verge of another country inhabited by beings of another order. There is genuine power in the description of the slow encroachment of the sea upon an old church and churchyard: the passage (beginning "Here is all the end of all their glory") is too long to quote, but the reader who turns to it will find it vigorous and curiously macabre. The effect of the phenomenon upon the poet's imagination may be better appreciated if we realize that within the modern period more than thirty towns along this coast have been swallowed by the sea.[1]

The miscellaneous poems included in the "Tristram" volume of 1882 are in the main of second-rate interest, but among them is the strictly regular Pindaric ode "Athens" which Swinburne ranked with the later less classically regulated ode on the Armada at the summit of his work, declaring in his Dedicatory Epistle that "By the test of these two poems I am content that my claims should be decided and my station determined as a lyric poet in the higher sense of the term." The desire to emulate Pindar has been the rock upon which many a vessel of modern verse has sunk. Swinburne's estimate of the worth of "Athens" is certainly far too high; despite the formal excellence of strophe, antistrophe and epode in regular sequence, the ode is rhetorical rather than truly poetic; studied, self-conscious, pompously magniloquent. The drama of Athens was the drama of human liberty; on the fate of the violet-crowned city hung the fate of humanity. This is the theme of the ode: Athens the mother of civilization. Swinburne's Hellenism and republicanism mingle in a sort of counterpoint. In the opening an analogy is at once drawn between

[1]The same phenomenon is described in "A Forsaken Garden" and is turned to magnificent account at the close of "Tristram of Lyonesse." Watts-Dunton, in whose "Aylwin" it is described elaborately, may have drawn Swinburne's attention to it.

Athens and England; and then an appeal is abruptly introduced to the modern Greeks to be worthy of their forefathers and to defend themselves against the Turks without depending upon the Cossacks. The spirit of ancient Greece endures in Song: thus is introduced a survey of the tragedies of Æschylus and Sophocles, followed by a disproportionately brief passage on Aristophanes. At the close the poet turns anew to the analogy between Hellas and England. A new note sounds through the ode: the *motif* of British imperialism, arrogantly expressed.[1]

Various personal, memorial and "literary" poems were published along with "Tristram." Carlyle's death inspired a sonnet on "the stormy sophist with his mouth of thunder"; and after the publication of the "Reminiscences" Swinburne's prejudice against Froude[2] and his fury at Carlyle's defamation of Coleridge and Lamb moved him to write the sonnets "After Looking into Carlyle's 'Reminiscences'." The sonnet "A Last Look" closes with something like magnanimity:

[1] This jingoism appears in many other poems in this collection: in a sonnet attacking the proposal to construct a Channel tunnel; in renewed expressions of hatred of Russia, inspired by Russian Anti-Semitism and by the assassination of Alexander II; in sonnets on the German *Kulturkampf*; and in a sonnet in which Swinburne congratulates England on Victoria's escape from an attempted assassination. "The calm crowned head that all revere" is a quaint phrase to come from the pen of the author of "The Eve of Revolution."

[2] Swinburne's intense dislike of Froude was partly inspired by the historian's interpretation of the character of Mary Stuart. He seems also to have believed that Froude had spread scandal about him. In 1866 he wrote for insertion in "Notes on Poems and Reviews" a Dryden-ish satire entitled "A Study" which he suppressed and which is published in Mr. Wise's "Bibliography."

Now, for all ill thoughts nursed and ill words given
Not all condemned, not utterly forgiven,
Son of the storm and darkness, pass in peace.
Peace upon earth thou knewest not; now, being dead,
Rest, with nor curse nor blessing on thine head,
Where high-strung hate and strenuous envy cease.[1]

There are also brief elegies on Dickens, Trelawny and Dante Rossetti. The baby-worship and child-worship first received full expression when Watts-Dunton's little nephew, Herbert Mason, came to live at Putney. The poems on Bertie's birthday and such pieces as "Herse" and "A Child's Laughter" are not without charm; but quite intolerable is "A Dark Month" in which the poet records day by day his loneliness during Bertie's absence. From this mawkishness one turns with relief to the "Sonnets on the English Dramatic Poets." Several of these, on Marlowe, Shakespeare and Webster,

[1] At Oxford Nichol brought Carlyle to Swinburne's special attention; a little later the poet's letters contain laudatory allusions to "Frederick the Great." But in 1866 he wrote the posthumously published essay entitled "Of Liberty, and Loyalty," prompted by Carlyle's Edinburgh inaugural and less directly by Ruskin's writings on social economy. Here he attacks the opinion that "by obedience instead of self-reliance, by drill instead of devotion, by force and not by faith, the world must find its redemption." In 1876 Carlyle's denunciation of the Turkophile policy of Disraeli occasioned Swinburne's "Note of an English Republican on the Muscovite Crusade" which attacks also Gladstone's policy as expressed in "The Bulgarian Horrors and the Question of the East." Swinburne's prose diatribe is supplemented by a satiric skit "The Ballad of Bulgarie" in which he depicts Gladstone, Bright and Carlyle sallying forth to do battle for the sake of Bulgaria. This satire is unfortunately not included in the Bonchurch Edition. About 1879 a series of unpublished and very indelicate pieces were written against Carlyle: "Old Malignity", "Les Mille et Une Crachats", and so forth. Many harsh allusions to the dead philosopher occur in the prose essays of the eighteen-eighties. Swinburne's last words on the subject, a brief apologia, are in the preface to the "Miscellanies" of 1886.

are well known; and the subtle characterization of plays and playwrights — Beaumont and Fletcher, who "sound like moonlight, mingling moan and mirth"; Ford, who "carved night and chiselled shadow"; Lyly, who resembles "a goldfinch in a twisted cage" — is decidedly pleasant. The appeal of such work cannot be wide, nor can such material, remote from life, ever form the substance of great art; yet such enthusiasms, when justified, carry with them something of the charm that inspired them. The fine flower of a like enthusiasm is the "Adieux à Marie Stuart" in which Swinburne recaptured for almost the last time all the old romantic fervor and beauty of his earlier verse. Lovely in form, tender in sentiment, gallant and chivalrous is this farewell to the "red star of boyhood's fiery thought", the "Queen once of Scots and ever of ours", to whom the poet had dedicated the most arduous labors of twenty years of his life.

CHAPTER FIVE

The Arthurian Poems

The story of Tristram is on the verge or fringes of "the Matter of Arthur" with which it had originally little if anything to do, but for centuries it has been loosely attached to Arthurian lore. Tristram and Iseult had haunted the imagination of Swinburne since boyhood. Even at Eton he seems to have made some sort of a beginning of a poem on the subject, and at Oxford, the influence of Morris turning his thoughts to the Middle Ages, he wrote the long fragment of "Queen Yseult." Morris, as his contribution to the Pre-Raphaelite decorations of the Oxford Union, had chosen the subject of the lovers, and from him Swinburne undoubtedly derived new inspiration, for his poem is painstakingly in the manner of Morris, the most elaborate, indeed, of the various bits of *pastiche* which survive to prove Swinburne's discipleship. Quaint and chaotic, studied and precious, tinged with an artificial ingenuousness that is totally foreign to Swinburne's mature style, labored in its color and decoration, "Queen Yseult" is of interest to-day only as a curiosity. It begins with the story of the fatal loves of Roland and Blanchefleur, the father and mother of Tristram; continues through Tristram's mission to Ireland; and comes to the accidental drinking of the fatal love-draught:

So the chaliced wine was brought,
And the drink of power that wrought
Change in face and change in thought . . .

As they drank in love and truth,
Lo, there grew in heart and mouth
As a hot and bitter drouth.

Then he bent towards her there,
And he knew that she was fair,
And he stooped and kissed her hair . . .

So was their great love begun,
Sitting silent in the sun,
Such a little thing was done.

The fragment continues through the years of Tristram's amorous delight with his lady, to the "maiden marriage" after his banishment, and breaks off after the vigil of Yseult of Ireland at Tintagel. Swinburne's faculty of self-criticism was sufficiently alert to detect the falsity of the poem and its derivative nature; and somewhat later in his Oxford years he began another version (of which a fragment called "Joyeuse Garde" survives) which shows that if still hesitating and uncertain (as the use of *terza rima* proves) he was at any rate freeing himself from the impediment of Morris' impetuous and overshadowing example. Thereafter the theme seems to have been "dropt into the deep well of unconscious cerebration" where it remained for many years. An awareness of the fact that Morris continued for long to dally with the idea of composing a poem on this subject may have caused Swinburne to withhold his hand. But his loyalty to Iseult, though for so long obscured, was not dead.

After the publication of Tennyson's "Holy Grail" in 1869 Swinburne wrote to Rossetti:

> I fell tooth and nail upon "Tristram and Iseult", and wrote an overture of the poem projected, all yesterday. My first sustained attempt at a poetic narrative may not be as good as "Gudrun", but if it doesn't lick the Morte d'Albert, I hope I may not die without extreme unction.[1]

It was not, then, Tennyson's version of the Tristram legend ("The Last Tournament", published December, 1871) but an earlier installment of "The Idylls of the King" that prompted Swinburne to return to his long-neglected subject. It is possible, however, that advance information as to the approaching publication of "The Last Tournament" led Swinburne to consent to the publication of his own "Prelude to an Unfinished Poem" in a holiday volume at the end of 1871; and it is certain that Tennyson's adoption of the debased form of the story found in Malory and his general degradation of the story confirmed Swinburne in his

[1]This letter to Rossetti of December 22, 1869, as printed by Hake and Compton-Rickett, is drastically expurgated. A passage promising to insert into "Tristram" anecdotes of "larks illustrative of the Alberto-Victorian purity of the court" of King Arthur has been omitted, as has an amazing torrent of eloquence on the subject of birching. A little later (February 12, 1870) he wrote to Rossetti that he hoped "to make the copulative passages of the poem more warm . . . than anything my chaste Muse has yet attempted."

decision to treat the great legend worthily. In the Dedicatory Epistle he says:

My aim was simply to present that story, not diluted and debased as it had been in our own time by other hands, but undefaced by improvement and undeformed by transformation, as it was known to the age of Dante wherever the chronicles of romance found hearing from Ercildoune to Florence; and not in the epic or romantic form of sustained or continuous narrative, but mainly through a succession of dramatic scenes or pictures with descriptive settings or backgrounds.

The episodic structure of "Tristram of Lyonesse" was, despite this assertion, probably not part of Swinburne's original design but rather the result of the intermittent fashion in which the poem was composed during more than a decade.[1] It was published in July, 1882. It should have been published alone; but the cautious Watts-Dunton, fearful of the effect of the amatory passages upon the public, insisted on the inclusion of a quantity of miscellaneous verse which deadened the impact of the title-poem.

Into the unplumbed depths of the controversy which has raged around the origin and rival versions of the Tristram legend it is fortunately unnecessary to descend here. Swinburne seems to

[1] In 1874 he busied himself with it; in March, 1877, the first canto appeared in the *Gentleman's Magazine;* and after "Mary Stuart" was off his hands (1881) he occupied himself with the poem whole-heartedly till its completion in April, 1882.

have made no direct use of either Eilhart or Gottfried, a fact that consorts with his lack of interest in German literature. The Anglo-Norman versions he seems to have known. He wisely rejects the Malory-Tennyson form of the death scene in favor of the earlier accounts, but he follows Malory in including the tale within the general Arthurian theme and from him he borrows several details. The Middle English "Sir Tristrem", in Sir Walter Scott's edition, was his primary source.[1]

The "Prelude" to "Tristram of Lyonesse" stands with "Ave atque Vale" and "Siena" at the summit of Swinburne's lyrical achievement. It is like nothing else in English poetry. It has been compared to "Epipsychidion", but though there is in it a tinge of Platonism reminiscent of Shelley and though the sensual rapture reaching through very fervor a supersensual plane is Shelleyan also, the dissimilarities are more marked than the resemblances. The theme of Swinburne's poem is Love, and Love is glorified in its opening, as it is in the Prelude to Wagner's "Tristan"[2]—Love, "the first and last of all things made"; the "blood within the veins of time"; the "root and fruit of terrene

[1] Paul de Reul suggests the possibility that Swinburne may have made use of the "Poëmes relatifs à Tristan", a collection published by Francisque Michel in 1835–1838.

[2] "Tristan und Isolde", finished in 1859, was performed entire for the first time in 1865; but the first London performance did not take place till 1882, a month only before the appearance of Swinburne's poem. Yet there are certain parallels between the poem and the music-drama that are astonishingly close if they are ascribed to coincidence only. I think Swinburne must have known Wagner's libretto. The roundel which he wrote upon "Tristan", accompanying another roundel on "Lohengrin", belongs to the following year, 1883.

things." This *motif* modulates into the torrential rhapsody on the zodiac of Love, the succession of constellations each presided over by a heroine of romance and each shining with various lights — the rose-red sign of Helen, the gold of Hero, the sapphire light of Alcyone, the opal of Iseult (set with beautiful appropriateness in April, the poet's birth month), and so on through the year.[1] Then, the music deepening, the poet, elaborating the old Propertian theme: *Sunt apud infernos tot milia formosarum*, seeks to pierce the mystery that has closed around these and all fair lovers:

They have the night, who had like us the day;
We, whom day binds, shall have the night as they.
We, from the fetters of the light unbound,
Healed from our wound of living, shall sleep sound.

From the wreck of time the poet will salvage something, and will give

From out my life to make their dead life live
Some days of mine, and blow my living breath
Between dead lips forgotten even of death.

In such a mood Browning began his master work:

The life in me abolished the death in things,
Deep calling unto deep: as then and there
Acted itself over again once more
The tragic piece.

The self-consciousness with which Swinburne begins his poem strikes a note which, despite the characteristically medieval list of women's names,

[1] Swinburne may have been aware of ancient traditional associations of the signs of the zodiac with various precious stones, but in the absence of any definite evidence it is useless to speculate upon his probable "sources" for the idea.

is distinctly modern. He aimed deliberately at creating a *magnum opus*, a more substantial achievement, greater in theme, in manner and in length than anything he had yet attempted, "the best", as he said in dedicating "Tristram" to Watts-Dunton, "I have to give." In the result there is an impression of strain, of constant effort after large effects, of attempting to sustain the whole at a consistently lofty level, in meter, diction, imagery and idea. At times success crowns this display of effort and energy; more often the faults of redundancy, flamboyance and incontinence which had been growing upon him mar the work. An insufficiency of purely narrative talent leads him to presuppose on the reader's part knowledge of the legend, the successive phases of which glimmer confusedly through the obscure though flaming magnificence of the style. In contrast to the ingenuous encyclopedic manner of the medieval story-tellers he presents a series of salient episodes, the significant moments in the love story, connected by narrative passages. The fundamental purpose is to sustain the theme of the "Prelude" which is Love: in the first canto, the dawn of passion; in the second, the fulfillment of love-longing; in the third, the yearning of Iseult for her absent lover; in the fourth, reunion; in the fifth (the marvelous "Iseult at Tintagel" which is the climax of the poem), the renewed yearning of Iseult to the choral accompaniment of wind and sea. The sixth canto, like much of the third, is pitched in a lower key. In the seventh a new *motif* — Fate — is introduced, but here also the theme of Love continues, this time the love of Iseult of the Fair Hands, love changed to jealousy and hate. The eighth canto is devoted to the life of Tristram in absence from Iseult of Ireland; and the last to Love-in-Death. Throughout, the interest is thus centered upon the love theme with a directness and exclusiveness equalled only by Wagner.[1]

All the resources of his flushed and brilliant imagery are employed by Swinburne to steep the poem in amorous rapture. The resolution with which the lovers embrace their doom, whole-

[1]Dramatic "relief" is sought but not very well obtained by introducing one or two unrelated episodes such as the story of King Arthur's incestuous love. In itself this passage is interesting as an indirect attack upon the Tennysonian conception of the "blameless king" but in the context it forms an irritating interruption of the narrative. In general Swinburne avoids needless complications. Thus, he barely touches on the story of Roland and Blanchefleur which he had treated lavishly in the early "Queen Yseult." He ignores the ingenuous marvels and picturesque anecdotage of the medieval romances, and refuses to become involved in details of antiquarian exactitude. He passes in silence over Tristram's adventures during the third visit to Ireland: the fight with the dragon and the second illness when he was nursed by Iseult. The dog which keeps Iseult company at Tintagel is a reminder that in early versions Tristram gives Iseult a hound which has the magical power to keep her from harm. He wisely omits the grotesque ordeal by fire to which Mark subjects his wife to test her innocence and through which by a trick Iseult passes unscathed. When omission of subsidiary detail is impossible, Swinburne sometimes resorts to retrospective narrative. Thus in the first canto, narrating the voyage of Tristram with Iseult to Cornwall, there is a "throw-back" to Tristram's first visit to Ireland, when he received the poisoned wound, and to his second visit, when he sought a cure. Swinburne did well to envelope these preliminary journeys within the folds of his main narrative. On the other hand, the reader of the sixth canto will note that Swinburne here allowed himself to become heavily involved in a long accessory episode dealing with Tristram's brother-in-law Ganhardine. This is the weakest part of the poem, though it is clear that Swinburne's purpose was to relieve the tension at the point where the earlier joyous episodes are about to yield place to the later tragic phases of the story.

souled in the joy of the hour, with full awareness of the sorrows that must be born of their love, yet with no hesitation and no regret, has in it a certain bracing quality that lifts the story of their love above that of the love of Jason and Medea whose raptures, in Morris' poem, are sicklied o'er with the pale cast of future woe. But in Swinburne's poem all nature is absorbed in the same passion; birds and beasts, sea and woodland, even swords and spears are full of love. The wave is "a sharp sweet kiss" upon Tristram's arm; the leaves are "full of sweet sound, full of sweet wind and sun." The "exalted eroticism" of the second canto has been praised by various critics; but the least prudish reader may be inclined to feel that in the perfervid elaboration of this and similar episodes the effect which reticence would have supplied is lost.

Of his "Laus Veneris" Swinburne had written: "Once accept or admit the least admixture of . . . modern thought, and the whole story collapses into froth and smoke." Yet in his "Tristram", a tale as typically medieval as is that of Tannhäuser, he did admit "an admixture of modern thought." A reviewer in the *Athenæum* at the time raised what Swinburne later called "a plausible objection" to the poem on this score.[1] When Tristram, banished

[1] That Swinburne condescended to notice and discuss this objection in his Dedicatory Epistle is an indication that the author of the review was Watts-Dunton.

from King Mark's court, wanders for three years about the world, in his loneliness his thoughts dwell much upon the mysteries of life, revolving around the conception of those firm laws in obedience to which the firmament moves and to which man, too, must perforce be obedient, since from them he cannot escape. How should those laws be altered to suit man's desires? how should Fate

> turn from its great way to give
> Man that must die a clearer space to live? . . .

Thus musing, Tristram goes about the wolds and finds everywhere the evidence of unalterable law, until, gaining a sense of fellowship with nature, he is content to be in obedience even as are all natural forces:

> The heart of the ancient hills and his were one;
> The winds took counsel with him, and the sun
> Spake comfort;

and he became

> one that saw
> Not without reverence and sweet sense of awe
> But wholly without fear or fitful breath
> The face of life watched by the face of death.

"The objection of an irreconcilable incongruity between the incidents of the old legend and the meditations on man and nature, life and death, chance and destiny" which are assigned to the hero, might, Swinburne admits, "be unanswerable if the slightest attempt had been made to treat the legend as in any possible sense historical or capable of either rational or ideal association with history." But since his hero belongs to "an impossible age in an imaginary world", his chronicler has a right, should it please him, "to reason in the pauses of action and philosophize in the intervals of adventure." This misses the point of the reviewer's strictures, for it is not the introduction of philosophic meditations but their wholly modern tone which is incongruous. It was questionable tact to introduce thoughts reminiscent of "Hertha" into the mind of a hero of medieval romance.

Three passages from the poem may be taken as representative of its highest qualities. The first, of swift and simple narrative, illustrates the prosodic characteristics of the whole. It is drawn from the close of the first canto, at the moment of drinking from the fatal cup, when Iseult,

> With light lips yet full of their swift smile,
> And hands that wist not though they dug a grave,
> Undid the hasps of gold, and drank, and gave,
> And he drank after, a deep kingly draught:
> And all their life changed in them, for they quaffed
> Death; if it be death so to drink, and fare
> As men who change and are what these twain were.
> And shuddering with eyes full of fear and fire
> And heart-stung with a serpentine desire
> He turned and saw the terror in her eyes
> That yearned upon him shining in such wise
> As a star midway in the midnight fixed.
> Their Galahault was the cup, and she that mixed;
> Nor other hand there needed, nor sweet speech

To lure their lips together; each on each
Hung with strange eyes and hovered as a bird
Wounded, and each mouth trembled for a word;
Their heads neared, and their hands were drawn in one,
And they saw dark, though still the unsunken sun
Far through fine rain shot fire into the south;
And their four lips became one burning mouth.

The metrics of this passage deserve careful study. A heavily stressed trochee as the first foot of a line (with feminine cæsura) occurs frequently in Swinburne's verse. In the sixth line of this passage the resounding emphasis upon the word "Death" and the long pause which follows it are tremendously effective; the word reverberates across the sea. Again, in the seventeenth line there is a scarcely less remorseless emphasis upon the word "wounded." The pause after the seventh syllable in lines 5, 11, 14 and 15 is one of Swinburne's favorite devices, the feminine cæsura suggesting hesitation and uncertainty before the rhythm sweeps onward again. The daring "substitutions" employed in line eight are not so typical of Swinburne. The preponderant employment of words of one syllable is remarkable throughout his poetry; no other poet has achieved such wonderful effects with monosyllables. Here, in a passage of 186 words, 167 are of one syllable. Equally characteristic is the disregard of line-pause as the sense rushes on, a disregard extending even to the paragraphs, the episode beginning and the paragraphs dividing in the middle of a couplet. Through this large use of run-on lines and through his bold and very successful pauses upon syllables that do not usually carry the stress (especially the first and seventh), Swinburne imparts a lyric impetus to a meter which has traditionally the qualities of strength, conciseness and lucidity — "fittest for discourse and nearest prose" — but that is seldom associated with passion.

That passion reaches its height in the fifth canto, "Iseult at Tintagel." In a high tower overlooking the sea, while Mark revels in the hall below, Iseult watches through the night and to the accompaniment of wind and waves prays for Tristram: now for his eternal salvation though it be bought at the price of her own soul; now for his prompt return to her here on earth; now for one hour of reunion at no matter how remote a time; again for his pardon by God; and finally a second time for reunion here and now. More than anywhere else in the poem Swinburne here achieves genuine dramatic "objectivity" without forfeiting lyrical *élan*. The fluctuations of passion, the conflict of desire and love and loneliness and guilt, are portrayed with true insight and power. The figure of Iseult, until now vague and unsubstantial beneath the garments of romance, becomes living, palpitating and individual. Moreover the Celtic atmosphere of the wild passion-haunted tale is best suggested here, as is the background of gray sea and rocky shore and mist-laden wind. While Iseult watched and prayed,

All their past came wailing in the wind,
And all their future thundered in the sea.

With variations, this is the recurring refrain or burden of the canto, a refrain made up not of a separate couplet but of a pair of lines in which the first rhyme harks back to what has gone before and the second leads on to the renewal of Iseult's prayer. The persistent rhyme upon the word "wind" comes through recurrence to symbolize the indifference of Fate to human passion. The cadences in the refrain change and are subdued as gradually wind and sea subside.

The theme of Fate, sounded gradually more vehemently, becomes the dominant motive at the beginning of the last canto. Here, with an art which might have been no better than metrical ingenuity, but which is raised by sincerity above the level of mere cleverness, Swinburne returns, as in a symphonic composition, to the opening movement of the "Prelude"; through forty-four lines the rhymes of the "Prelude" are employed again, but the rapturous praise of Love has changed to a meditation upon Fate.[1] In the immortal closing lines of the poem Swinburne turns to the account of high poetry the theme of "A Forsaken Garden" and "By the North Sea": the gradual and inevitable encroachment of the sea upon the land. In this,

[1]The same device had been employed less elaborately in the contrasted openings of the sixth and eighth cantos.

his final treatment of this sublime subject, Swinburne touches sublimity:

> And the king
> Built for their tomb a chapel bright like spring
> With flower-soft wealth of branching tracery made
> Fair as the frondage each fleet year sees fade,
> That should not fall till many a year were done.
> There slept they wedded under moon and sun
> And change of stars: and through the casements came
> Midnight and noon girt round with shadow and flame
> To illume their grave or veil it: till at last
> On these things too was doom as darkness cast:
> For the strong sea hath swallowed wall and tower,
> And where their limbs were laid in woeful hour
> For many a fathom gleams and moves and moans
> The tide that sweeps above their coffined bones
> In the wrecked chancel by the shivered shrine:
> Nor where they sleep shall moon or sunlight shine
> Nor man look down for ever: none shall say,
> Here once, or here, Tristram and Iseult lay:
> But peace they have that none may gain who live,
> And rest about them that no love can give,
> And over them, while death and life shall be,
> The light and sound and darkness of the sea.

All competent judges agree, whatever the qualifications they feel compelled to make, that Swinburne's is incomparably the finest rendering of the legend in English literature. In Arnold's version the characters are endowed with a self-control that is far removed from the passion of the old story. Arnold shifts the center of interest to Iseult of Brittany and, discarding the story of the virgin marriage, gives her two children by Tristram. To these children, as the curtain falls upon the scene, she is telling the old tale of Merlin and Nimuë. This quiet close suggests beautifully the restoration of the poise and norm of nature when the tragedy has worked itself out. A lovely poem, it is certainly far more satisfying than is Tennyson's unfortunate mishandling of the theme. By removing the motive of Fate, by suggesting that Tristram's love for Iseult is frivolous, by following Malory's version of Tristram's character and his manner of death at the hands of Mark, and by associating the legend with his general picture of the degenerate last days of the court of King Arthur, Tennyson (though complacently unaware of the fact) reduced one of the great love stories of the world to the level of a vulgar amour, fit matter for a divorce court or for a murder trial where the cuckolded husband pleads the "unwritten law." This so-called "idyll" cannot enter into comparison with Swinburne's great poem. There are several versions of later date: Hardy's "Queen of Cornwall" is an ingenious but unconvincing attempt to reconcile the two conflicting stories of the lovers' end; while Mr. Masefield's and Mr. Robinson's are too recent to be judged unprejudicedly.

In "The Tale of Balen"[1] (1896) Swinburne again challenged comparison with Tennyson. The Laureate, who had turned the story of Tristram

[1] Swinburne employs the earlier and better form of the name "Balen", whereas Tennyson, following Malory, uses the form "Balin".

and Iseult into a sermon on the seventh commandment, had preached in his "Balin and Balan" (1885), the latest of the "Idylls", on the even triter topic: "Do not lose your temper." By a strange perversity of judgment the poet who had followed Malory in his miserable version of the Tristram story, departed from the "Le Morte D'Arthur" when (if we ignore the unavoidable puerilities of Balin's adventures) Malory is at his noblest. The thought of the adulterous cancer at the heart of the Round Table had become an obsession in Tennyson's mind. Balin, according to his conception of the tale, was a knight with a very bad temper ("My violences! my violences!"). One day he held converse with Vivien[1] from whom he heard gossip (the word precisely suggests the tone) about the Queen and Lancelot; and believing these charges against Guinevere, he smashed to pieces the shield upon which she had permitted him to bear her arms. Later, meeting his brother whom he did not recognize and who did not recognize him with his strange new shield, he fought with him and each slew the other, making a very theatrical end, enveloped in each other's arms. Had Morris made this story the subject of a poem, as he at one time planned, he would have accomplished something

[1] There are critics who discover in this second portrait of Vivien a "pagan sensuality and charm" indicating that Tennyson had profited by Swinburne's criticism of her in "Under the Microscope"; but she appears to me to be still, despite the "paganism", heavily draped in Victorian vulgarity.

better; and here, as in "Tristram of Lyonesse", Swinburne is in a way Morris' heir.

Tennyson, anxious to avoid medieval puerilities and determined to impart a "modern" meaning to his antique material, omitted what is the very heart of the old story: the absurd and irrational but typically medieval motive of "the Custom of the Castle" which compelled a knight to guard a certain path until he was slain by a stronger knight who in turn had to remain on guard. Swinburne boldly accepts the circumstances of the original story, and with an art finer than Tennyson's turns these and other childish bits of fable to good account as symbols of the irrational Fate which encompasses human life. For the rest, he follows the narrative in "Le Morte D'Arthur" very closely, often practically word for word.[1] His additions are chiefly in the way of beautiful elaborations of the setting, especially at the beginning of each canto where the time of year is indicated, from the spring-

[1] Only Paul de Reul among previous writers on Swinburne has recognized the extent of the verbal indebtedness, and even he has given but a tithe of the evidence in the parallels which he cites. It is possible to trace almost every narrative stanza to its source in Malory. Swinburne omits a few of Malory's digressions which would have interrupted the course of his narrative, such as the details of the funeral of King Lot and his followers, and the three prophecies of Merlin which, since they allude to later phases of the history of the Round Table, would, if included, have transgressed the unity of action which Swinburne preserves. A few other minute changes have been made with reason. Thus, the absurd name of Lot's brother — Nero — is suppressed. At the final parting between Merlin and Balen it is the former (who has the gift of prophecy) and not the latter (as in Malory) who says, "In this world we meet no more."

tide to winter, in harmony with the development of the human tragedy and in strict accord with a familiar and pleasing medieval theme. The tradition that Balen was a knight of Northumberland seems to have moved the poet strongly. From the plushy suburban comforts of Putney he looks back to his own childhood in the north of England. Northumbrian words — "whin", "scaur", "bole", and so forth — are appropriately introduced to enhance the atmospheric effect, and many of Malory's archaisms are retained. At the very end Swinburne uses with exquisite tact two incidents of the original narrative. When Balen and Balan lay dying, slain by one another, Malory tells how "Balan yede [went] on all four feet and hands", crawling to his brother. The poet makes the situation more poignant by a sudden flash of recollection of their childhood and of every childhood:

So
Beneath their mother's eyes had he,
A babe that laughed with joy to be,
Made toward him standing by her knee,
For love's sake long ago.

In Tennyson's version the brothers die in each other's arms. But Malory had told that though Balan died soon, "Balin died not till the midnight after." As Swinburne elaborates this simple record, recollections of his own childhood mingle with Balen's last memories:

Then anon
Died Balan; but the sun was gone,
And deep the stars of midnight shone,
Ere Balen passed away.

And there low lying, as hour on hour
Fled, all his life in all its flower
Came back as in a sunlit shower
Of dreams, when sweet-souled sleep has power
On life less sweet and glad to be.
He drank the draught of life's first wine
Again: he saw the moorland shine,
The rioting rapids of the Tyne,
The woods, the cliffs, the sea.

The joy that lives at heart and home,
The joy to rest, the joy to roam,
The joy of crags and scaurs he clomb,
The capture of the encountering foam
Embraced and breasted of the boy,
The first good steed his knees bestrode,
The first wild sound of songs that flowed
Through ears that thrilled and heart that glowed,
Fulfilled his death with joy.

"The Tale of Balen" is certainly the finest achievement of Swinburne's later life, an extraordinarily fresh evocation of the spirit of adventure, of chivalry, and of the wild northern country to come from a man of sixty shut up for many years in a semi-detached villa near Putney Bridge. Not the least admirable feature of the poem is the disappearance, in the presence of a great story, of Swinburne's usual magniloquence. The tale never lags nor wanders off into mazes of philosophic meditation or of nature description for its own sake. The stanzaic scheme, reminiscent of Tennyson's "Lady of Shalott", but with a longer fourth line and without the refrain in the concluding line, would have weighed heavily upon the rhyming powers of almost any other poet; but Swinburne bears the burden so effortlessly that the reader is hardly conscious of the metrical feat, and the stanza is varied in tone and color to suit the sense, now light and dancing, now swift, trenchant and severe, and at the close relying for its solemn appeal upon the bald fact of this tragedy of irrational Fate.

CHAPTER SIX

The Tragedies

No portion of the broad field of modern English literature is more thickly strewn with failures and with that sort of half-failure which is euphemistically called a *succès d'estime* than the infrequently visited corner where lie the rusty wrecks of many a poetic drama. From Wordsworth to Masefield, almost all the considerable poets and many poets who are seldom considered cherished ambitions to write for the stage, and many of them covered their failure to win popularity on the boards by calling their productions dramas for the library or "closet-dramas." The history of this department of modern imaginative literature is too long and too complex to be entered upon here, but it needs to be noted at once not only that Swinburne's tragedies form part of that history but that he was in one way or another connected with most of the poets who tried their hand at poetic plays. Thus, after the loyal friendship and tactful skill of Sir Henry Irving had made Tennyson's historical and romantic plays not entirely unacceptable in the theater, we find Swinburne consulting with the same actor-manager about the possibility of producing "Bothwell" at the Lyceum. It is a striking fact that links are discoverable between Swinburne and each of the dramatists of the so-called "Elizabethan Revival" — Thomas L. Beddoes, George Darley, Charles Jeremiah Wells, and Sir Henry Taylor. Some of these links will be indicated in the course of this chapter.

Swinburne was twelve years old when he first read, in Campbell's "Specimens of the English Poets", some passages from "The Duchess of Malfi." A little later he read Lamb's "Specimens of the English Dramatic Poets." In dedicating his last book, "The Age of Shakespeare" to Lamb's memory he wrote:

> A child it was who first by grace of thine
> Communed with gods who share with thee their shrine.

Dyce's edition of Marlowe he was given when he was thirteen years old. Just when he became acquainted with "Dodsley's great old plays" is not known; but it is on record that before he was fifteen he had read not only all the major dramatists but many of the most obscure. In later life he always insisted that his technique was Elizabethan or, as he put it, that his plays were designed for performance at the Fortune or the Red Bull. At Eton, after reading "The Revenger's Tragedy", he wrote a tragedy, as he told Churton Collins,

> into which, with ingenuity worthy of a better cause, [he] contrived to pack twice as many rapes

and about three times as many murders as are contained in the model, which is not noticeably or exceptionally deficient in such incidents.

There is no other record of experiments in dramatic form till the year 1858, when he composed the earliest of three experiments in the manner of John Fletcher.[1] These plays, which remain unpublished, are of interest solely as evidence of the strict discipline in style and prosody to which Swinburne subjected himself. The earliest in date and least in merit is "The Laws of Corinth", a bit of Fletcherian *pastiche* of no independent interest whatever, "Laugh and Lie Down" is better — and worse; better in that some suggestions of originality in style are imposed upon the Fletcherian groundwork; worse in that the choice of the lowest, laxest and coarsest of models seems deliberate. Both these experiments are fragments; but shortly after leaving Oxford he turned again to Fletcher and composed "The Loyal Servant" with an increased mastery of technique that would warrant the publication of this play had the style been more individualized and the theme more interesting. This play marks a transition between the two earlier experiments and the two plays which Swinburne published in 1860, for instead of reproducing Fletcher's simple, lucid English the

[1]The manuscripts of these plays are in the collection of Mr. Thomas J. Wise, to whom I am indebted for permission to examine them.

language is now slightly archaistic in tone, betraying the Pre-Raphaelite influence.

At Oxford he had other plans for dramas in mind; and in 1858 he had composed the first draft of "Rosamond", now lost. Just when "The Queen-Mother" was written is not clear — apparently not until after he had left the university and had developed his style considerably beyond the point reached in the second version of "Rosamond." The two plays were published together in 1860. They are of very different merit; the earlier a promising piece of apprentice-work, the later giving evidence of approaching maturity.

The action of "Rosamond" passes at Woodstock; the characters are Henry II, his fair mistress and his jealous wife. With the exception of a few of the shorter *juvenilia* none of Swinburne's other poems shows so clearly the influence of Pre-Raphaelite poetry. As in "The Defence of Guenevere", hazy, indefinite figures move before an elaborately wrought, colorful background. The character drawing is of less than no consequence. The pitiable Rosamond, when confronted by Queen Eleanor, contradicts the proud boast which (in the only oft-quoted passage in the play) she has made to her attendant:

> I that am
> Part of the perfect witness for the world
> How good it is; I chosen in God's eyes
> To fill the lean account of under men,
> The lank and hunger-bitten ugliness
> Of half his people; . . .

I that have held a land between twin lips
And turned large England to a little kiss;
God thinks not of me as contemptible.

Another passage in the same scene anticipates those reveries upon the previous incarnations of Dolores and Faustine which were presently to shock and fascinate the Mid-Victorians; anticipates, too, the meditation of another romanticist upon La Gioconda who, "as Leda, was the mother of Helen of Troy, and, as Saint Anne, the mother of Mary":

Yea, I am found the woman in all tales,
The face caught always in the story's face;
I Helen, holding Paris by the lips,
Smote Hector through the head; I Cressida
So kissed men's mouths that they went sick or mad,
Stung right at brain with me; I Guenevere —

and so forth.

A painstaking quest of color effects in the manner of Rossetti and Morris is evident in many places, as in the following passage which is no more than a translation of one of Rossetti's dream-women into the terms of another art:

Why once the king spake of my hair like this,
"As though rain filled and stained a tress of corn
Loose i' the last sheaf of many slackened sheaves;
Or if" (ay, thus) "one blew the yellow dust
That speckles a red lily off both cheeks
Held in the sun, so if in kissing her
I let the wind into her hair, it blows
Thin gold back, shows the redder thread of it,
Burnt saffron-scented."

The delicate and luscious verse has a languor and morbidity that prompt the comment with which Rosamond herself receives Constance's song: "The sick sweet of it taints my mouth through." Despite the underlying more vigorous Elizabethan cadences and the sudden, sharp, allusive bits of dialogue that are reminiscent of Browning, the little play lacks energy and vitality. King and wife and mistress are in a dream world of love and jealousy and death. Only a more spacious canvas, showing the connection of the episode at Woodstock with the larger issues of Henry's reign, could have enabled the poet to intellectualize the subject, as is evident from a comparison of Swinburne's purely sensuous treatment of the theme with the firmer grasp exhibited in George Darley's earlier "Thomas à Becket" and Tennyson's later "Becket."[1]

"The Queen-Mother" is a more substantial piece of work. The principles of dramatic blank verse are apprehended and there is a larger appreciation

[1] An interesting comparison, for which there is no room here, might be made of these three tragedies; a few words on the three versions of the central scene (the meeting of Eleanor and Rosamond) will suggest the contrast. In Darley's play the jealous queen scolds her rival like a termagant, and Rosamond, after pleading for pity, drinks the poison handed to her and dies. Swinburne endows the queen with more restraint and dignity, presents in Rosamond an even more pitiable figure, and brings King Henry upon the scene after his mistress has taken poison but before she dies. In Tennyson's version Becket enters in the nick of time to save Rosamond from Eleanor's dagger, and — in this following the probabilities of history rather than the imaginative truth of the legend — Rosamond is left alive at the conclusion of the drama. Viewed more largely, Swinburne's play might be compared with other versions of the story: in the early chroniclers, in Drayton's "Heroical Epistles", in John Bancroft's "Henry II", and elsewhere. A yet wider view would embrace tragedies and poems founded upon the stories of other royal mistresses, such as Jane Shore.

of history. The play is no mere romantic episode but an attempt to portray an entire society. It is much marred by obscurity of motivation, by undue attention to subsidiary issues, by an apparent lack (in the earlier acts) of a well-defined purpose, and by a great deal more talk than is required by the action; but towards the close it moves with swiftness and strength. The Pre-Raphaelite influence is yielding to the Elizabethan. In particular there is evidence of a close study of Chapman. The subject is Chapmanesque; the brilliant and corrupt court which forms the background of "The Revenge of Bussy d'Amboise" is here depicted with a like "proud full sail" of verse. Less fortunate is Chapman's influence as seen in the over-weighted sententiousness of much of the dialogue. This influence is crossed with that of Shakespeare and Webster. Bold enjambment and violent but effective metaphor are frequent, as in the following magnificently phrased anticipation of the inevitable remorse which follows crime:

> I will not do it;
> Lest all that regiment of muffled years
> Now huddled in the rear and skirts of time
> I must walk through, take whips into their hands
> To bruise my shame withal.

The Websterian "gnomic" quality of some of the verses might have developed, if harmonized with Swinburne's idiosyncrasies of style, into a valuable instrument for his more mature poetry and might have helped to hold in check his volubility. Such a sentence as the following is an early example of the sharp and sudden turns of thought that occur infrequently, unexpectedly and always effectively in Swinburne's poetry:

> It is the custom and grey note of age
> To turn consideration wrong way out
> Until it show like fear.

There are some signs in "The Queen-Mother" of the influence of "Joseph and His Brethren", a play with which Rossetti had acquainted Swinburne in the early months of 1860.[1] But more profound is the influence of Beddoes.[2] Rossetti discovered in both "Rosamond" and "The Queen-Mother" "a

[1] This huge and shapeless dramatic poem by Charles Jeremiah Wells won no notice when published in 1823, and its author relinquished the pursuit of literary fame and retired to a drowsy existence in Brittany, to be aroused many years later by the enthusiasm of Rossetti, the ardent discoverer of unappreciated masterpieces. Rossetti and Swinburne determined to gain for the poem belated recognition. They got into touch with Wells; and there is something a little pathetic in the bemused gratification of the old man at the enthusiasm of two young strangers, the very name of one of whom he could not, in Swinburne's sprawling autograph, decipher. About 1860 Swinburne wrote a laudatory essay on Wells but had no fit medium of publication at his command. The scheme slumbered for many years; in 1875 the essay, in revised form, appeared in the *Fortnightly;* and in the following year, yet further revised, it served as an introduction to a reprint of "Joseph." The "grand Elizabethan echo" which Swinburne heard in the play was what chiefly inspired his enthusiasm.

[2] In his essay on George Chapman, Swinburne commends Beddoes' "brilliant correspondence on poetic questions which to me gives a higher view of his fine and vigorous intelligence than any other section of his literary remains." In the same essay he remarks that Beddoes' "noble instinct for poetry could never carry him in practice beyond the production of a few lofty and massive fragments of half-formed verse" and that he was incapable "of reducing under any law of harmony to any fitness of form his own chaotic and abortive conceptions of a plot." On the dramatic works of Swinburne's maturity Beddoes exerted no influence whatever.

decided dash of 'Death's Jest-Book'." It is not very apparent in the first play save in the grotesque song which Queen Eleanor overhears in the second scene. But "The Queen-Mother" is steeped in Beddoes. Cino, the fool, is another such bitter gnomic commentator on life as is Isbrand. The reek of the Medicean French court is suggestive of the similar atmosphere in Grüssau. In both plays love and death, rivalry and revenge, public motives and private, jostle together on an overcrowded stage of complex intrigue. The supernatural is, however, avoided as in practically all Swinburne's work; and the taste for the macabre he may have acquired from Rossetti.

When all allowances have been made for influences, imitations and echoes, "The Queen-Mother" remains the work of no mere student and imitator. It stands upon its own feet; and its author was furnished with an instrument for the composition of his most ambitious work in the dramatic form — the trilogy on Mary Queen of Scots.

"The Queen-Mother" is, indeed, a sort of antechamber to the Scots trilogy. Though its central event, the massacre of Saint Bartholomew, occurred at a later date than the events set forth in "Chastelard", the setting prepares the way for the dramas on Queen Mary. There is portrayed (with a sympathy that is repellent to many readers) the cruel and lustful life of the court in which Mary Stuart was bred, the life vividly characterized in the article on her which Swinburne contributed to the "Encyclopædia Britannica":

The society in which the child was thenceforward reared is known to readers of Brantôme as well as that of imperial Rome at its worst is known to readers of Suetonius or Petronius — as well as that of papal Rome at its worst is known to readers of the diary kept by the domestic chaplain of Pope Alexander VI. Only in their pages can a parallel be found to the gay and easy record which reveals without sign of shame or suspicion of offence the daily life of a court compared to which the court of King Charles II is as the court of Victoria to the society described by Grammont. Debauchery of all kinds and murder in all forms were the daily subjects of excitement or of jest to the brilliant circle which revolved around Queen Catherine de'Medici.

It is probable that when Swinburne began "Chastelard" he scarcely realized that he had set himself to a task which was to command his attention and exercise his intellectual powers to the full for two decades. His original intention was apparently to make "Chastelard" complete in itself, embracing an action that is rounded out to a tragic close and while fitted, as he subsequently perceived, to become the first part of a trilogy, not merely or necessarily that first part. It is important to note that though Mary Beaton is the link that binds the three parts together, since her undying loyalty to the memory of Chastelard is the direct cause of the Queen's execution, this highly dramatic *motif* occurred to Swinburne at a late stage in his work upon the trilogy. In 1879, while engaged on "Mary Stuart", he wrote to Lord Houghton: "I have hit on a dramatic *motif* which will serve at once as a connecting link between this and the two parts preceding, and as a good solid hinge for the dramatic movement of the third." Indisputably he refers to this conception of Mary Beaton's part in the tragedy, she who is the witness alike of the initial crime and the final retribution.

Though with increasing knowledge of the history of the period the scope of his dramas immensely widened during the two decades in which the trilogy was composed and though the full realization of the essential theme — retributive justice — is a late growth, his conception of the character of Queen Mary was unfaltering and clear-cut from the first. He never wavered in the portrayal of his heroine; unfortunately, while not abandoning his central subject, he suffered it to become obscured by a cloud of irrelevant detail, ambitious as he was to be true to historical as well as to poetic fact. The result is that in the two later parts the historian has overlaid and almost smothered the poet, who appears from time to time struggling in the mass of documentary evidence, charge and countercharge, rumor, gossip and hearsay. Swinburne's pride that he had not to accuse himself "of any voluntary infraction of recorded fact or any conscious violation of historical chronology, except . . . in two instances: the date of Mary's second marriage, and the circumstances of her last interview with John Knox" is the pride of the historian rather than of the dramatist; and it would have been better had he called to mind the frequent occasions on which he himself insisted upon the contrast between the facts of history and the truths of imagination. It is significant that while composing "Bothwell" we find him studying "Anthony and Cleopatra" in an effort to wrest from Shakespeare the secret of his manipulation of history. A more dangerous model could not have been chosen.

The "Britannica" article on Mary Stuart and the "Note on the Character of Mary Queen of Scots" are helpful to an understanding of his purpose, but the essentials of his interpretation are exquisitely suggested in the "Adieux à Marie Stuart" in which he celebrated the completion of his trilogy:

> Strange love they have given you, love disloyal,
> Who mock with praise your name,
> To leave a head so rare and royal
> Too low for praise or blame.
>
> You could not love nor hate, they tell us,
> You had nor sense nor sting:
> In God's name, then, what plague befell us
> To fight for such a thing?

"Some faults the gods will give," to fetter
Man's highest intent:
But surely you were something better
Than innocent!

No maid that strays with steps unwary
Through snares unseen,
But one to live and die for; Mary,
The Queen.

That is, the apologists for Mary — and Swinburne was thinking especially of Hosack's "Mary Queen of Scots and Her Accusers" (1870–1874) — in seeking to extricate her from the accusations heaped on her by Froude and other historians, impaled her upon the other horn of the dilemma by portraying her as a coward, a fool and a dupe. That she was so her poet refused to believe, and he boldly accepted the alternative which he implied in the motto from Maundeville prefixed to "Chastelard" which declares that Mary was one of those women of the North who, if any man behold them, slay him with their eyes as doth the basilisk. The tragedy is that of the victims of *une belle dame sans merci*, beautiful, generous, wayward, terrible, before whom successively Chastelard, Rizzio, Darnley, Bothwell and Babington lay down their lives. The determination with which Swinburne held to this conception is shown in "Mary Stuart" where, completely disregarding the more obvious situation which the clash between Mary and Elizabeth put within his grasp as within Schiller's, he portrays the devotion and death of the last of Mary's lovers. The clue to the dissatisfaction with which the reader completes the trilogy is thus found in the third part; for therein the poet has clung to the old theme of "all for love and the world well lost" at the same time that he has endeavored to bring within the compass of that high and passionate but narrow *motif* a survey of all the historical issues of Mary's reign and its aftermath. The intensification and enlargement of his interest in sheer history is the prime cause of his esthetic failure. The choice of self-immolating adoration as the dominant theme throughout the trilogy carried with it the absolute necessity to conduct the action of the two later parts along the lines of, and within the limits of, "Chastelard."

For "Chastelard" is the most successful of all Swinburne's plays. The conception of love that it reveals is not one to appeal to most modern minds, the less so because of the disconcerting signs of more than normal sympathy with that conception. Aspects of Mary's character, for the understanding of which the broad background of public policy is needed, are disregarded or half-unconsciously postponed for future treatment; and she is revealed as the enchantress, queenly, warm, tender, heartless, desiring to save her lover, willing to sacrifice him. Chastelard is another Chevalier des Grieux, caught in snares more insidious than those of Manon;

he is — an analogy which Swinburne himself suggests — another Tannhäuser, poet and lover, delured into the Horselberg. He gives all for love, deliberately presenting to his mistress the choice between his death and the continuance of her favors. He is a brave, amorous, fantastic and romantic gentleman. "Sir," says the Queen's half-brother Murray to him:

> Sir, in all things
> We find no cause to speak of you but well:
> For all I see, save this your deadly fault,
> I hold you for a noble perfect man.

This tribute agrees with his character as sketched by Brantôme:

> *Bref, il estoit Gentil-Homme tres-accomply: et quant à l'ame, il l'avoit aussi tres-belle; car il parloit tres-bien, et mettoit par escrit des mieux, et mesme en rime, aussi-bien que Gentil-Homme de France, usant d'une poesie fort douce et gentille en Cavalier.*

This debonair culture and reckless romanticism contrast very bravely with the sophisticated courtiers among whom Chastelard moves; and his figure stands out in sharp bright outline against the dour Scotch background.[1] Intoxicated by the Queen's love, his fond presumption flares up to the

[1]The contrast is heightened by the French songs. Swinburne never again caught so entirely the spirit of French verse as in Mary Beaton's opening song and in Queen Mary's "J'ai vu faner bien des choses." The former, "Le navire est à l'eau" (afterwards set to an appropriate melody by Tosti), borrows its form from several of Hugo's lyrics, but it is shot through with a delicate archaism appropriate to the generation of poets who followed Ronsard and preceded Malherbe.

point of hiding himself in her chamber on her wedding night to the intent of being discovered and slain at her feet.[1] When her lover is apprehended Mary hesitates, but in the end she suffers him to go to his death. This betrayal is witnessed by Mary Beaton. Earlier in the play she had been shielded by Chastelard after he had mistaken her for the Queen one night.[2] This incident had aroused the Queen's jealousy and had plunged her into the marriage with Darnley.[3] In thus emphasizing the Queen's betrayal of her lover Swinburne introduces the *motif* of retributive justice which bides its time but which is unescapable.[4] Not until many years later did it occur to him (as we have seen) to embody this theme in the person of Mary Beaton, who had witnessed the execution of Chastelard whom she had loved unrequitedly, who had remained by the Queen through all the fluctuations of her fortunes, and who is present at the final tragedy of Fotheringay.

[1] According to Brantôme, Chastelard hid twice in Mary's chamber. The first offence she pardoned; and who can blame her — so runs Brantôme's apology — if after the second she surrendered him to justice? Swinburne, partly to avoid undramatic repetition, partly to lessen Mary's justification, suppresses the first indiscretion.

[2] Swinburne here makes use of the well-worn theatrical device of "the trick in the dark" (compare Massinger's "The Guardian" and Otway's "The Orphan," among many other plays).

[3] It is here that Swinburne allows himself one of his two liberties with historic fact: he moves up the marriage two years, thus bringing it within the action of "Chastelard" and accounting for it dramatically.

[4] It is likely that a passage in Brantôme is primarily responsible for this idea. Brantôme defends Queen Mary, but notes that after her execution many people declared that by her death she paid the penalty for her betrayal of Chastelard: "*Par vengeance divine, elle avoit justement pâty comme elle avoit fait pâtir autruy.*"

"Chastelard" may be regarded as a sort of glorified libretto of some Italian opera. The setting is Northern, but the color, the passion, the diction, the theme itself are of the South; and all would lend themselves well to the interpretation of orchestra and song. So regarded, two scenes stand out: the midnight meeting in the Queen's bedchamber and the wonderful *duo* in the last act, when the Queen, cravenly repenting of the reprieve sent to Chastelard, visits him in prison to beg it of him again. To imagine what Verdi or Puccini would have made of such material is to sense at once the beauty, the passion and the limitations of the play.

Though history is subordinated to romance, Swinburne seems to have had already a wide acquaintance with source-materials when he wrote the play.[1] Yet this first effort gives but a superficial portrait of the central figure, a portrait of Queen Mary which is brilliant indeed but whose lines and shadows the poet had to deepen as his conception of her character became more profound.

Other subjects occupied the forefront of Swinburne's consciousness for several years after the publication of "Chastelard" (1865), but Queen Mary was not forgotten. He worked intermittently on his second part between 1869 and 1872

[1] He owes much to Brantôme's character of his hero in the "Discours" on Mary Queen of Scots. Other details he found in Laboureur's "Additions" to the "Mémoires" of Castlenau, and he drew also upon Knox's "History of the Reformation in Scotland."

and made it his chief occupation in 1873.[1] In March, 1874, "Bothwell" appeared, dedicated to Victor Hugo in a French sonnet of admirable workmanship in which Swinburne describes:

Mon drame épique et plein de tumulte et de flamme,
Où vibre un siècle éteint, où flotte un jour qui fuit.

He never forgot the master's reply: "To occupy these two summits [*i.e.*, of epic and dramatic poetry] is granted to you only" — high praise had Hugo been able to read English! In the Dedicatory Epistle to his Collected Works Swinburne writes of "Bothwell" as "an ambitious, conscientious, comprehensive piece of work." It is: he was ambitious

[1] In November, 1869, he made "an analysis of all the events and situations in Mary Stuart's life from Rizzio's murder to her flight to England" and was "choked and stifled with the excessive wealth of splendid subjects and dramatic effects." He set to work to "carve or weave" something out of them; and sometime before August, 1871, the first act of "Bothwell" in a preliminary form was completed and privately printed by Frederick Locker. At that time he writes: "I feel at times crushed under the Tarpeian weight of my materials." In February, 1873, he writes: "I am making gradual way with 'Bothwell', but am yet far from sight of harbour", and he finds comfort in the thought that "the book must be either an utter failure" or else "not merely by far the greatest work I have done . . . but a really great poem and fit to live as a typical and representative piece of work." In December, 1873, he writes to Morley: "I am working hard and steadily at my gigantic enterprise of 'Bothwell', which dilates in bulk and material at every step. If ever accomplished, the drama . . . will be the biggest, I fear, in the language. But having made a careful analysis of historical events from the day of Rizzio's murder to that of Mary's flight into England, I find that to cast into dramatic mold the events of those eighteen months it is necessary to omit no detail, drop no link in the chain, if the work is to be either dramatically coherent or historically intelligible; while every stage of the action is a tragic drama of itself which cries aloud for representation. The enormity of the subject together with its incomparable capability (if only the strength of hand requisite were there) for dramatic poetry assures me, as I proceed, more and more forcibly of the truth which I suspected from the first, that Shakespeare alone could have grappled with it satisfactorily, and wrung the final prize of the tragedy from the clutch of historic fact."

to make his epic-drama (or "chronicle-play", as he later preferred to call it) the final word on Mary's character and career; conscientious in his historical documentation and accuracy; comprehensive in suffering no detail to escape him that might shed light upon the complexities of the theme. Admirable qualities in a historian; less admirable, certainly not essential, in a dramatist. "Bothwell" has been much praised by most of Swinburne's critics and little read, even by lovers of that difficult form of literature, the poetic drama; and the probability is that in the future it will be less praised and even less read. It carries too heavy a mass of impedimenta to travel easily down the years.

What Swinburne attempted and the measure of success that followed that attempt can best be indicated by an analysis of the action with some illustrative quotations.

The events between the death of Chastelard (1563) and the day of the murder of Rizzio (March 9, 1566) are omitted from Swinburne's scheme. When "Bothwell" opens we find Darnley committed to those leaders who oppose the policy of Mary and her Italian secretary. The first act is devoted in part to establishing the background of the fanatic Kirk in Edinburgh, in part to the plans and conferences culminating in the murder of Rizzio. An interview between Mary and John Knox is the most memorable scene. In Knox only does Mary meet her match:

He hath a tongue to tame a tiger with,
Fright into fierce and violent reverence
The fearfulest earth's monsters. I do think
I like him better than his creed-fellows
Whose lips are softer toward me.

To the Queen Knox says:

Lo, here I stand
A single soul and naked in [God's] eye,
Constrained of him, to do what thing he will,
And dare and can no other. Hath he sent me
To speak soft words of acceptable things
In ladies' chambers or kings' courts? I wot, no.
I am to bring God's gospel in men's ears,
And faith therein, and penitence, which are
The twain parts of it.

Then, turning to the Queen's women, he continues:

Ah, fair ladies,
How fair were this your life and pleasurable
If this might ever abide, and so in the end
With all this gay gear we might pass to heaven:
But fie upon that knave, Death, that will come
Whether we will or will not: and being come,
When he hath laid on his assured arrest,
The foul worms will be busy with this flesh,
Be it never so fair and tender; and the soul,
The silly soul shall be so feeble, I fear,
It can bring with it neither gold nor pearl,
Painting of face, garnish, nor precious stones.

The old refrain, "This is the end of every man's desire", sounds through Knox's eloquence; and in this interview between the fair frail creatures of the French court and the rugged preacher (the typical Swinburnean antithesis) the two contrasting elements in his temperament are juxtaposed. His thought fluctuates between the delight of the eyes and the pride of life on the one hand and on the other the realization that the end of these things is death; between a Renaissance Cyrenaicism and a puritanical renunciation.

Knox has not long been gone when the truth of his words is brought home to the Queen. As Rizzio sings to her of how "Lord Love went maying" the weak treacherous Darnley and the brutal Ruthven enter with their fellow conspirators and dragging away the shrieking, terrified secretary butcher him outside the door.

The huge second act is devoted to the rapid ascendency of Bothwell; the contemptuous acceptance by Mary of Darnley's false affirmation of innocence of Rizzio's murder; his consequent isolation from both parties; his thwarted attempt to escape to France; the birth of Mary's son; the suspiciously sudden illness of Darnley; his practical imprisonment at Glasgow and removal thence to Kirk o' Fields; Mary's last visit to him; and the preparations for his assassination. This barest summary indicates how much is crowded into these twenty-one scenes; and the confusion is deepened by the involved, allusive, contorted, parenthetical and highly figurative style beneath which we recognize with difficulty the poet's attempts to individualize the speeches of the different characters. Three scenes stand out in memory: the first, in which Mary exercises upon her husband her powers of fascination and so lulls his suspicions against her; the nineteenth, the dream of Darnley written in obvious emulation of the dream of Clarence; and the last, which closes at the utmost reach of Swinburne's power, exhibiting Mary's wretched consort in a frenzy of weak, guilty terror that is comparable to the last sight of Guido Franceschini.

> I say I hear their feet —
> Thou hast no ears — God hath no ears for me
> Nor eyes to look upon me — hands he hath,
> Their bloody hands to smite with, and her heart
> Is his toward me to slay me. Let them come;
> How do men die? but I so trapped alive —
> O, I shall die a dog's death and no man's.
> Mary, by Christ whose mother's was your name,
> Slay me not! God, turn off from me that heart —
> Out of her hands, God, God, deliver me!

The opening of Act III finds the Scots openly accusing Bothwell of the murder of Darnley, while Mary's devotion to the murderer is becoming a public scandal. The pretense of a trial results in Bothwell's acquittal, the presence of his troops in Edinburgh terrorizing his accusers. After Bothwell's divorce from his wife,[1] he and the Queen are married and proceed to Borthwick Castle, which is besieged by the Protestant lords, Bothwell escaping,

[1]Swinburne, replying to Lord Houghton's objection to the superfluity of the part of Jane Gordon, Bothwell's divorced wife, stated that it had been "very considerably curtailed in order not to make the poem any longer than was absolutely necessary"; but even so it is too long. Jowett is said to have persuaded Swinburne to reduce the length of "Bothwell" by several thousand lines.

accompanied by the Queen disguised as a page. In no other part of the drama is Swinburne so enmeshed in his cumbrous and heterogeneous material as in this act. The one solution, had he divined it, was to discard ruthlessly and slash his way through the mass of archives and testimony. As it is, nobly dramatic situations are obscured in an uncontrolled passion to be exhaustive.

From this point the drama rises in power to its impressive close. The fourth act is much shorter than any of the earlier acts and is correspondingly more effective. After conferences between the Queen's party and the lords confederate against her, Bothwell is permitted to leave Scotland and she is handed over to her enemies. With Mary a prisoner comes the astonishing four-hundred-line diatribe against her spoken by Knox in the streets of Edinburgh. This is the climax of the clash between the Catholic Queen and the reforming minister. She is, as Swinburne pointed out to Lord Houghton, "the representative of the past — of monarchy and Catholicism — as Knox, the only person then living of courage and intelligence equal to her own, is in effect, beneath the outer shell of Protestant bigotry, the prophet or at least the precursor of democracy and the popular spirit of the future." For once a speech of enormous length is not out of place. It seems to overwhelm the victim. The clouds are gathering thickly and a sense of doom hangs over the protagonist.

The fifth act opens with the escape from Lochleven. Grandly eloquent is Mary's address to her followers on the shore of the lake. Then comes the ruin of all her hopes at Langside, and she must choose between England and France as a place of refuge. Spurning the latter alternative, she turns rather to England, whence she may rally her people and wreak vengeance on her enemies. With magnificence of diction beyond the power of any English poet since Shelley and comparable to the most exalted flights of rhetoric in Victor Hugo, "Bothwell" closes. On the shore of Solway Firth, Queen Mary, setting out for England, looks back upon Scotland and her seven troubled years therein and declares that she will return to make "from sea to sea one furnace of the land."

The last part of the trilogy was published in 1881. Between the close of "Bothwell" and the first scene of "Mary Stuart" eighteen years have elapsed.[1] From Bolton, her first asylum, the royal prisoner was moved to Tutbury and thence to Sheffield, where she remained fourteen years. Plot and counterplot surged round her until, with or without her consent, there was formed the con-

[1]Among the events which Swinburne omits is the inquiry into the charges brought against Mary of complicity in the murder of Darnley. In "Bothwell", as we have seen, her guilt is accepted unquestioningly; and in the "Britannica" article Swinburne accepts almost unquestioningly the genuineness of the celebrated "Casket Letters" upon the authenticity of which the charges against her mainly rest. Swinburne leaves out of his scheme the conspiracy and execution of the Duke of Norfolk, who planned to overthrow Elizabeth, marry Mary, and set her upon the throne of England.

spiracy of Anthony Babington (the last victim of her fascination) to assassinate Queen Elizabeth. It is at this point that Swinburne resumes his task of dramatizing her history.

"Mary Stuart" is a good deal less than half so long as "Bothwell"; but the lessened length is due to paucity of material fitting into the poet's scheme rather than to deliberate compression. The great dramatic opportunity inherent in this latest phase of Mary's story is that chosen by Schiller: the clash between the two queens; and that subject Swinburne puts almost completely aside.[1] He felt it necessary to concentrate attention upon Babington, Mary's last lover, as attention in the first part had been concentrated upon her first lover, Chastelard. But the conspiracy is quickly foiled, and the whole second act is devoted to what is unavoidably a side issue — the trial and execution of the conspirators. Then follows the trial of Mary on the charge of plotting against the life of Elizabeth. She is shown defending herself without counsel against the array of English lawyers.[2] She is pronounced guilty, but Elizabeth is reluctant to put her to death. Mary Beaton now comes forward into the action

[1]He does indeed touch on it in the fourth act where Elizabeth repels the intervention of France, but in doing so he involves himself in a serious error of technique, since the implication is that Mary's death or pardon is to depend upon the chances of high politics, whereas it hangs upon a very different issue.

[2]Did the poet have in mind the trial of Vittoria in Webster's "White Devil"? I think it likely, for in an essay on Webster he compares Vittoria's courage in the court scene with Mary's and suggests that Webster may have had Mary in his mind

again, and at this point where Swinburne dares to sacrifice the facts of history to the truths of imagination his play comes to life. Mary Beaton has in her possession a letter which Mary Stuart believes to have been long since destroyed, a letter in which Mary Stuart had repeated the infamous charges which the Countess of Shrewsbury had brought against Elizabeth. If shown to Elizabeth it will seal the fate of the prisoner. Shall it be delivered? The decision shall rest upon whether Mary gives any sign of remembrance of the long-dead Chastelard and of repentance for her betrayal of him. Mary Beaton sings to her mistress his song: "*Après tant de jours, après tant de pleurs*" — a song so tender and now so bitterly apt — and the Queen's only comment is:

> Nay, I should once have known that song, thou say'st,
> And him that sang it, and should now be dead:
> Was it — but his rang sweeter — was it not
> Rémy Belleau?

Mary Beaton thereupon sends the fatal letter to Elizabeth who upon reading it signs the death warrant. Throughout her last days Mary Stuart comports herself as becomes the woman whom Swinburne has portrayed from the time, a quarter of a century earlier, when she arrived in Scotland. She is not, as in Schiller's tragedy, the doomed heroic queen of romance, concerned to forgive her enemies. Her thoughts are still upon the Catholic ascendency and upon revenge. The closing scene is managed as in "Chastelard." The setting is in an upper chamber; at the window stands a woman who witnesses the execution in the courtyard below and describes it to Mary Beaton who cowers in the room. On hearing the cry below: "So perish all found enemies of the Queen!" Mary Beaton says, speaking with the voice of Nemesis:

> I heard that very cry go up
> Far off long since to God, who answers here.

The motto of the play, taken from the "Choëphoræ", declares that the voice of Justice claims the payment of debt for wrong.

Swinburne's conception of Mary Stuart's character is in the main that accepted by most modern historians. But it errs, from the point of view of the historian, in a too free handling of the probabilities of the situation with too little regard for testimony at variance with the poet's own conclusions. That, for example, Chastelard was Mary's accepted lover has never been proved. That she was guilty of complicity in her husband's murder is one of the most hotly contested problems in history. As a poet, Swinburne was of course free to make his own decisions; the difficulty is that he asked and expected to be judged also as a historian. He differs from Froude in his analysis of Mary's character chiefly in emphasizing the good qualities which Froude ignores, but he is quite as frank as Froude in admitting the evil. He is at many points widely divergent from such partisan biographers as Andrew Lang and John Skelton. The trilogy is, of all imaginative reconstructions of the story, that of most ambitious scope, firmest grasp, and most convincing vitality. Beside it Scott's treatment of the Lochleven episode seems thin and facile. Alfieri's "Maria Stuarda", which centers in the murder of Darnley and portrays the Queen as guiltless of the crime, is scarcely more than an episode. Schiller's "Maria Stuart" concentrates upon the final days at Fotheringay.[1]

The trilogy cannot be "placed" logically among Swinburne's other works. The appeal of a fascinating, beautiful and romantic woman, reinforced by boyhood associations with the traditions of the Border country, made him accept Mary, succumb to her fascination, and dedicate twenty years of arduous toil to the story of her life and death. Yet she embodied many of the qualities and states of mind most abhorrent to him: disregard of the public welfare, scorn of the people, assertion of absolute monarchical rights, and devotion to the Roman Catholic Church. His theme ruled out the possibility of any celebration of liberty, save by implication and half-heartedly in the person of John Knox. Mary's charm, exercised with all its old potency three centuries after her death, drew

[1]It would be interesting to know whether Swinburne in old age read Maurice Hewlett's "The Queen's Quair." A quaint analogy is suggested by this book. Just as Swinburne the dramatist desired to be judged as a historian, so Hewlett the novelist insisted that his romance be read as history.

her rapt and adoring poet far out of the course within which his convictions usually guided him.

The train of thought is obvious that now led Swinburne to undertake a tragedy on the subject of Lucrezia Borgia.[1] Hers was a story of lechery and crime, passion and revenge, such as had inspired those famous Jacobean dramas, "The White Devil" and "Women Beware Women." The Borgia legend had something in common with the Cenci legend. And Hugo's "Lucrèce Borgia", which Swinburne considered "the most perfect in structure as well as the most sublime in subject" of the master's plays, was nevertheless in plot "a pure invention of tragic fancy", leaving the way clear for a dramatist who should limit himself to the opportunities afforded by history. Nat Lee's ranting tragedy of "Cæsar Borgia"[2] may have prompted him to essay anew a tragedy on a theme which an earlier English playwright had attempted and spoiled in the attempt. In September, 1882, he wrote to Churton Collins:

[1] In a letter from Mentone in 1861 he tells Lady Trevelyan that he is engaged on a prose story "about my blessedest pet which her initials is Lucrezia Estense Borgia. Which soon I hope to see her hair as is kept at Milan in spirits in a bottle." The "Gampishness" of this statement does not hide the seriousness of his intention. In or about 1862 he wrote the *canzone* called "A Ballad of Life", his original intention being to place under the title this inscription: "In honorem D. Lucretiae Estensis Borgiae" and under the title of the companion "Ballad of Death" a similar inscription. In the "Birthday Ode" to Hugo (1880) he put into an allusion to Hugo's drama on Lucrezia (Epode iii) something more of genuine feeling than is to be found in most of the allusions in that critical eulogy.

[2] Swinburne had read this play; I have seen his annotated copy of it.

I rather want something big to do, or at least attempt. The one great subject for historic tragedy which I have always thought of and recoiled from or put by[1] — "The Life and Death of Cæsar Borgia" — seems no less magnificent but more and more unmanageable the more I think of it. The catastrophe — if his own reported words be accurate[2] — is about the most *moral* thing I ever read of in history, and ought to be dramatized accordingly, to conciliate the suffrages of the religious reading world: but what between triple incest, and the bisexual harem of the Vicar of Christ . . . even I feel conscious of something like the sentiment called "funk" in face of the inevitable difficulties. Yet the triumph and fall (through his own triumphant wickedness) of the greatest warrior and statesman of his age might and should be an almost incomparable argument of tragic poetry.

The only portion of his tragedy that Swinburne completed — it would seem the only portion of any length that he wrote — is the episode of "The Duke of Gandia", published in 1908.[3] Its brevity is but partial compensation for the repulsiveness of its lustful and murderous theme. It may well have

1 Fragments of a tragedy on the subject begun at Oxford in 1858 are still extant.

2 The reported "last words" were not Cæsar Borgia's, as Swinburne implies, but Alexander VI's. The reference is of course to the old tradition (so admirably retold by John Addington Symonds and so miserably mangled in Barnabe Barnes' "The Devil's Charter") that the Pope, having long since sold his soul to the devil, murmured on his death bed: "I will come; it is but right; wait yet a little while."

3 Sir Edmund Gosse, in a letter to the present writer dated nearly a decade ago, concurs with me in believing that "The Duke of Gandia", though published so late in Swinburne's life, belongs to 1882.

been that the poet was appalled by the subject he had undertaken and put it by. But its evil glitter fascinated him.

Swinburne turned next to a subject admirably suited to his genius. It is curious that there is no allusion to the composition of "Marino Faliero" in his letters. The play was published and probably written in 1885. It is legitimate therefore to regard it in part as a product of the anti-Byronism which in 1884 had moved him to compose the celebrated diatribe on the "noble poet." In that diatribe Swinburne had presented a formidable arraignment of Byron's historical plays. That "Marino Faliero" was written in direct rivalry with Byron and was inspired by a desire to do justice to a great subject which had been previously mishandled, Swinburne himself admitted.[1]

Byron's tragedy, for all its faults, is not the despicable performance which Swinburne considered it. A whole-hearted championship of liberty breathes through every page; and his own personal experience of association with conspirators imparts a note of authenticity to the energetic scenes in which he depicts the plot against the Venetian

[1] He was probably also acquainted with Casimir Delavigne's miserable vulgarization of Byron's play; but there is no indication that he knew the several German dramas on the subject which had appeared shortly before his own tragedy. He may have made use of such contemporary accounts of the conspiracy as those by Nicolo Trevisan and Pietro Giustinian, but his chief "source" was the full, though somewhat simplified, account in Marin Sanudo's "Vitae Ducum Venetorum."

government. Swinburne the republican could not but acknowledge the grandeur of this enthusiasm, but Swinburne the artist was justified in regarding the play as, artistically, a failure. Byron's willful obedience to the unity of time limited the action to a single day and rendered the motive of the tragedy obscure.[1] Instead of gradually unfolding the situation and thus developing an interest in his protagonist, he chose to thrust the reader into the very conclusion of the whole matter. Swinburne's first technical object was to place the beginning of the action much earlier and thus to reconstruct the play on truly dramatic lines. The point in the story where Byron's play commences is not reached in Swinburne's till the opening of Act III. What precedes that point in the latter tragedy accounts dramatically for matters and motives of which we learn only incidentally, if at all, in Byron's.

Swinburne's attention and sympathy are concentrated upon Faliero.[2] The character of the Doge is more complex than in Byron's drama where the insult offered by Steno to Faliero and his wife is the

[1] Byron showed his awareness of this difficulty when he urged John Murray to print a translation of one of the Italian chronicles of Faliero's rebellion along with his play. "Recollect," he wrote, "that without previously reading the 'Chronicle', it is difficult to understand the tragedy."

[2] The Duchess, as Swinburne portrays her, is a not altogether happy combination of traits drawn from Byron and (apparently) Delavigne. She is courageous and conscious of her purity, and regards slander with an indifference which she vainly strives to make her husband emulate. Her relationship to the aged Doge is more that of a daughter than a wife. Byron prided himself on the fact that there was no "love-interest" in his play; Swinburne, I think mistakenly, introduces such an interest in the relationship of the Duchess and Bertuccio who loves her and is loved by her despite her fidelity to the Doge.

drop that makes the cup of the Doge's wrongs, full already, run over. Byron portrays him as prompted to conspire against the State of which he is the titular head by indignation against the oppression of the people by the all-powerful *Dieci*. At first thought, the qualities of pride, jealousy and revengefulness which Swinburne attributes to Faliero (on good historical grounds) seem to render him a less appropriate protagonist for a drama of liberty than is Byron's noble hero; but Swinburne's intention is clear. For when the conspiracy has been discovered and thwarted, the Doge, in prison, reasons with himself and justifies on public grounds the course of action into which he had been led by passionate resentment of private wrongs. These self-communings make clear to him his own imperfections which had rendered him unworthy to be the leader of his people towards liberty. Thus, most movingly, the poet, in Faliero's last long speech, modulates his theme into a prophecy of the ideal leader who shall one day arise:

I

Have erred, who thought by wrong to vanquish wrong,
To smite with violence violence, and by night
Put out the power of darkness; time shall bring
A better way than mine, if God's will be —
As how should God's will be not? — to redeem
Venice. I was not worthy — nor may man,
Till one as Christ shall come again, be found
Worthy to think, speak, strike, foresee, foretell,
The thought, the word, the stroke, the dawn, the day,

> That verily and indeed shall bid the dead
> Live, and this old dear land of all men's love
> Arise and shine forever.[1]

While Faliero thus meditates, his words are interrupted ever and again by the Latin chants of the penitents outside the prison. Here, as in the antithesis between Mary and Knox, the contrast of the Catholic past and the republican future is suggested. No threats of punishment in another life can move Faliero from his steadfastness:

> Die we may
> From record of remembrance: but, being sons
> Whose death or life, whose presence or whose dust,
> Whose flesh or spirit is part of Italy,
> What mean these fools to threaten us with death? —

an echo of "Tiresias" and "The Pilgrims."

Nowhere else in his poetry did Swinburne clothe loftier thoughts in nobler verse than in the final words of the Doge to the little group around him:

[1] Here the doctrine of the rejection of violence, the spirit of Mazzini, confident in the slow but sure progress of the world towards liberty, triumphs over the doctrine of tyrannicide which Swinburne inherited from Landor. Swinburne expressed the same recantation in his sonnet for a Portrait of Orsini, who had attempted to assassinate Napoleon III and who

> thought to vanquish wrong with wrong,
> Erring, and make rage and redemption meet.

Mr. W. B. D. Henderson in his study of Landor's influence on Swinburne fails to remark these significant recantations of Swinburne's early opinions. — "Marino Faliero" is appropriately dedicated to Aurelio Saffi, who with Mazzini and Armellini had formed the triumvirate during the short-lived Roman Republic of 1848–1849. This dedication should be read side by side with "After Nine Years", a poem in which Swinburne pays homage to the memory of Mazzini.

Fare thee well,
And thou, my wife and child, all loves in one,
Sweet life, sweet heart, fare ever well, and be
Blest of God's holier hand with happier love
Than here bids blessing on thee. Hark, the guard
Draws hither: noon is full: and where I go
Ye may not follow. Be not faint of heart:
I go not as a base man goes to death,
But great of hope: God cannot will that here
Some day shall spring not freedom: nor perchance
May we, long dead, not know it, who died of love
For dreams that were and truths that were not. Come:
Bring me but toward the landing whence my soul
Sets sail, and bid God speed her forth to sea.[1]

The ambition to do well what another poet had done badly again inspired Swinburne when he selected the subject of his next tragedy: "Locrine" (1887). This curious piece of misapplied ingenuity is a dramatization of the myth of the son of King Brutus who fell in love with the wife of his enemy and was at last routed by the forces of his own wife Guendolene. The classic allusion to the story is of course in "Comus", where Sabrina, who loosens the spell cast upon the Lady, is the "virgin daughter of Locrine." In the dedicatory stanzas prefixed to his play Swinburne alludes beautifully to Milton's use of the subject:

No part have these wan legends in the sun
Whose glory lightens Greece and gleams on Rome.
Their elders live; but these — their day is done,

[1]It is worth noting that in this passage of 128 words 118 are monosyllables.

Their records written of the wind and foam
Fly down the wind, and darkness takes them home . . .
Yet Milton's sacred feet have lingered there,
His lips have made august the fabulous air,
His hands have touched and left the wild weeds fair.

About 1595 the myth had been dramatized by a playwright whose identity still remains, after much discussion, uncertain. The subject (that of "Rosamond" in a more complex form: the rivalry of wife and mistress in a king's affections) offers fine opportunities for tragic treatment, opportunities which the anonymous Elizabethan dramatist, bungler though he was, did not entirely miss, but which Swinburne has deliberately obscured for the sake of a dizzying exhibition of metrical tightrope walking. Never was a command of the resources of prosody so misused. The ten scenes are written in nine different and often highly complex stanzaic schemes. The first scene is written in couplets; the second in Petrarchian sonnets; the third in a nine-line stanza rhyming *aabaabbab;* the fourth in *ottava rima;* the fifth in what Swinburne called *quarta rima;* the sixth in the Chaucerian stanza; the seventh in the stanza of "Venus and Adonis"; the eighth in *terza rima;* the ninth in Shakespearean sonnets; and the tenth in couplets. This bewildering metrical *tour de force* passes beyond all allowable limits of art. Petrarch would have shuddered at the sight of sonnets cut into scraps of dialogue and ending in the middle of a sentence!

The forms used were not intended for such purposes and Swinburne is for once unable to bend the measures to his own devices. If the reader takes pains to note the prosodic schemes he finds it impossible to follow the sense of the dialogue. If he reads with his mind upon the speaker's meaning he loses all sense of the metrical forms. The attempt to attend to form and substance at the same time results in hopeless confusion.[1]

Not even agility of technique distinguished "The Sisters" (1892), the most deplorable failure in the canon of Swinburne's writings. Here he ventures, protected by the rusty armor of romance, into the field of "realism" and modern life. The story is of a young soldier, Reginald Clavering, back from Waterloo, who is loved by two sisters, one of whom he loves. The other, taking in jealous grief a hint from the play which Reginald has written and which they perform together, poisons him and her sister and herself. The play-within-the-play (a quaint transference of an Elizabethan *motif* to the period of "Vanity Fair") is written in the full and heightened style of Swinburne's blank verse. The main drama is composed in blank verse so simple

[1]Something similar had been attempted long before in Fulke Greville's monstrously tedious plays, and an approximation to Swinburne's feat occurs in the anonymous Elizabethan play "Selimus." In one of his essays Swinburne comments upon this feature of "Selimus", adding that it "may have been an exceptional experiment due merely to the caprice of one eccentric rhymster." By implication he writes himself down as an "eccentric rhymster"; and no more need be said.

as to be insipid. We have already seen that Swinburne intended his hero to be a self-portrait. Apart from that point, the piece is of interest only as a curiosity.[1]

The last tragedy — which Gosse does not so much as mention in his biography of Swinburne and which has in general been slighted by critics — is "Rosamund, Queen of the Lombards" (1899). The story of the Donna Lombarda who married her father's slayer, was forced by her husband to drink from a cup fashioned from her father's skull, and through the instrumentality of a young warrior brought about her husband's death, occurs in many literatures.[2] As a small boy Swinburne had been fascinated by the tale when he read Alfieri's "Rosmunda" with his mother.[3] From one or two

[1] It is but fair to add that in one fragment of North country lyric Swinburne recaptures for a moment a suggestion of the old beauty and pathos.

[2] This curious chapter in literary history has never been completely told. The chief facts are these. There are several earlier narratives before the tale of Rosamund is found in the "De Gestis Langobardorum" of Paul the Deacon. Gregory of Tours retells it in the "Historia Francorum." It occurs twice in the poetry of John Gower. Giovanni Rucellai, the earliest but one of the pseudo-classic dramatists of Renaissance Italy, combined it with the story of Antigone in his tragedy of "Rosmunda" (1515). It is found in Machiavelli's "History of Florence", in Bandello, and in Belleforest. Overlaid with a confused welter of blood and lust it may be detected by the careful reader of Middleton's "The Witch." In even more repulsive form it occurs in D'Avenant's "Albovine, King of the Lombards." It is an episode in Prevost's "Mémoires d'un Homme de Qualité", whence Alfieri derived hints for his "Rosmunda." There is an Italian ballad on the subject, at least one opera, and the theme is found as far afield as Scandinavia.

[3] In a letter to Mrs. Leith, Swinburne records his reading of "Rosmunda" with his mother. It has been suggested that he refers to Rucellai's tragedy, but it is far more likely that Lady Jane Swinburne read Alfieri with her small son. A cancelled prose introduction to Swinburne's play exists in manuscript in Mr.

other earlier versions he derived suggestions for his play; but the evident immediate source has not hitherto been indicated. A striking piece of narrative verse by the accomplished and too little known poet, Paul Leicester Warren, Lord De Tabley, is "Rosamund." This tells of the barbaric banquet of Albovine, the proffered cup, and the king's remorse, but barely hints at the wife's vengeance to come. De Tabley was on several occasions a guest at "The Pines", both Swinburne and Watts-Dunton being admirers of his poetry. It is more than likely that his poem prompted Swinburne to write the play, which, opening just before the banquet and depicting the final episodes, thus fills in the tale as related by De Tabley.

That the terrible barbaric theme had never had justice done to it by earlier dramatists was an incentive to Swinburne. But he is himself scarcely equal to the demands of the difficult subject. His Albovine is a weak creature, his Rosamund a confused conception. The drama is of more interest for what the poet seems to have been attempting than for what he accomplishes. We see him exercising a severe restraint upon his congenital volubility. He aims at a swift development of the action to a foreordained catastrophe. The versification is plain, the diction almost bald; but when

Wise's collection. In it Swinburne gives the argument of the tragedy and notes Middleton's, D'Avenant's and Alfieri's use of the theme but does not refer to Rucellai.

the end comes it somehow misses fire. The means employed are too "literary"; the play comes from the library, not from life.[1]

"When I write plays it is with a view to their being acted at the Globe, the Red Bull, or the Black Friars." So Swinburne reminded Watts-Dunton in his Dedicatory Epistle. The Elizabethan audience was constantly in his mind, and in his critical essays he refers often to the temper of that audience.

> Nothing in the age of Shakespeare is so difficult for an Englishman of our own age to realise as the temper, the intelligence, the serious and refined elevation of an audience which was at once capable of enjoying and applauding the roughest and coarsest kinds of pleasantry, the rudest and crudest scenes of violence, and competent to appreciate the finest and the highest reaches of poetry, the subtlest and the most sustained allusions of ethical and political symbolism.

The drama, he says elsewhere, was "the most natural and representative form" of English genius until it "shrivelled up and shuddered into everlasting inanition under the withering blast of Puritanism." Elsewhere still he remarks upon "the obvious fact that in the modern world of English letters the novel is everywhere and the drama is

[1] The only comment invariably made by critics of the tragedy is upon the fine effect produced by the frequent allusions to the somber oppressive heat of the Italian June which lowers over the action. To Mrs. Leith Swinburne wrote: "I wrote it all in the month of June," adding: "You will recognize my Norse abhorrence of hot weather and southern climate."

nowhere." To the end of his life he was completely unaware of the rebirth of English drama, in altered guise and adapted to new requirements of subject and taste, which was being accomplished within a few miles of Putney. In an isolation from his age astonishingly complete he wrote his tragedies for performance in Finsbury Fields or on the Bankside.

In the course of a critique on John Nichol's historical drama "Hannibal" which Swinburne, for old friendship's sake, wrote in 1872 there occurs this passage:

> There are two ways in which a poet may treat a historic subject: one that of Marlowe and Shakespeare, in the fashion of a dramatic chronicle; one, that of the greatest of all later dramatists [Hugo], who seizes upon some point of historic tradition, some character or event proper or possible to the time chosen, be it actual or ideal, and starting from this point takes his way at his will, and from this seed or kernel develops as it were by evolution the whole fabric of his poem. It would be hard to say which method of treatment requires the higher or the rarer faculty; to throw into poetic form and imbue with dramatic spirit the whole body of an age, the whole character of a great event or epoch, by continuous reproduction of historic circumstance or exposition of the recorded argument scene by scene; or to carve out of the huge block of history or chronicle some detached group of ideal figures, and give them such form and colour of imaginative life as may seem best to you.

The former method, he goes on to say, has been

almost completely neglected by English dramatists since the time of Ford's "Perkin Warbeck"; and the modern age has produced "but one workman equal to that task" — Sir Henry Taylor.[1]

Generally speaking, Swinburne's tragedies belong in the same class with "Perkin Warbeck" and "Philip van Artevelde." He does not detach a group of ideal figures but throws into poetic form "the whole body of an age" by "continuous reproduction of historic circumstance." His wide perspective and close grasp of history are qualities of a fine order. He has an understanding of motive — of motive rather than of character. In a manner reminiscent of Browning's *dramatis personæ* the men and women in his plays dissect and disentangle the reasons for action. The atmosphere of high-wrought emotion, particularly the emotions of love and patriotism, is often convincingly suggested. But there is generally a singular diffuseness, an unwillingness to sacrifice irrelevant details, a want of power to select the essential elements in a situation. In the rare cases where this sacrifice is made, the process of selection is generally carried too far and the situation is reduced to the barest

[1]To "Artevelde" Swinburne alludes frequently in his critical essays and always in laudatory terms, calling it "the noblest of all modern historical plays." But the theme of Taylor's once so celebrated masterpiece bears no relation to any of Swinburne's plays; the method of treatment is different; and the rare passages of genuine poetry are pitched in a key of subdued Wordsworthian melancholy with a somber dignity and restraint that Swinburne could admire but could not imitate. Swinburne knew Taylor in his extreme old age and was proud to quote his praise of "Mary Stuart."

outline. In one sense Swinburne's dramas possess unity: the unity of a great central idea; but this center is too often hidden by the elaboration of semi-detached or unrelated side issues. The basic defect in all the tragedies (allowance being made for splendid exceptions in individual scenes) is technical incompetence. He planned his plays for performance at some Elizabethan theater; but he models them from the externals inward, not *vice versa*, thus reproducing some of the superficial characteristics of the old drama without ever discovering the secret of the method of the old dramatists — a method formulated with due regard for the requirements of the actual and definite theaters in which their plays were produced.

Swinburne's plays are therefore properly to be interpreted as the culmination and conclusion of the movement known as the "Elizabethan Revival" which had begun with Darley, Beddoes, Wells and Taylor. In ability to wrestle with difficult problems of structure, to arrange great masses of detail, and to persevere to the end he is far superior to the author of "Death's Jest-Book." In eloquence and passion he is far above Taylor. But his dramas reach back to the works of these and the other "closet" dramatists of the earlier nineteenth century. In this department of imaginative literature he represents the setting of the sun of Romanticism.

CHAPTER SEVEN

"The Noble Pleasure of Praising"

Criticism and controversy, the two major departments of Swinburne's prose work, are not completely separate; in his most violent diatribes there are digressions on general principles of criticism, and conversely, in the midst of serene appreciation of great work he may flame up into angry and disputatious denunciation. Every reader of his prose has experienced bewilderment when without warning the tone suddenly changes and the critic, enjoying and teaching us to enjoy some play or poem or novel, is transformed into a hysterical person who shrieks and rages, pouring forth a cataract of ugly and redundant adjectives. Such a phrase as "the chattering duncery and the impudent malignity of so consummate and pseudosophical a quack as George Henry Lewes", followed by the declaration that "not even such a past master in the noble science of defamation could plausibly have dared to cite in support of his insolent and idiotic impeachment" such and such testimony, makes us smile at the egregious example of the pot calling the kettle black. But more often we are merely bewildered by these outbursts. For often he does not condescend to name the object of his attack. When he declares that "any Helot of culture whose brain may have been affected by habitual indulgence in the academic delirium of complacent superiority" knows this or that, we refuse to follow further the course of his argument, distracted by a desire to know what particular "Helot" he has in mind. The violent essays of his later years are strewn with phrases like "No one above the intellectual level of an Ibsenite or a Zolaist will doubt or deny" that such and such a proposition is true. These sporadic allusions to abhorrent persons totally unconnected with the issue in hand account in part for the difficulty of reading Swinburne's prose. Sometimes a fragment of autobiography lies hidden in the chaos of hard words. But one must possess a clue to the secret. In the essay on Dickens there are two examples of these hidden meanings. When we read that Dickens' fame is great enough to deserve "the thanksgiving of all men worthy to acclaim it, and the contempt of such a Triton of the minnows as Matthew Arnold", we are distressed by the needless sneer, but when we go on to read the description of Arnold as "a man whose main achievement in creative literature was to make himself by painful painstaking into a sort of pseudo-Wordsworth" the puzzle is solved, for we remember that after Arnold's death it became known that he had called Swinburne "a sort of pseudo-Shelley." In the same essay occurs this passage:

> The publishers of the beautiful and convenient Gadshill Series are good enough to favor us with the prefatory importunities of a writer disentitled to express and disqualified to form an opinion on the work of an English humorist. The intrusive condescension or adulation of such a commentator was perhaps somewhat superfluous in front of the reprinted Waverley Novels; the offence becomes an outrage, the impertinence becomes impudence, when such rubbish is shot down before the doorstep of Charles Dickens.

What's the matter now? Why, not only had Andrew Lang differed from Swinburne on the question of the character of Mary Stuart but in his "Letters to Dead Authors" he had likened Swinburne attacking Byron to a bantam crowing over a dead eagle. The animus is clear. Again, what is the explanation of this onslaught in another essay?

> The volumes of Dodsley's "Old Plays" in their very latest reissue are encumbered with heaps of such leaden dullness and such bestial filth as no decent scavenger and no rational nightman would have dreamed of sweeping back into sight or smell of any possible reader.

The editor of the new "Dodsley" was W. Carew Hazlitt, grandson of William Hazlitt, who, because of his attacks on Coleridge, was anathema to Swinburne. Everyone remembers the anecdote of the innocently indiscreet visitor to "The Pines" whose remarks on Hazlitt were received by Swinburne in frozen silence and by Watts-Dunton with the whispered warning "We don't mention Hazlitt here." Examples of such side thrusts at objectionable persons might be multiplied indefinitely. Nor are they the only obstacles in the reader's path. The mode of progress is not straightforward but zigzag, and from many a bypath we must return to the main road.

A somewhat extended analysis of the "Note on Charlotte Brontë" will serve as an illustration of Swinburne's methodless method. With heavy irony he begins by commending the *Spectator's* opinion that the works of Charlotte Brontë will one day be again regarded as evidence of exceptional intellectual power, and venturing to commit himself further, he affirms that they will be read when the works of the female immortals of the present hour have fallen into oblivion, "when even 'Daniel Deronda' has gone the way of all waxwork, when even Miss Broughton no longer cometh up as a flower, and even Mrs. Oliphant is at length cut down like the grass."[1] Then, coming to grips with his subject, he comments upon the twin-born genius of Charlotte and Emily Brontë who have this in common with Mrs. Browning, that they possess that rarest form of imagination which is

[1]The clever use of the title of one of Miss Broughton's most popular novels is probably lost upon a reader of to-day.

the gift of genius. His taste for antithesis leads him to consider the differences which divide pure genius from mere intellectual power. Intellect is constructive, genius creative; and as examples of the kind of character produced by each he adduces Tito Melema and Edward Rochester. Genius invariably gives a sense of something inevitable.

Perhaps we may reasonably divide all imaginative work into three classes; the lowest, which leaves us in a complacent mood of acquiescence with the graceful or natural inventions of an honest and ingenious workman, and in no mind to question or dispute the accuracy of his transcript from life or the fidelity of his design to the modesty and the likelihood of nature; the second of high enough quality to engage our judgment in its service, and make direct demand on our grave attention for deliberate assent or dissent; the third, which in the exercise of its highest faculties at their best neither solicits nor seduces nor provokes us to acquiescence or demur, but compels us without question to positive acceptance and belief.

From the enunciation of this general law (if law it be)[1] Swinburne begins to work back gradually to his subject. He is constrained to admit that even in almost all the work of Fielding, Scott and Thackeray

[1] We are here reminded of Watts-Dunton's theory of the distinction between "absolute" and "relative" vision in poetry, an idea which must have been frequently discussed by him and Swinburne and which may be traced back to the old romantic discussions of the distinction between the Imagination and the Fancy.

at most we find the combination of event with character, the coincidence of action with disposition, the coherence of consequences with emotions, to be rationally credible . . . We rarely or never feel that given the characters, the incidents become inevitable; that such passions must needs bring forth none other than such action.

We are confident that the stage is now set for the appearance of Charlotte Brontë. But no; he chances to recollect that Sydney Dobell had once published a commendation of Emily Brontë; and we must, before reaching our subject, push our way through a commendation of the commendation written by the late admirable Dobell, which commendation was regrettably omitted from the posthumous collection of Dobell's admirable essays admirably edited by Professor John Nichol. Emily Brontë is praised; Dobell is praised; Nichol is praised. Surely it is time for Charlotte to appear; and she does so for a moment side by side with George Eliot. Swinburne compares the knowledge and culture of George Eliot with the passion and spiritual force and fervor of inspiration evident in Charlotte Brontë. The former he defines as "a type of intelligence vivified and coloured by a vein of genius"; the latter as "a type of genius directed and moulded by the touch of intelligence." Impatient with the antithetical seesaw of this pronouncement, we are likely to miss the truth of the contrast. The long digression which follows on the contrasting kinds of error into which genius and intelligence may be led is occupied with remarks upon George Eliot to the almost entire exclusion of the subject of the "Note." Yet once more the truth of what Swinburne says has to be acknowledged.

Where genius takes one false step in the twilight and draws back by instinct, intelligence once misguided will take a thousand without the slightest diffidence.

The insignificant slips in the painting of the social background of "Jane Eyre" are examples of the venial errors of genius; but the marriage of Maggie Tulliver and Stephen Guest is due to the irretrievable errors of the intellect. We penetrate one layer of digression only to reach another, for the mention of "The Mill on the Floss" introduces a discourse on the limits of realism in art. Swinburne is now hovering on the brink of one of his many denunciations of Zolaism, but he recovers himself with the comment that

there are characters and emotions which may not lie beyond the limits of degraded nature, but do assuredly grovel beneath the notice of undegenerate art.

The last third of the story of Maggie Tulliver serves to illustrate this assertion; and then the critic, knowing the value of generous concessions, admits that the critical judgment of genius is more liable to error than the critical judgment of trained intelligence (instances cited) and that George Eliot's earliest imaginative work attained at once a perfection far beyond the floundering tread of Charlotte Brontë's immature and tentative genius. He then turns to the character of Paul Emmanuel as an example of the triumph of moral insight and dramatic imagination, comparing him with Don Quixote. Have we at last reached the "Note on Charlotte Brontë"? No; in a moment we are in the midst of a digression on the weakness of Thackeray's good characters; and from that we proceed to some excellent comment on the landscape in the novels of the Brontës, especially in "Wuthering Heights." "There was a dark, unconscious instinct as of primitive nature-worship in the passionate great genius of Emily Brontë"; in her poetry there sounds "the pure note of absolutely right expression for things inexpressible in full by prose." The transition is not obvious that leads us from this digression to the question of direct transcripts from life in the work of the two sisters. Emily, Swinburne writes,

would probably have said, or at least presumably have felt, that such study after the model was to her impossible — an attempt but too certain to diminish her imaginative insight and disable her creative hand; while Charlotte evidently never worked so well as when painting more or less directly from nature.

"Painting from nature" — creative work based upon the author's own actual experiences! The train of thought carries Swinburne to the old infamous comment on "Jane Eyre" that its author must be a woman who long since had deserved to forfeit the society of her own sex; and with startling suddenness he breaks into an attack of the utmost violence upon the *Quarterly Review*. Thereafter he is, not unnaturally, out of breath, and the "Note" closes with some rather chaotic comments on Shakespeare's unfinished "Timon" and "Two Noble Kinsmen", Thackeray's unfinished "Denis Duval", and Forster's unfinished "Life of Swift." It takes an effort to understand that all this is *à propos* of Charlotte Brontë's unfinished "Emma."

I have entered into this much detail about the "Note" because it is representative of many of the qualities, both bad and good, in Swinburne's critical work. Not all his critiques are so badly put together as is this, but in almost all there is an evident lack of ability to arrange and compose; and the curious welter of warm appreciation and hot denunciation, of general principles and particular instances, of ability to make a point and inability to keep from straying away from it — these qualities, though exaggerated to the point almost of caricature in the "Note", are typical of all his prose work.

Swinburne's analysis of the three classes of imaginative literature is one of several "laws" which he attempted to set up. He took a delight that was almost childish in his "discovery" that great writers fall into one of two categories, on the one hand "the gods of harmony and creation", on the other, "the giants of energy and invention."[1] To thrust all the great poets into one or another of these classifications was a task neither practical nor profitable, and Swinburne, though he continued to toy with the notion, never carried it out completely. Yet when he sets Shakespeare over against Jonson, Milton over against Dryden, and Shelley over against Byron, we cannot but see what he intends. His scheme is no infallible guide but it has the value of suggestiveness. It encourages him, however, in his favorite method of criticism by comparison and contrast. No other critic ever resorted more frequently to the aid of analogy, often reinforced by antithesis. Here is a typical sentence: "As humorist rather than as poet, Pope is to Dryden what Sheridan is to Congreve." The analogy is a sound one, as is that which places Shirley between Fletcher and Etherege in the relation which Brome occupied between Jonson and Wycherley. Sometimes the formula attains a

[1]The notion is set forth with greatest elaboration in the essay on Coleridge: "In all times there have been gods that alighted and giants that appeared on earth; the ranks of great men are properly divisible not into thinkers and workers, but into Titans and Olympians. Some times a supreme poet is both at once: such above all men is Æschylus; so also Dante, Michel Angelo, Shakespeare, Milton, Goethe, Hugo, are gods at once and giants; they have the lightning as well as the light of the world, and in hell they have command as in heaven; they can see in the night as by day." In the "Study of Ben Jonson" and elsewhere Swinburne returns to the idea.

complexity almost algebraic: as is Massinger to Tourneur, so is Tourneur to Webster, and so is Webster to Shakespeare. Even here, apart from the somewhat eccentric undervaluation of Massinger, the comparison is suggestive, But occasionally the method is overstrained, as when Tennyson is compared with Musset, poets whom Swinburne would not have brought into relationship had not Taine already done so. In this case the desire to equate carries him even farther, and having compared a famous English poet with a famous French poet, he must needs discover another pair, and we have Browning and Leconte de Lisle thrown into juxtaposition and contrast. The same instinct leads him to the wearisomely reiterated comparisons of Æschylus and Shakespeare, Shakespeare and Hugo, Dante and Milton. Often it is a contrast rather than a resemblance that he seeks to indicate; and of all his critical comments of this kind that to which he returns most often and with most gusto is the distinction between Dante, Chaucer and Villon, all representative of the Middle Ages, but Dante the expression of the aristocracy, Chaucer of the bourgeoisie, and Villon "the first vocal voice of the dumb painful people." In this perilous kind of criticism he is least happy when he undertakes to compare poets with painters. To equate Chaucer and Benozzo Gozzoli is to reveal a want of understanding of the profundities beneath Chaucer's simplicities, for there is no such depth underlying

Benozzo's delightful ingenuousness. Again, to compare Morris' treatment of the story of Jason and Medea with Carpaccio's treatment of the legend of Saint Ursula is to ignore the distinction between studied and genuine simplicity.

In the "Notes on Poems and Reviews" Swinburne stated emphatically his view of the function of criticism:

> I can enjoy and applaud all good work . . . I have never been able to see what should attract men to the profession of criticism but the noble pleasure of praising.

This, the oftenest quoted sentence in all Swinburne's prose, is echoed again and again in later essays. In the "William Blake" he declares that "to recognise their equal, even their better when he does come, must be the greatest delight of great men." Just as Blake himself had declared that "the worship of God is, honoring his gifts in other men, each according to his genius, and loving the greatest man best", and as Ruskin had laid down the law that "all good critics delight in praising, as all bad ones in blaming", so in one of his prefaces Swinburne writes:

> My chief aim, as my chief pleasure, in all such studies as these has been rather to acknowledge and applaud what I found noble and precious than to scrutinize or to stigmatize what I might perceive to be worthless or base.

Elsewhere he formulates the critic's function as "to do homage wherever it may be due; to let nothing great pass unsaluted or unenjoyed." He admits that the sincere critic cannot always avoid a painful duty; but:

> When full honour has been done and full thanks rendered to those who have done great things, then and then only will it be no longer an untimely and unseemly labour to map and mark down their shortcomings for the profit or the pleasure of their inferiors or our own.

The intensity of his conviction of "the greatness of great men" makes plausible and tolerable the exaggerations of his praise; and these exaggerations, as expressed in his essays, should be correlated with such episodes in his personal life as the first meeting with Landor when he threw himself at the old man's feet, or the first meeting with Mazzini when he chanted the "Song of Italy" to him, or the dinner party in honor of Browning at which Swinburne appeared bearing a footstool that he might sit at Browning's feet. Such gestures are absurd but they are not ignoble. The same is true of his eulogistic criticism. Not infrequently, however, it is carried to an extreme well-nigh pathological, as when he defines this capacity for admiring as

> a righteous and a reverent delight in the sense of an inferiority which does not disable or deprive us of the capacity for adoration; a rapture of lowliness which exalts humility itself into something like

the gladness of pride — of pride that we can feel and exultation that we may acknowledge how high above us are men who yet are not too high for the loyal thank-offering, not only of our worship, but surely also of our love.

Only to readers who are not on the watch for the typical Swinburnian antithesis will this attitude of prostration before his "superiors" seem incompatible with the arrogance which he assumes when commenting upon his "inferiors." It was indisputably with a thought of his own controversies that he commended Pope for

fighting the good fight of sense against folly, of light against darkness, of human speech against brute silence, of truth and reason and manhood against all the banded bestialities of all dunces and all dastards, all blackguardly blockheads and all blockheaded blackguards, who then as now were misbegotten by malignity on dullness.

Yet, despite the testimony of some of his friends, I cannot believe that he was really happy in the scavenger work which engaged so much of his attention during his middle years. To some attacks he returned the best answer — silence.[1] In

[1] He made no reply to Mortimer Collins' "Two Plunges for a Pearl" (1871), a *roman à clef* which Rossetti called "an elaborately spiteful outrage." The book is feebly Peacockian in tone. Among the characters is Mr. Reginald Swynfen, "a little man, built like a grasshopper", who "firmly believed himself the greatest living poet . . . His excitable brain could stand but little wine . . . His poems, gentle reader, you may have read, or tried to read. They deal with effeminate heroes and somewhat masculine heroines, Rizzios and Messalinas." In the dialogue Swynfen boasts of his ancient blood and declares his poetry superior to "the soft silly sensuousness of Tennyson" and to "the bald Boeotian

the case of the quarrel with Robert Buchanan he was goaded into controversy, though it must be said that when once in the midst of it he enjoyed the fray.[1] It has been said that both he and Furnivall

stuff" of Browning. In one scene Swynfen makes passionate love to a young lady. He is unaware of their dangerous proximity to the coping of a well into which the resourceful lady topples the poet. In this mortifying situation we leave him. During the eighteen-seventies there were other scurrilities of like nature.

[1] The long-drawn-out quarrel with Buchanan has been so often narrated that the briefest summary will suffice here. Buchanan's squib ridiculing Swinburne but not ill-natured in tone, called "The Session of the Poets", appeared in the *Spectator*, September 15, 1866, during the excitement over "Poems and Ballads." W. M. Rossetti opened his "Criticism" of Swinburne's book with an allusion to the "poor and pretentious poetaster", Buchanan. Buchanan delayed his reply till January 29, 1870, when he published "a personal onslaught" on W. M. Rossetti in the *Athenæum*. Then followed the novel discussed in the preceding note; Collins was a friend of Buchanan's. In the *Contemporary Review* of October, 1871, Buchanan published under the pseudonym "Thomas Maitland" his notorious article "The Fleshly School of Poetry", attacking D. G. Rossetti and incidentally Swinburne. Rossetti replied (having suppressed an "open letter" to Buchanan and a burlesque ballad on him, both which might have exposed him to action for libel) in "The Stealthly School of Criticism" (the *Athenæum*, December 16, 1871). Buchanan enlarged his article into a pamphlet, "The Fleshly School of Poetry and other Phenomena of the Day" (1872). This, with Alfred Austin's "The Poetry of the Period" (1870), inspired Swinburne's "Under the Microscope" (1872), the most formidable of all the poet's exhibitions of vituperation and invective. Buchanan replied with some ineffective verses, "The Monkey and the Microscope", in *St. Paul's Magazine*. There the matter rested for three years. In 1875 there was published anonymously "Jonas Fisher: a Poem in Brown and White." In Part III (stanzas 188 *et seq.*) is a long diatribe against a nameless poet, a "prurient paganist" who "warbles a sick, putrescent, dulcet lay", hymning "the sensuous charms of morbid immorality." Swinburne thought he recognized the hand of Buchanan and published in the *Examiner*, November 20, 1875, an unsigned "Epitaph on a Slanderer", four lines of extreme bitterness never republished in his collected works. A week later the same newspaper, reviewing "Jonas Fisher", declared that it was by "either Mr. Robert Buchanan or the Devil." Upon which Swinburne published in the same journal (December 11) and also circulated in privately printed form his celebrated letter, "The Devil's Due." This was suggested by the reviewer's remark just quoted, upon which Swinburne comments: "Certainly it is inconceivable that the authorship of any work whatever should be assignable with equal plausibility to the polypseudonymous lyrist and libeller in question and to the Satan of Milton, the Lucifer of Byron, or the Mephistopheles of Goethe."

enjoyed the dirty game of slinging mud at each other.[1] No doubt each was excited by the competition, but Swinburne at any rate (as he wrote

Buchanan brought suit for libel against the *Examiner*. At the trial (June 29–July 1, 1876) the Earl of Southesk acknowledged his authorship of "Jonas Fisher." Buchanan won the verdict with damages of one hundred and fifty pounds against the *Examiner*. In Hall Caine's "Recollections of Rossetti" (1882) Buchanan published a retractation of his charges against Rossetti. See also the *Academy*, July 1, 1882. In Watts-Dunton's somewhat cryptic sonnet, "The Octopus of the Golden Isles", the isles are those of Romance; the man who dwelt therein was Rossetti; the inky squid, Buchanan. For further details see Mr. Wise's "Bibliography."

[1] The following is a succinct outline of the course of this noisy controversy. In 1875 Swinburne subjected Fleay's metrical tests of dramatic authorship to ridicule. In 1876 Furnivall controverted statements of Swinburne's regarding certain metrical features of "Henry VIII." Furnivall, though Gosse does not indicate it, was right in his facts, however ill-mannered in his way of presenting them. In the "Study of Shakespeare" Swinburne parodied the meetings of "The Newest Shakespeare Society", Furnivall's organization. During 1877 Furnivall, William Minto and Swinburne were engaged in controversy over a point in Chaucer in the *Athenæum*. See especially Swinburne's letter in the issue of April 14. In the *Gentleman's Magazine*, August and September, 1879, Swinburne adduced certain non-Shakespearean words in "Edward III" as evidence of non-Shakespearean authorship. Furnivall, again correct in fact but outrageous in manner, showed (in the *Spectator*) that an argument based on the presence of these words would deprive Shakespeare of the authorship of "The Tempest", "King John" and other canonical plays. This contribution Furnivall reprinted in a pamphlet, "Mr. Swinburne's Flat Burglary on Shakespeare." Gosse now appealed to Edward Dowden to use his influence on Furnivall to stop "this shocking scandal." Dowden replied mildly that so far as facts were concerned Furnivall was unquestionably in the right. (See Dowden's "Letters", where Gosse's letter is also printed.) Furnivall now heard that Swinburne's "Study of Shakespeare" was to be dedicated to the veteran scholar, J. O. Halliwell-Phillipps, to whom he wrote, demanding insolently that Halliwell-Phillipps refuse the dedication. This letter was very properly ignored. Furnivall's retort was a scurrilous reference to "the firm of Pigsbrook and Co." in his foreword to a facsimile edition of the 1604 "Hamlet." Halliwell-Phillipps wrote to Browning, the President of the New Shakespeare Society, complaining of this "phraseology of Billingsgate." Browning replied that his position was purely honorary and that he was not responsible for Furnivall's utterances. Halliwell-Phillipps then published his correspondence with Browning. Furnivall's rejoinder was the incredibly coarse brochure, "The 'Co.' of Pigsbrook and Co." In the *Academy* during the year 1880 there appeared several further letters from Swinburne and Furnivall. In the end the poet declined,

to a friend) soon became "sick of the subject." It is possible to read a certain measure of self-condemnation in the following remark:

> It is certainly no very dignified amusement, no very profitable expenditure of energy or time, to indulge in the easy diversion of making such curs yelp, and watching them writhe under the chastisement which an insulted superior may condescend to inflict, till their foul mouths foam over in futile and furious response, reeking and rabid with virulent froth and exhalations of raging ribaldry.

He is here writing of Milton's controversial pamphlets, but his thought is obviously of his own opponents; and it is noteworthy that he remarks that though Milton "did not hesitate to set his heel, when duly guarded by the thick-soled boot of prose" upon "things unmentionable", "he never permitted the too fetid contact of their stercorous feculence to befoul the sandal of his Muse." The garments of Swinburne's own "Muse" are kept almost wholly free from the mud and dust of controversy. But even the death of an opponent did not restrain his prose, for he characterized the old *Nihil nisi bonum* as "the liar's maxim and the

none too soon, to take further part in controversy. An undated pamphlet, certainly not by Swinburne, is in existence entitled "Furnivallos Furioso! and The Newest Shakespeare Society, A Dram-Attic Squib of the Period in Three Fizzes." This shows that the Society and its director were objects of ridicule to others besides Swinburne. It must be added that several vice-presidents of the Society resigned in protest against Furnivall's bad manners and methods of controversy. To them he wrote an extraordinarily censorious letter which is quoted in Mr. Munro's memoir of Furnivall.

traitor's plea, which forbids us to speak truth when to speak truth is to speak evil of the defeated, the dishonoured, and the dead.''[1] But in all such writing, if he found satisfaction at all, it was the satisfaction of wielding tremendous and overwhelming epithets. At this game his opponents were not his equals. Where Swinburne is Rabelaisian in his command of adjectives, Furnivall and Buchanan are merely vulgar.

The highest and hardest work of the critic, says Swinburne, is ''first to discover what is good, and then to discover how and in what way it is so.'' As a discoverer of the ''how'' and the ''why'' of excellence he is not so often successful as in the discernment of what is excellent. His task was really frequently that of an anthologist. In the elaborate, almost encyclopaedic essays on the early dramatists he is carrying on the work of Charles Lamb. Like Lamb he rejects preconceived and arbitrary standards. He takes no interest in the problem of fitting the ''man'' into his ''milieu'' and never accounts for poetic excellence by examining the political and social conditions in which a writer lived. His point of view is not moral nor

[1]The sonnets on the dead Napoleon III involved Swinburne in a controversy with R. H. Hutton, the editor of the *Spectator*, in 1873. The chief instance of an attack on the dead is, however, Swinburne's article "The New Terror" (*Fortnightly Review*, December 1892). This was prompted by William Bell Scott's ''Autobiographical Notes'' in which there are indiscreet allusions to Swinburne and Rossetti. This book had been published posthumously by William Minto.

religious nor philosophical nor social. He is an impressionist in that having received impressions from "good work" judged for the work's sake, his aim is to convey to his reader something of his own enthusiasm. Beneath the verbosity and extravagance there is almost always sound judgment and fine taste. It takes an attentive reader to detect the qualifications introduced into eulogy, but the qualifications are there and often form the most illuminating part of the critique.

How admirable, for example, are these comments on Ben Jonson: "Elaborate ostentation of effort and demonstrative prodigality of toil." And: "This crowning and damning defect of a tedious and intolerable realism." And again: "He was careful and troubled about many things absolutely superfluous and superogatory." And this of "Cynthia's Revels": "The Cyclopean ponderosity of perseverance which hammers through scene after scene at the task of ridicule by anatomy of tedious and preposterous futilities." And of the same play:

> The wildest, the roughest, the crudest offspring of literary impulse working blindly on the passionate elements of excitable ignorance was never more formless, more incoherent, more defective in structure, than this voluminous abortion of deliberate intelligence and conscientious culture.

Other playwrights are equally well characterized. Writing of "the clumsy and ponderous incompetence of expression" in the work of John Marston he remarks that Marston's

> vehement and resolute desire to give weight to every line and emphasis to every phrase has too often led him into such brakes and jungles of crabbed and convulsive bombast of stiff and tortuous exuberance, that the reader . . . feels as though he were compelled to push his way through a cactus hedge.

Some of Dekker's plays are described as "improvisations of inebriety"; Dekker's "besetting vice of reckless and sluttish incoherence" and his "reckless and shameless incompetence" are noted, and he is described as:

> A man of gentle, modest, shiftless and careless nature, irritable and placable, eager and unsteady, full of excitable kindliness and deficient in strenuous principle,

whose "slippery style and shambling licence" we pardon for the sake of his lyric note, his pathos, his tenderness and his fancy. In writing of Chapman, Swinburne admits his pedantry, his taste for bizarre instances and recondite allusions, and his "bombast and bulky vacuity." The citation of these adverse opinions may serve to correct the current impression that Swinburne's Elizabethan criticism is a confused mass of extravagant eulogy. As an encomiast he is not always so safe a guide. It is difficult to stomach the adjective "noble" applied to that repulsive production "Thierry and Theodoret." Few readers will find "overflowing fun and masterdom of extravagance" in that thin humor-study, "The Noble Gentleman." It may be asserted with some confidence that not one reader in a thousand shares Swinburne's experience in reading "The Silent Woman": "For whole scenes together . . . an inward riot or an open passion of subdued or unrepressed laughter." Few will agree that "The Alchemist" is marked by "serene inspiration" or that there is "unsurpassed ingenuity and dexterity" in the composition of "Bartholomew Fair." The sides of not many of us "shake with laughter" at that "drollest and liveliest" of comedies, "A Chaste Maid in Cheapside." Nor do we share his taste for "that brilliant and amusing play," "The Dutch Courtesan" whose underplot he thought worthy of Molière!

When Swinburne writes of dramatists with whom he is not in entire sympathy he is more judicious than when he writes about his favorites. Thus, the paper on Thomas Dekker is written in unusually simple, straightforward English. Another masterly study is that of Philip Massinger, "the most temperate, studious and conscientious of the successors of Shakespeare." He seeks to place this playwright midway between the depreciation of Leslie Stephen and the immoderate praise of Hartley Coleridge; and the need to keep a middle course has the happy effect of holding Swinburne's own enthusiasm in check. Again, in the two papers on Thomas Heywood, Swinburne admits, with proper professions of humility, a certain lack of sympathy which places him in opposition to Charles Lamb. The resulting tone is of a mellow quietness that permits the introduction of a tribute to Fleay's "prodigious monument of learning and labour" — that Fleay who had been second only to Furnivall in Swinburne's disesteem. He senses with precision Heywood's peculiar appeal when he describes it as "the quaint, homely, single-hearted municipal loyalty of an old-world burgess."

His criticism of the old dramatists is limited to certain strictly esthetic topics. Source-studies, verse-tests, archivistic and antiquarian scholarship of all kinds: the structure of the stage, the history and organization of the dramatic companies, the problem of the relationship of playwright, patron, actor and publisher — these things interest him not at all. The problem of authorship does concern him, but he ridicules all "scientific" criteria for its determination, relying upon "instinct — that last resource and ultimate reason of all critics in every case and on every question." The essay on Beaumont and Fletcher contains some striking examples of his success in arriving intuitively at results afterwards reached by other lines of argument by other scholars. His discrimination between Dekker's and Ford's shares in "The Witch of Edmonton" is a good example of his studies in the problem of composite authorship. On the other hand, modern scholarship has not substantiated his opinions regarding the authorship of "Arden of Faversham" and "The Second Maiden's Tragedy." In his discussion of "Appius and Virginia" he is on the verge of the theory of non-Websterian authorship propounded by a later poet-critic.

The old drama is the only subject that occupied Swinburne's attention as a critic throughout his life. His first published essay was on Marlowe and Webster; the unfinished critique on which he was working just before his last illness was on one of the lesser playwrights. This was the one field in which he claimed to speak with the authority of an expert. The essay on John Ford (1871) is the first of his major efforts in this department; and the most ambitious studies are those of Chapman (1875), Shakespeare (1875–1876) and Ben Jonson (1889). His hope was to compose a sort of encyclopedia of appreciative essays on the entire company of dramatists from the emergence of Lyly to the closing of the theaters. If we include the posthumously published essays there is scarcely a playwright, even of fourth rank, to whom he did not devote a laudatory critique. As the years passed it came about that the lower the rank of the dramatist and consequently the more nearly complete a "discovery" by Swinburne himself, the more extravagant became the praise. The latest essays cannot be read with patience. But in the more celebrated studies, such as the "Study of Shakespeare", what Swinburne offers is profound appreciative suggestiveness. We do not go to him for the "facts about Shakespeare"; but we leave his book with a larger sense of Shakespeare's greatness. The evident disproportion in the treatment of the plays — twenty pages devoted, for example, to "Henry VIII" and but four to "Macbeth" — is due to his avoidance of hackneyed criticism; where he has little to say he says little. Something will be said presently of Swinburne's prose style, but here it needs to be remarked that though the flamboyant redundance of his prose is marked in many of the studies of the dramatists, one discovers in them passages of noble eloquence such as the celebrated opening of the "Study of Shakespeare" and the penultimate paragraph of the article on "Beaumont and Fletcher."

It must be repeated that in this field Swinburne regarded his task as largely that of an anthologist. He delighted to discover the solitary excellence (such as the lovely lines on a cameo in "Doctor Doddypoll") which redeems some very minor poet from oblivion; it was his happiness to

> Mark where a bold expressive phrase appears,
> Bright through the rubbish of some hundred years.

But, as we have seen, his strictures against the dramatists can be as strident as his praise is vociferous. "The sun is strong and the wind sharp," he warns his readers, "in the climate which reared the fellows and followers of Shakespeare. The extreme inequality and roughness of the ground must also be taken into account." His purpose was to continue and broaden the work of Charles Lamb. He wished to widen the appeal of the greater dramatists and to introduce the minor playwrights to a modern audience. By ceaselessly and patiently selecting individual scenes for analysis and commendation, he did something very similar to Lamb's achievement in the "Specimens of the Dramatic Poets." To his influence is largely due the far greater general knowledge of the Tudor and Stuart dramatists to-day as compared with half a century ago. He sponsored Bullen's editions of the dramatists. Yet the failure of Bullen's "Beaumont and Fletcher" — abandoned, a splendid fragment, shortly before the Great War — is in some measure an indication of Swinburne's failure in his encyclopedic work of *haute vulgarisation*. He failed because his critiques are comprehensible only to those who have already read the plays which he discusses; and those who have read them are almost exclusively specialists who are impatient with the poet's errors in chronology and ascription, his impressionism, his want of training as an archivist, his want of balance; and are by temperament insensitive to his admirable compensating qualities.

Of the numerous essays on the English poets of the Romantic Period and his own day incomparably the finest is the "William Blake" (1868). This outstanding and influential book was begun as a review of Alexander Gilchrist's "Pictor Ignotus" but developed into an independent work. In the phrasing of some passages the review form still clings to it; the comparatively meager treatment of Blake's designs is due to Gilchrist's comparatively full discussion of them, while the large space devoted to the "Prophetic Books" is intended to atone for the biographer's almost entire neglect of them. Rossetti attempted to dissuade Swinburne from the task of interpreting the "Prophetic Books", but he was not to be turned aside. He profited from personal acquaintance with Kirkup, Palmer and other surviving friends of Blake. He examined original manuscripts and Blake's engraved books in the British Museum and elsewhere. He rummaged through the files of old newspapers and periodicals, discovering the *Examiner's* attack on Blake and Blake's letter in defence of Fuseli. As is usual in Swinburne's critical writings, there are digressions in his book indicative of the tastes and interests uppermost in his mind at the time of writing.[1] But in the main the work is admirably composed, well thought out and brilliantly set out.

[1]There are allusions to C. J. Wells, Baudelaire, and especially Walt Whitman; and certain curious references to the poetry, the heresies and the "paganism" of the Albigeois are explicable when we remember that Swinburne had been contemplating a long poem on the history of the Albigeois heresy and persecution.

The appeal of Blake to Swinburne was manifold. Blake's conception of the function of art and the place of the artist in the world (admirably expounded in Swinburne's second chapter) anticipated in part the doctrine of *L'Art pour l'art.* His advocacy of self-expression and joy as opposed to asceticism and abstinence supported the liberal continental ethic which Swinburne set up against the rigid Victorian code. His emphasis upon the One-ness of the human and the divine had something in common with the Comtist positivism which for a while influenced Swinburne's thought. The non-orthodox mysticism of Blake, though Swinburne rejected it intellectually, found its way into "Songs before Sunrise." He sympathized with Blake's dreams of a universal republic and with his doctrine of the duty of "holy insurrection" against false beliefs. The kinship between Blake and Shelley and Blake and Whitman were additional claims upon Swinburne's attention.

Yet Swinburne is ready to make many concessions. He avoids the error of inappropriately clear definition of doctrines and notions radically incoherent and obscure. "The huge windy mythology of elemental dæmons, and the capricious passion for catalogues of random names, which make obscure and hideous so much of these books" he was not troubled to extenuate. There is a wonderful description of the world of Blake's mythology:

Titans of monstrous form and yet more monstrous name obstruct the ways; sickness or sleep never formed such savage abstractions, such fierce vanities of vision as these: office and speech they seem at first to have none; but to strike or clutch at the void of air with feeble fingers, to babble with vast lax lips a dialect barren of all but noise, loud and loose as the wind.

He warns his readers:

The complete and exalted figure of Blake cannot be seen in full by those who avert their eyes, smarting and blinking, from the frequent smoke and sudden flame. Others will see more clearly, as they look more sharply, the radical sanity and coherence of the mind which puts forth its shoots of thought and faith in ways so strange, at such strange times.

He recognizes the anomaly of the mystic visionary, independent of creeds, living in the age of the "Enlightenment":

His ecstasy of study was neither on the one side tempered and watered down by faith in established forms and external creeds, nor on the other side modified and directed by analytic judgment and the lust of facts.

Ready to admit that the philosophy of freedom in "The Marriage of Heaven and Hell" might, "if translated into rough practice, and planted in a less pure soil than that of the writer's mind", "bring forth a strange harvest", Swinburne yet insists that, though Blake enjoyed "the high and subtle luxuries of exceptional temperaments", "he never found or felt out any way to the debatable land where simple and tender pleasures become complex and cruel", for "a temperament so sensuous, so receptive, and so passionate, is further off from any risk of turning unsound than hardier natures."[1]

In this critical essay there was made the first attempt to penetrate into the mysteries of the "Prophetic Books." That is the historical significance of Swinburne's work. Later explorers have pushed into the furthest recesses of the jungle; but all have been willing to acknowledge Swinburne as the pioneer. To attempt to follow him here would involve us in details of interpretation. The essence of his exegesis is contained in this sentence:

> The very root or kernel of [Blake's] creed is not the assumed humanity of God, but the achieved divinity of Man; not incarnation from without, but development from within; not a miraculous passage into flesh, but a natural growth into godhead.

The parts of Swinburne's study dealing with Blake's designs contain the finest of his attempts to

[1]To this radical sanity of outlook Swinburne discovers an exception in the latter part of that mysterious poem "The Mental Traveller." He interprets it as: "The perversion of love; which having annihilated all else, falls at last to feed upon itself, to seek out strange things and barren ways, to invent new loves and invert the old, to fill the emptied heart and flush the subsiding veins with perverse passion." This line of thought brings us close to some of the "Poems and Ballads" and to "Les Fleurs du Mal."

translate into words the impression produced by the graphic arts. In the famous description of "The Reunion of Body and Soul" (one of the designs in Blair's "Grave") the verbal image is as superb as the visual, and Swinburne surpasses the most magnificent passages in "Modern Painters":

None who have ever seen can well forget the glorious violence of reunion between body and soul, moving with fierce embraces, with glad agony and rage of delight; with breasts yearning and eyes wide, with sweet madness of laughter at their lips; the startled and half-arisen body not less divine already than the descending soul, though the earth clings yet about his knees and feet, and though she comes down as with a clamour of rushing wind and prone impulse of falling water, fresh from the stars and the highest air of heaven.

We may take leave of Swinburne's greatest prose work with this wonderful picture of the mystic poet-artist's daily life:

About his path and about his bed, around his ears and under his eyes, an infinite play of spiritual life seethed and swarmed or shone and sang. Spirits imprisoned in the husk and shell of earth consoled or menaced him. Every leaf bore a growth of angels; the pulse of every minute sounded as the falling foot of God; under the rank raiment of weeds, in the drifting down of thistles, strange faces frowned and white hair fluttered; tempters and allies, wraiths of the living and phantoms of the dead, crowded and made populous the winds that blew about him, the fields and hills over which he gazed.

As surely the finest as it is indisputably the most famous of the shorter essays on nineteenth-century poets is that on Byron (1865), a landmark in the history of criticism since it ushered in the revival of appreciation of the poet. By no means indiscriminate praise — for Swinburne deplores Byron's bad ear, the falsetto note in much of his verse, the histrionic affectations, the failure of the dramas — it is nevertheless essentially a tribute to Byron's greatness, a greatness which became manifest when Byron came to realize his power in the departments of comedy and satire. Over against the three impediments, "youth, genius, and an ancient name", Swinburne sets "his splendid and imperishable excellence . . . of sincerity and strength" and "his glorious courage, his excellent contempt for things contemptible, and hatred of hateful men." The celebrated concluding paragraph of this essay has been so often quoted that it need not be given here. It deserves its fame, for never again did Swinburne achieve such delicate rhythms, such restrained dignity of style, such perfect harmony.

The subsequent onslaught upon Byron in the notorious essay "Wordsworth and Byron" (1884) was prompted by Arnold's prophecy that "when the year 1900 is turned" the chief poetic glories of the nineteenth century would be these two poets. Swinburne's diatribe exhibits the disciple of Shelley resenting in a highly irascible way the slight put upon his master. The virulence of epithet is scarcely to be matched in English criticism, but if we disregard the violent phrases that overcloud the thought it will be apparent that the change from the essay of 1865 is one of tone and emphasis rather than of opinion. Byron's commonplace metrical talent had been stressed in the earlier critique; this view is now elaborated with accompanying ridicule and parody. That his triumphs were in the Bernesque vein, "a province outside the proper domain of absolute poetry", is an opinion heavily reinforced in the later essay. The former praise of Byron's sincerity is now whittled down to the bare admission that when he wrote on political subjects he was sincere.

If the tone of the estimate of Byron is extravagantly unjust, that of the estimate of Wordsworth is grudgingly laudatory. Nevertheless at various points Swinburne penetrates to the heart of Wordsworth's appeal: his tenderness, his sympathy with suffering, the spontaneity of his best work, his occasional sublimity, "the felicity of his instinct" which so far transcended the guidance of his theories. A good instance of Swinburne's rare reliance upon succinctness is the remark: "The frequent vapour that wraps his head and the frequent dust that soils his feet [fill] the simpler sort with admiration of one so lofty at once and so familiar."[1]

Swinburne's critiques on his elder contemporaries are among the least satisfying of his prose writings. He passed through adolescence during "the melancholy generation of the eighteen-fifties"; and the "poetry of doubt" characteristic of that period made upon him an impression lastingly unfavorable. "The fretful and fruitless prurience of soul which would fain grasp and embrace and enjoy a creed beyond its power of possession" was incomprehensible to him; the "letch after gods dead or unborn, such as vexes the nerves of barren brains and makes pathetic the vocal lips of sorrowing scepticism" inspired his scorn; and he turned in disgust from "the small troubles of spirits that nibble and quibble about beliefs living or dead" and "the sickly moods which are warmed and weakened by feeding on the sullen drugs of

[1]The essay on Coleridge (1869) is not one of Swinburne's more substantial contributions to appreciative criticism. The theory of "gods" and "titans" is here set forth at considerable length. There are some interesting comments upon prosody, such as the insistance on the importance of assonance and alliteration no less than of rhyme as "requisite components of high and ample harmony." The following is a fine example of that rare succinctness of which I have spoken: "Coleridge was the reverse of Antaeus; the contact with earth took all strength out of him." — It is curious that to his master Shelley, Swinburne never consecrated an essay surveying his entire work. "Notes on the Text of Shelley" contain emendations, some of which have passed into the established text, but they are of no general interest. The preface, written in French, which he contributed to a French translation of "The Cenci" (1883) is in the main a character study of Beatrice Cenci with a comparison of Shelley's and Landor's treatment of the theme. — The article on Keats contributed to the "Encyclopædia Britannica" seems to me to be profoundly inadequate.

dejection." In the essay on Matthew Arnold he says finely:

> Nothing in verse or out of verse is more wearisome than the delivery of reluctant doubt, of half-hearted hope and half-incredulous faith. A man who suffers from the strong desire to believe or disbelieve something he cannot may be worthy of sympathy, is certainly worthy of pity, until he begins to speak; and if he tries to speak in verse he misuses the implement of an artist . . . Nothing which leaves us depressed is a true work of art. We must have light though it be lightning, and air though it be storm.

Thirty years later, in a paragraph on Arthur Hugh Clough, he returned to the same thought:

> Nothing is to be made by an artist out of scepticism, half-hearted or double-hearted doubts or creeds; nothing out of mere dejection and misty mental weather.

On the other hand, he is ready, generously over-ready, to celebrate any distinguished achievement in contemporary literature, for, as he says, "there has never been an age that was not degenerate in the eyes of its own fools"; and his own function as critic is to recognize greatness, not deplore degeneracy.

To Browning Swinburne did not devote a separate essay, but allusions to him are fairly numerous and almost always favorable. Tennyson he assailed again and again in prose and verse. To indicate the points of contrast between the two poets would be to labor the obvious. It is sufficient to say that while the Laureate let his disapproval of the younger school of poets be known on various occasions,[1] Swinburne on his part saw in Tennyson the opponent of those principles which he had expounded in his early manifestos and had exemplified in his poetry. He seized upon the least admirable portion of Tennyson's work, the "Idylls of the King", and ignoring the allegorical significance of the character of Arthur, paraded the "blameless king" before the British public as a wittol and a prig.[2] But apart from the "Idylls" he often dealt generously with the Laureate, particularly in later years; and the essay "Tennyson and Musset" is an amazing farrago of old prejudices and new enthusiasms.

The cool and modulated tone of Swinburne's review of Arnold's "New Poems" (1867) is appropriate to the subject, but he does not let his pleasure in praising silence his protests against the poetry of sterile doubt, against Arnold's experiments in unrhymed irregular verse, against Arnold's eccentric opinions of French literature and his lack

[1] The story goes that Tennyson, after reading privately to a little company his narrative of the love-frenzy of Lucretius, looked around complacently and said, "Think what a mess little Swinburne would have made of this!" The anecdote may be apocryphal but it points the contrast.

[2] The most notorious of these attacks is in "Under the Microscope." According to an anecdote which deserves to be better known, Swinburne, meeting Tennyson one day at the house of a friend, said, "We understand, of course, that Arthur is Prince Albert and Guenevere is Queen Victoria. But, Tennyson, who is Launcelot?" The Laureate's reply has not been recorded.

of appreciation of French poetry. He doubts the validity of Arnold's "mission" to wage warfare against the "Philistines", and questioning the famous assertion that Oxford has never given herself to the Philistines, wittily depicts Arnold himself as Samson a prisoner in Gaza. In the main, however, the review is a generous tribute. "I cannot reckon the help and guidance in thought and work which I owe to him," writes Swinburne, proceeding to contrast the lucidity and equality of Arnold's style with "the clatter of the chaotic school."

> The supreme charm of Mr. Arnold's work is a sense of right resulting in a spontaneous temperance which bears no mark of curb or snaffle, but obeys the hand with imperceptible submission and gracious reserve . . . His verse bathes us with fresh radiance and light rain, when weary of the violence of summer and winter in which others dazzle and detain us.

The long remainder of Swinburne's studies in English literature must be passed over with the briefest notice. The articles on Rossetti and Morris are reviews undertaken as acts of friendship. The essay on William Collins has been influential in directing new attention to that poet's lyrical gift, though there is a suspicion that Swinburne's enthusiasm was in part due to Collins' youthful and quite insignificant republicanism. The diatribe called "Whitmania" is a recantation of the allegiance expressed in "Songs before Sunrise." Whitman's comment upon the attack was a noble one: "Swinburne has his own bigness; he is not to be drummed out of all camps because he does not find himself comfortable in our camp." An article on Dickens[1] is marked by an unexpected ability to estimate the relative worth of the novels and to indicate their shortcomings; but it is marred by more than ordinary truculence.

Apart from a few papers of minor importance and the early essay on Baudelaire, Swinburne's French studies are devoted to the praise and glory of Victor Hugo. Most of this material was originally a series of reviews of Hugo's successive volumes. The most noteworthy is that on "L'Homme qui rit" which opens with the celebrated likening of the genius of Hugo to that storm which had so much impressed Swinburne on his first crossing of the English Channel. This paragraph has been selected by Professor Saintsbury (in his "History of English Prose Rhythm") as a specimen of Swinburne's prose at its best. It is too long and too familiar to quote here, but it may be remarked — since it is generally overlooked — that the passage is no mere purple patch but firmly wrought into the texture of the essay, since the *motif* of the storm at sea recurs again and again, and one phase and

[1]The *Quarterly Review*, July, 1902; republished together with a brief paper on "Oliver Twist" in a posthumous volume, 1913.

then another of Hugo's genius is likened now to the thundercloud, now to the high indifferent moon, and now to the broad expanse of sea.

Swinburne for long meditated a general survey of Hugo's work; but "A Study of Victor Hugo" was put forth as a partial expression of the "infinite and worldwide sorrow" at the master's death. Here the rapture of devotion exceeds even that in the notices with which Paul de Saint Victor had followed the stages in Hugo's career. It soon cloys; and the reader, with flagging attention, is likely to miss passages of fine criticism hidden away beneath the transports. "Studies in Prose and Poetry" contains no less than eight papers on as many posthumous works of Hugo. They occupy half the volume. The laudation is more extreme than ever and the subjects are in the main not so worthy of it.

Swinburne's essays on the fine arts are insignificant in number, but one — "Notes on Designs of the Old Masters at Florence" — is of historical importance as anticipating the subjective meditative mood of Walter Pater, who admitted that it had influenced him in forming his style and method. At the time of Swinburne's visit to Florence (1864) the vast collection of drawings in the Uffizi and Pitti was in most admired disorder, uncatalogued and unarranged. Through the influence of Seymour Kirkup, the young poet obtained permission to examine them. The resulting "Notes" are upon two hundred and twenty-six drawings by forty-five different artists. The mere arrangement of so many scattered impressions into an essay which for all its variety manages to preserve a unity of tone was an extraordinary feat. The painters of the High Renaissance are not ignored, but there is an emphasis, not so common in Swinburne's day as it afterwards became, upon the Quatrocento, with special attention to Paolo Uccello, Filippino Lippi, and Botticelli. The following passage is quoted not only because it illustrates Swinburne's work in this kind but because it clearly anticipates Pater:

Of Leonardo the samples are choice and few; full of that indefinable grace and grave mystery which belongs to his slightest and wildest work. Fair strange faces of women full of dim doubt and faint scorn; touched by the shadow of an obscure fate; eager and weary as it seems at once, pale and fervent with patience or passion; allure and perplex the eyes and thoughts of men. There is a study here of Youth and Age meeting; it may be, of a young man coming suddenly upon the ghostly figure of himself as he will one day be; the brilliant life in his face is struck into sudden pallor and silence, the clear eyes startled, the happy lips confused. A fair straight-featured face, with curls falling or blown against the eyelids; and confronting it, a keen, wan, mournful mask of flesh: the wise ironical face of one made subtle and feeble by great age. The vivid and various imagination of Leonardo never fell into a form more poetic than this design. Grotesques of course are not wanting;

and there is a noble sketch of a griffin and a lion locked or dashed together in the hardest throes of a final fight, which is full of violent beauty; and again, a study of the painter's chosen type of woman: thin-lipped, with a forehead too high and weighty for perfection or sweetness of form; cheeks exquisitely carved, clear pure chin and neck, and grave eyes full of a cold charm; folded hands, and massive hair gathered into a net; shapely and splendid, as a study for Pallas or Artemis.

Pater's ultra-refinement of taste and more exquisite sense of prose rhythm would have subtilized the cadences in this paragraph and have eliminated the alliterations and the balanced pairs of verbs, substantives and epithets; but his method is here in germ.[1]

Five or six passages from Swinburne's prose have been quoted and re-quoted, passing from book to

[1] The "Notes on Some Pictures of 1866", written in collaboration with W. M. Rossetti and the "Notes" on Simeon Solomon published in *The Dark Blue* in 1871 are ephemeralities. The article on "Mr. Whistler's Lecture on Art" (1888), which provoked Whistler's cruel and witty reply, is, though heavily ironical in tone, in the main laudatory in substance. Swinburne protests against three doctrines expounded by the lecturer. He denies that art appeals only to the sense of beauty. He is no longer, as in youth, in sympathy with the doctrine of the "aristocracy" of art; and he denies that "all efforts to widen the sphere of appreciation . . . must needs be puny or unprofitable." And he denies that all great art must needs be joyous, citing Whistler's portrait of his mother in which he discerns "an intensity of pathetic power, which gives to that noble work something of the impressiveness proper to a tragic or elegiac poem." These opinions need not have occasioned any quarrel. Unfortunately, trespassing upon a province with which he was entirely unfamiliar, Swinburne ventured to satirize Whistler's praise of Japanese art, affecting to regard the portraits of Carlyle and the painter's mother as betrayals of Whistler's loyalty to Japan. It is a well-known fact that Watts-Dunton persuaded Swinburne to write this article.

book.[1] Instead of yielding to the temptation to transcribe them here I have preferred to cite a large number of brief critical judgments. Of the splendor of the "great" passages there can be no question; but the real reward for the undeniable effort which is demanded of the reader of Swinburne's prose is the discovery of passages such as those I have quoted. There are scores of them and they prove that the frenzied and fantastic superstructure of his style was built upon a firm foundation of critical judgment. Of the intolerable vices and redundances and hysterical exaggerations of his prose enough has been written elsewhere.[2] His euphuistic manner, alliterative, antithetical, redundant, grew worse as he grew older, and is the more offensive because he could, when he would, free himself of its most disagreeable traits, as his private letters and several inti-

[1] These passages are: the last paragraph of the essay on Byron; the last paragraph of the review of Rossetti's "Poems"; the opening of the review of "L'Homme qui rit"; the opening of "A Study of Shakespeare"; the description of the Lac de Gaube in "Studies in Prose and Poetry"; and the penultimate paragraph of the essay on Beaumont and Fletcher.

[2] His style lends itself easily to parody and the parodists have not been merciful. See, for example, the cruel but amusing skit, "The Appreciations of Algernon", a parody of the essay on Dickens, in *Punch*, August 6, 1902. Edward Dowden, in a review of "A Study of Shakespeare" (the *Academy*, January 3, 1880), makes good-natured fun of Swinburne's style and of his ridicule of Fleay's verse tests. Dowden expresses the wish to quote some passages from Swinburne's book; — "But when one comes to transcribe such passages the pen drives heavily amid the radiant riot of flower-soft speech and the supreme spilth of starry syllables. One whose understanding has been darkened by verse tests finds himself, too, as he copies, half unconsciously at work on a painful series of prose tests, including the alliteration test, the abusive-epithet test, the triple-redundant-adjective test, and the never-ending-hyperbole test."

mate essays[1] prove. The problem of the "sources" of his style does not admit of any very definite solution. The late Edward Thomas remarked wittily that "had De Quincey and Dr. Johnson collaborated in imitating Lyly they must have produced Swinburnian prose." More seriously Gosse pointed to analogies in the critiques of Paul de Saint Victor. There are obvious signs also of the influence of Carlyle, Ruskin and Hugo; and evidence of an attempt to imitate the elaborate loftiness of Landor as well as his arrogance in controversy. Mr. T. E. Welby finds echoes of Charles Lamb and of Emily Brontë. But when the *quellenstudien* have all been finished, Swinburne's prose remains individual in its virtues and in its defects, without progenitors and without offspring.[2]

This chapter may appropriately conclude with a brief summary of what the Germans would call Swinburne's *Belesenheit*. His keen critical enthusiasm was expended upon a limited number of

[1] For example, in the "Recollections of Professor Jowett" and "The Journal of Sir Walter Scott," both in "Studies in Prose and Poetry."

[2] Of Swinburne's letters I have written at length in the *Nation* (New York), April 5, 1919. It is unnecessary to say much about them here. The warning is required, however, that the letters included in volume xix of the Bonchurch Edition are merely those published by Sir Edmund Gosse and Mr. Wise in 1919; the collection does not include the family letters published in whole or in part by Mrs. Disney Leith, nor those letters to Rossetti, Watts-Dunton and other correspondents published by Messrs. Hake and Compton-Rickett. Other sections of his correspondence remain still unpublished; some batches of letters have been destroyed.

subjects. Theological disputations were a barren waste to him. His vague acceptance of a sort of Absolutism was unaccompanied by any definite interest in modern idealistic metaphysics. With the growth of the "new" mysticism he had, in marked contrast to Watts-Dunton, little sympathy. He shows no such large, if loose, grasp of the general tendencies of modern scientific thought as is exhibited in the poetry of Tennyson. The entire realm of the natural sciences was closed to him. A few poems and fewer essays were devoted to the fine arts, but though in his early maturity he gave signs of ability as an art critic, his accomplishment in this department is almost negligible. That he was unable to appreciate music has been affirmed, though there is some conflict of testimony here. To a degree to which Keats alone among modern poets affords a parallel his life was devoted to literature. Yet there were great bare spaces in his interest and knowledge. With Oriental literature and thought — a subject to which Watts-Dunton devoted some attention — he had little or no concern. The mythology of Scandinavia, in which his friends Morris and John Payne found material for many poems, was a blank to him. That nostalgia for the great centuries of medievalism which is so marked a characteristic of many nineteenth-century writers is entirely absent from Swinburne's writings, and though he went to the Middle Ages several times for themes, his essential and intense modernism made him regard the epoch as "the shambles of faith and of fear." Among modern European literatures, that of Germany influenced him scarcely at all. He distrusted Germany, and there is no evidence that he was thoroughly acquainted with her language or her literature.

Even within the fields of literature over which he had a mastery there were portions into which he rarely strayed. Greek literature meant to him Homer and Sappho, Pindar and the dramatists (among whom Euripides is never mentioned save with whimsical contempt); not the historians or orators or philosophers. No other English poet of modern times and equal rank has been so little influenced by Plato. In Latin, Vergil, the lyrists (especially Catullus) and the satirists are within the range of his sympathies; but he had, and after his first phase, could have little appreciation of the nihilism of Lucretius; and he recorded his dislike of Horace. With Spanish literature he was apparently unacquainted at first hand. Italian poetry he knew well. Allusions to Dante are frequent in his poetry and are introduced with exquisite effect. To the "Decameron" he turned more than once for a subject. Petrarch and Tasso were farther removed from his sympathies; Ariosto attracted him in moderate measure; but the school of Berni and Pulci he ruled out of "the domain of absolute poetry." Of Goldoni he speaks in contempt. To Leopardi he was drawn by their common dedication to the cause of Italian liberty. Of the greatest Italian poet of his own day, one who had so much in common with himself — Carducci — he very strangely never speaks.

He was as intimately acquainted with French as with English literature. Villon, Hugo and Baudelaire stood first in his estimation, though in later life he retracted what he came to consider his over-praise of "Les Fleurs du Mal." Many allusions make it evident that he was steeped in Rabelais. Molière he appreciated, but with the great tragedians of the seventeenth century he had little in common. Between him and Voltaire there was an intellectual rather than an esthetic bond. Among novelists Balzac is supreme. For that phase of realism that is called "Naturalism" he had no sympathy; he respected Flaubert but is loud and repetitious in his denunciations of Zola. The men of *Mille-huit-cent-trente*, save Musset, are his masters. Among his immediate contemporaries he probably ranked first — but on grounds of personal friendship rather than of entire understanding or identity of aims and taste — Mallarmé. To Verlaine he never alludes.

His width of range, depth of knowledge and catholicity of taste in English literature require no further illustrations than have been given in the course of this chapter.

CHAPTER EIGHT

Last Phases as Lyrist

Our narrative of the events in Swinburne's life has been for long interrupted because of the need to consider the poetry of his middle years, the Arthurian narratives, the tragedies, and the critical essays. But when due account has been taken of his work in other departments of literature it becomes the more apparent that it is by his achievement as a lyric poet that he must be judged; and it is appropriate therefore to devote our final chapter to the lyrical, meditative, elegiac, satiric and political poetry of the long last period of his life. But first it is necessary to resume the few external events of these thirty years and to take some account of the conditions in which he lived.

The loneliness, ill health and hard drinking of the middle years brought the poet to a desperate pass in 1879. In June of that year his mother made a last despairing effort to save him from himself, but no sooner had he left home and returned to his London chambers than he began a drinking bout which by September had reduced him to a state not far from death's door. Lady Jane Swinburne then appealed by telegraph to Watts-Dunton; and that faithful solicitor hurried to Swinburne and by force and persuasion bundled him into a cab and drove him out to Putney. There he was Watts-Dunton's guest, and a guest he remained for thirty years. He was put upon a strict regimen whose results were manifested in the sudden renewal of poetic and critical work in the following year. Stories are told of how Watts-Dunton gradually, tactfully and firmly weaned him from the brandy bottle and through the intermediate stages of port and sherry brought him to the ration of one bottle of ale each day. These tales may be apocryphal, but as allegories of Watts-Dunton's influence they are sufficiently near the truth.

Two years after the death of Watts-Dunton Mr. E. V. Lucas set the fashion, in an article entitled "A Visit to 'The Pines'", of indulging in more or less ill-natured witticism at the expense of Swinburne's friend. His example has been followed by other writers. Only Mr. Max Beerbohm has had the taste and tact to combine in just the proper proportion wit, admiration, graciousness and light mockery in describing the quaint household where dwelt the singular and celebrated pair of friends. It is the more difficult to form a definite estimate of Watts-Dunton because of the tradition established by writers who accepted his hospitality and then wrote in derision of him.[1]

[1]The essayist who devoted a volume to Watts-Dunton during his subject's lifetime unfortunately maintained throughout his monograph a tone of uncritical eulogy which makes the book valueless. This fault was not repaired by the "official" "Life and Letters" (1916), an ill-planned and gossipy book.

Walter Theodore Watts came to London to practise as a solicitor at a time when the "new poetry" was at the height of celebrity. He was ambitious to win for himself a place in literature and in the early eighteen-seventies began to contribute to the *Examiner* and the *Athenæum*. He became chief literary critic on the staff of the latter journal. Meanwhile he had met Rossetti and Swinburne in a professional capacity, and his wise management of their affairs gained for him their friendship. By 1879 this friendship with Swinburne was so close that, as we have seen, it was to Watts-Dunton — not Gosse, nor Jowett, nor Nichol, nor any other — that the Swinburne family turned in time of dire need.

In his "Life of Swinburne" Sir Edmund Gosse is elaborately and guardedly hostile in his allusions to Watts-Dunton. Other critics have usually dismissed him with indulgent smiles and self-indulgent facetiousness. But the man who won the confidence of Tennyson, upon whom Rossetti came to rely, who was the close friend of so self-contained a person as William Morris, and who became the "best and dearest friend" of Swinburne is not thus lightly to be set aside. What won him the intimacy of these poets? Certainly not his own poetry, for though a few pieces have some charm,[1] as a

[1] For example, "The Last Walk from Boar's Hill" (in memory of Jowett); and the "Doppelgänger" sonnet and the hay-making chorus in "The Coming of Love."

whole his verse is negligible. "Aylwin", after enjoying for many years a coterie-celebrity in manuscript, was, when published in 1898, received by the critics as a new birth of romance. It is now sinking out of sight, remembered if at all as a curiosity for the sake of the inserted portraits of the writer's friends. Swinburne, with an extravagance of generosity which in this case imposed itself upon public opinion for a while, pronounced him the foremost critic of the age. As an observer and recorder of *personalia* he may still be read with pleasure,[1] though his literary reminiscences have not the sharp pictorial quality of those of Sir Edmund Gosse. The wide generalizations in his article on Poetry in the "Encyclopædia Britannica" and in the essay on "The Renaissance of Wonder" in Chambers' "Cyclopædia of English Literature" have been, I think, unduly depreciated of late years, for the distinctions between relative and absolute vision, between lyric and dramatic imagination, between ages of acceptance and ages of wonder, and the like have the value of suggestiveness. But it is as the friend of poets that he will be remembered.

"I am content," he said, "to be overshadowed by such men and such poets as they." He was no mere hero-worshipper, for he managed to consort with them as an equal. Nor is it just to charge him

[1] In the posthumous collection of papers entitled "Old Familiar Faces" or in the many still unassembled essays and reviews buried in the files of the *Athenæum*.

with motives exclusively of self-interest, for if he gained by these intimacies they burdened him with responsibilities and anxieties and an enormous expenditure of time and energy. He watched over Swinburne with a care that was almost feminine and that, if it was "fussy" (as has been said), was also efficacious. And in contrast to the men of great reputation whose friend he was must be set scores of obscure and struggling men of letters whom he befriended and assisted. Nor was there any sycophancy in his relationship with Swinburne; witness the gentle manly reproof addressed to the poet in the midst of the Furnivall controversy. Indeed, far from being sycophantic, he assumed a kind of overlordship of the poet which was vastly irritating to other friends of longer standing who had either not troubled, or had been powerless, to rescue him from drink. In the abundant accumulated evidence of Watts-Dunton's mastery over Swinburne there is much that is amusing and something that is pathetic. He probably saved the poet's life; but he schooled him with soft assurance in an alien way of life. He became Swinburne's other self, his counsel's consistory; and Swinburne as a child went by his direction. He checked with an austere regard of control the poet's familiar smile towards objects of old affection. He kept "Bohemian" acquaintances away from "The Pines"; and the sturdy little old man into which the flaming portent of the eighteen-sixties had developed by insensible degrees submitted meekly. The two men seldom went far from home, and more seldom independently. An occasional holiday in Norfolk; a visit to the Channel Islands; a not very successful visit to Paris in 1882 to attend a celebration in honor of Victor Hugo — these were the only breaks in the humdrum regularity of the life at Putney, where walks on the Common, long hours of study and writing, solemn receptions of visitors, and evenings of reading aloud to each other made up the daily and yearly round. As the years passed and Swinburne's deafness and isolation increased, Watts-Dunton came more and more into the foreground; and visitors who came to offer the tribute of their reverence to the great poet were disillusioned and disappointed to find that it was "Aylwin" and not "Atalanta," "The Renaissance of Wonder" and not "Songs before Sunrise", which were the subjects of conversation at "The Pines."

In the stuffy atmosphere and among the plushy comforts of the semi-detached villa at the foot of Putney Hill Swinburne composed five more volumes of miscellaneous verse, published at widening intervals. These are: "A Century of Roundels" (1883), "A Midsummer Holiday and Other Poems" (1884), "Poems and Ballads: Third Series" (1889), "Astrophel and Other Poems" (1894), and "A Channel Passage and Other Poems" (1904).

The first of these stands somewhat apart from the

From the photo. by Poole, reproduced in "The Life and Letters of Theodore Watts-Dunton," by permission of the publishers, G. P. Putnam's Sons

SWINBURNE AT SIXTY-FIVE

other four. A "roundel" is a tiny poem in a *forme fixe* of Swinburne's own invention, a modification of the rondeau, with no precise limitation in line-length but rigidly limited to two rhymes and eleven lines (including a twice recurring refrain). One hundred of these little pieces were written with too swift facility by way of disciplining the loose fluency of the Pindaric manner which had of late engaged the poet's attention. It is obvious that some remedy more drastic than easy obedience to fixed rules should have been adopted to check the fatal fluency. To read the collection through is an exhausting experience; the studies of babyhood are particularly trying. But several of the poems have something of a quiet charm. There are memorials to Wagner, to George Powell (Swinburne's friend and one of the first interpreters of Wagner in England), to Rossetti (associated very beautifully with Villon), and to other departed friends. There are various nature poems (notably several on the Channel Islands); impressionistic sketches from painting and music (including the delicately wrought "Flowerpiece by Fantin"); meditations upon the passage of the years; and memorials of the past. Some of these are of biographical interest for the wistfulness with which the caged sea-mew recollects the wild free life of old.

Instead of examining each of the remaining four collections independently I shall take this large body of verse as a whole, for there are no lines of development to be traced separately. What has to be done is to indicate the leading classes into which this later lyric, meditative, elegiac, personal, political and satiric poetry falls, and to call attention to the comparatively few pieces that have some lasting interest, attractiveness and individuality.

Watts-Dunton has been blamed for turning the genius of his friend into the channels of nature poetry. It is quite true that for such subjects Swinburne's temperament was not suited. Mingling though he did, or seemed to do in the earlier years, with the elements; steeping himself in sky and wind and sun and sea; watching the recurring seasons of "white rain" and blossom, of foliage and fruit, of mists and snows; evoking, as on occasion he could do, the *genius loci*, he nevertheless did not possess the talent of observation, the feeling for the concrete and detailed. Movement, and the play of light and shadow upon waves or leaves — these large vague phenomena held his attention; but not the Wordsworthian details of countryside. The earth may be "a wide sweet smile"; the great wind may "grapple" with the sea; March laugh gladly; "the flower-soft feet of refluent seasons" glide beside the mill stream — but never in all Swinburne's poetry have we one picture so concrete, definite, intimate, so firmly attached to earth as, for example, the opening lines of "Tintern Abbey." Yet during the earlier years at Putney he wrote many poems descriptive of nature. For this misdirection of talent Watts-Dunton was doubtless responsible; but the question must in fairness to him be asked: How else would Swinburne have occupied himself? What else would he have written? There was no need (in Doctor Johnson's phrase) "to endow his purposes with words", but there was a real need to endow his words with purposes. The quest of a subject bore hard upon him, as it had done upon Tennyson in old age; and Watts-Dunton spread before him an illimitable range of poetic themes.

Thus it comes about that we have "A Midsummer Holiday", the chronicle of an excursion through the country in the form of nine ballads. Only twice in these tedious pieces does Swinburne recapture for a moment something of his old energy: once in "On a Country Road" in praise of Chaucer; and again in "On the Verge" where looking out across the broad expanse of sea he reads into the experience the obvious and commonplace symbolic implication, expressed, however, with genuine power and emotion:

Friend, who knows if death indeed have life or life have death for goal?
Day nor night can tell us, nor may seas declare nor skies unroll
What has been from everlasting, or if aught shall always be.
Silence answering only strikes response reverberate on the soul
From the shore that hath no shore beyond it spread in all the sea.

In "March: an Ode" he puts the question in springtime: What has become of the raging winds which a month ago roared around us? Where has gone that energy? In the answer there is a hope of the survival somewhere in the universe of the influence of all great vanished power. The idea is Arnoldian; and in "Neap-tide", too, we are again reminded of Arnold; but while Arnold, in "Dover Beach", sees in the ocean's "melancholy, long, withdrawing roar" a symbol of the receding tide of faith, Swinburne accepts joyfully the *lowest* high tide of the month, confident that high water will return. Often a nature poem is but the decorative surface of a thought connected with literature or history. Thus, "On the South Coast", a description of a stately church which fronts the sea, is really a meditation upon the eight hundred years of England's greatness, whose memories are stored within its walls; and "An Autumn Vision" draws an analogy from a magnificent rainbow seen among the clouds above the stormy sea to the sweetness and love set amid the terror and evil in the plays of Shakespeare. Sometimes we feel that the poet is employing a nature theme as the medium for a metrical exercise; "The Palace of Pan", for example, is of technical interest as an example of his ability to turn an old jingle into music, for it is composed in the meter of M. G. Lewis' silly old ballad of "Alonzo the Brave." Sometimes, again, we are uncomfortably aware that he has chosen a subject through sheer inability to find another, as in "A Channel Passage" where he narrates for the third time the experience of the storm at sea as he returned from Ostend in 1855. Occasionally there is frank bright joy in the actual intimate contact with the natural world; and of such poems the finest is "A Swimmer's Dream" in which he associates the memories of far-past swimming days with like delights which yet remain. Like Meredith Swinburne never "measures our lean humanity against yonder sublime and infinite" — a morbid and Byronic gesture; nor does man, in his poetry, sink to forlorn insignificance as does Clym Yeobright, faced with the impassivity of Egdon Heath. Rather, the poet is the more conscious of man's worth as he rejoices in "the great heart of life beating round him."

A purer passion, a lordlier leisure,
A peace more happy than lives on land,
Fulfils with pulse of diviner pleasure
The dreaming head and the steering hand.
I lean my cheek to the cold grey pillow,
The deep soft swell of the full broad billow,
And close mine eyes for delight past measure,
And wish the wheel of the world would stand . . .

A dream, and more than a dream, and dimmer
At once and brighter than dreams that flee,
The moment's joy of the seaward swimmer
Abides, remembered as truth may be.
Not all the joy and not all the glory
Must fade as leaves when the woods wax hoary;
For there the downs and the sea-banks glimmer,
And here to the south of them swells the sea.

A more profound experience, one transcending the sensation of mere physical contact and reaching to those depths where "spirit and sense" are one, is recorded in "A Nympholept."[1] In this poem the sophisticated ideas which mystics and sentimentalists have read into Nature are discarded; and man confronts, as he confronted in primeval ages, with passion and terror and exaltation, the universal Pan. For a moment one is reminded of Arnold Böcklin's celebrated painting of "Pan in the Forest" where a shepherd is seen fleeing in terror from an enormous and monstrous apparition which looms up from behind the farther slope of a near-by hill; but whereas Böcklin's picture, for all its sense of wonder, is a product of debased romanticism, Swinburne's poem has in it nothing of the meretricious. The poet describes the silence of the brooding sultry noon in the mid-forest, heavy with the sense of an august presence:

> The naked noon is upon me: the fierce dumb spell,
> The fearful charm of the strong sun's imminent might,
> Unmerciful, steadfast, deeper than seas that swell,
> Pervades, invades, appals me with loveless light,
> With harsher awe than breathes in the breath of night.
> Have mercy, God who art all! For I know thee well,
> How sharp is thine eye to lighten, thine hand to smite! . .
>
> In thee is the doom that falls and the doom that stands:
> The tempests utter thy word, and the stars fulfil.

[1]This astonishing poem is contained in "Astrophel and Other Poems", a volume which Mr. Nicolson (without so much as mentioning "A Nympholept") dismisses as "redeemed from absolute dullness" by a few personal and elegiac pieces. Mr. Welby, on the other hand, accords to it the admiration which is its due.

Not in sleep, for "never in sleep has man beholden this", but in a condition of clairvoyance bordering upon hallucination, he beholds "a form, a face, a wonder" grow as the moon grows through the month; and the initial terror and dread change to desire, and desire to delight and love. The sense of wrath and imminent ill yields to uncertain joy which yet prompts the doubtful question of Nature's kindliness to man. Is it sufficient to love her without yearning for a reciprocated love?

> Thee, therefore, thee would I come to, cleave to, cling,
> If haply thy heart be kind and thy gifts be good,
> Unknown sweet spirit.

Man shares the helplessness of all things in this presence; but his consciousness renders him of more worth than the stars or winds, seas or forests around him:

> The skies that scorn us are less in thy sight than we,
> Whose souls have strength to conceive and perceive thee, Pan.

Metrically the poem is as admirable as it is in its emotion and exaltation; for Swinburne has managed to convey in harmonies that are clangorous and almost strident an effect after which other poets (Mallarmé, for example) have groped hesitatingly in faltering rhythms and images suggested in tones barely above a whisper.

The humanism with which "A Nympholept" closes — and by humanism I mean the sense of the preëminent significance allotted to humanity in the universe — is the theme of "The Interpreters" in which the poet voices his belief (not so clearly, however, but that some commentators have misunderstood the poem) that Nature had been purposeless had not man been in the world to give her "sense and soul by song." This idea is elaborated in the lyric idyl entitled "Pan and Thalassius", a piece noteworthy also for its original and exquisite meter.

In some of the simpler nature poems — "Heart's-Ease Country", for example, or "Northumberland", or the touchingly wistful and self-revelatory verses "To a Sea-Mew" — Swinburne recalls past scenes and loved places in the same mood that inspires many of the later elegies. The affectionate "Dedication" of "Astrophel" to William Morris and the melancholy "Dedication" of "A Channel Passage" to the memory of Morris and Burne-Jones[1] are more intimate in tone than the magnanimous "Birthday Ode" addressed to the aged Tennyson and the "Threnody" which Swinburne composed upon the Laureate's death. No less than twelve poems commemorate the unfortunate blind poet, Philip Bourke Marston. In these; in "A

[1] In volume vi of the Bonchurch Edition the "Dedication" of "Astrophel" to Morris is omitted; and the "Dedication" of "A Channel Passage" to the memory of Morris and Burne-Jones is put in front of "Astrophel" and called a dedication to Morris alone. Since this poem refers to both friends and to both as among the departed, the result of this error is grievous nonsense. So also, in volume iii, the "Dedication" to William Bell Scott, which belongs to "Poems and Ballads, Third Series", is omitted. These blunders have resulted from the unwarrantable transference of Swinburne's various dedications from their original places at the end of each volume of poems to the front of the volume.

Sequence of Sonnets on the Death of Robert Browning"; in "A New Year's Eve" (in memory of Christina Rossetti); in "Barking Hall" (in memory of his mother); and in other late elegies there is voiced a straining hope after the possibility of personal immortality. Of these memorials to "precious friends hid in death's dateless night" the most beautiful in depth of tenderness is the elegy "In Memory of John William Inchbold", the painter-poet with whom Swinburne had sojourned at Tintagel many years before. Memories now return of

> Tintagel, and the long Trebarwith sand,
> Lone Camelford, and Boscastle divine.

The elegiac conventions are swept aside; the "pathetic fallacy" is repudiated. Of old, men fancied that Nature mourned for the dead; that dream is now over:

> Not for our joy they live, and for our grief
> They die not. Though thine eyes be closed, thine
> hand
> Powerless as mine to paint them, not a leaf
> In English woods or glades of Switzerland
>
> Falls earlier now, fades faster. All our love
> Moves not our mother's changeless heart.

There is no affirmation of belief in immortality, but there is a clear admission of the possibility:

> And joy for thee, if ever soul of man
> Found joy in change and life of ampler birth
> Than here pens in the spirit for a span,
> Must be the life that doubt calls death on earth.

For if, beyond the shadow and the sleep,
A place there be for souls without a stain,
Where peace is perfect, and delight more deep
Than seas and skies that change and shine again,

There none of all unsullied souls that live
May hold a surer station.

The austerely controlled grief for this friend "beloved in life and death" changes to plangent passion in the "Elegy" on Sir Richard Francis Burton. Here the poet recalls with splendid power and *élan* his memories of Auvergne, that "wild and woeful land" through which he had wandered long since with his friend: the precipices and peaks and crags, the narrow valleys and the rushing river; and from these memories he draws a metaphor of the soul's progress through life; and from Burton's adventures in the Orient a metaphor of the departing soul confronting the dawn.

Not all these elegies are prompted by such genuine emotion, for in later years Swinburne came to feel it almost a duty to celebrate in fitting terms the achievement of this or that person illustrious and lately dead. More often than not it is a man of letters who is thus honored, a fact which leads us from these "occasional" pieces to poems on subjects from literature among which we may read, or attempt to read, those in honor of Sir Philip Sidney ("Astrophel"), of Marlowe ("Inscriptions for the Four Sides of a Pedestal"), of Dante ("The Festival of Beatrice"), of Bruno, of Burns, and of others among the great departed. The verbose and tiresome "Prologues" to various Elizabethan dramas are even more "derivative" and remote from the sympathies of almost all conceivable readers; and "The Altar of Righteousness", the most ambitious poem of Swinburne's latest years, though its theme is the eternity and immutability of the moral order as compared with the fleet passage of rival religions, resolves itself, long before its close, into a sort of catalogue of the Great Dead — Christ, Mahomet, Æschylus, Shakespeare, Bruno — which reminds one of the "Positivist Calendar."

From the congenial but stagnant air of his study at "The Pines" the poet passed each day out into the High Street, down to the river, and on to Putney Common, where then as now the children played and the nursemaids watched the babies. The unreasoning and slightly fantastic tenderness which Swinburne lavished upon the young objects of his devotion is a late development in his emotional life, scarcely appearing before 1876 and not reaching full expression till several years later. The example of Landor's love of children may have guided his thoughts in this direction; certainly the author of "L'Art d'être Grandpère" taught him much. The silliness of Swinburne's baby worship has been a broad mark for the shafts of criticism; on the whole, however, despite the monotony of the subject matter, these pieces reveal the poet in an attractive aspect, bathed in "the light of little children and their love." Only a very cynical generation could find matter for ridicule in such verses as "In a Garden."

To Putney came distant reverberations of events in the larger world. Cut off from association with men of broad vision from whom he had derived impressions of public affairs in the pre-Putney period; subjected incessantly to the provincial Toryism and truculent insularity of Watts-Dunton; half informed or misinformed, Swinburne frequently wrote unwisely on questions of the day. Occasionally in the early years at "The Pines" the old radicalism flared up stridently. In December, 1883, he was lashed into fury by Tennyson's acceptance of a peerage and especially by the comments of the Tory press upon the exalted honor thus done the Laureate. He wrote "Vos Deos Laudamus"; and at a later date, when the House of Lords rejected Gladstone's Reform Bill, "The Twilight of the Lords" and "A Word for the Country", in which he demanded the abolition of the Upper House. These pieces he published in the radical *Pall Mall Gazette*, the very heart of Home Rule agitation in England. The Irish Question was now looming large upon the political horizon, and opposition to Home Rule makes its appearance in Swinburne's political verse in 1883. During 1886–1887 it became his most vital interest. Partly through the resurgence of innate aristocratic instincts, partly through the influence of Watts-

Dunton, he became allied with the Unionists. He developed an intense hatred of Gladstone. "The Union", "The Question", "Apostasy", and other poems are vituperative against Gladstone and Parnell. "See the man of words embrace the man of blood!" he shrieked, and did not hesitate to libel the Prime Minister as "the hoary henchman" whose hands could never be cleansed from Gordon's blood.[1] John Morley, in the midst of many cares,

[1] With these diatribes it is interesting to compare John Payne's contemporary attacks on Gladstone: the astonishing "Chant Royal Prolongé" and the equally amazing prose note attached to the poem "Areopagitica." This note contains what is, I believe, the longest sentence in English literature. — The only one of Swinburne's Unionist poems of lasting interest is "The Ballad of Truthful Charles", published in the *St. James's Gazette*, July 18, 1889. When reprinted in the "Posthumous Poems" of 1917, Clement K. Shorter and other critics, ignorant of the occasion that had prompted this satire, objected so strenuously to it that, apparently as a result of these complaints, it has been most unfortunately omitted from the Bonchurch Edition. Swinburne hails Parnell as "the crownless king . . . of holy Liarland"; and the refrain of the ballad, put into Parnell's mouth, is "I meant to cheat you when I said it." The point of the accusation is lost upon those who do not remember that during the inquiry growing out of the forged Parnell letters published in the *Times*, Parnell was asked why he had told the House of Commons in 1881 that secret societies had ceased to exist in Ireland and had replied, "It is possible that I was endeavoring to mislead the House of Commons on that occasion." The cynicism of this reply is what inspired Swinburne's by no means inexcusable "Ballad." — Home Rulers sought to embarrass Swinburne by reminding him of his "Appeal" on behalf of the condemned Fenians in 1867. In a letter headed "A Retrospect" (the *Times*, May 6, 1887) the poet sought to contrast the murders for which the Fenians were executed and the assassinations in Phoenix Park. He denied that Mazzini, had he lived, would have favored Home Rule; and in a second letter (May 11) he quoted Karl Blind to the effect that Mazzini, "the champion of the Unionist principle in nationality matters, was utterly opposed to the dissolution of the Legislative Union between England and Ireland." Swinburne failed to see that if this was Mazzini's position, it proved nothing save his lack of logic, for the situations in Italy and Ireland as opposed respectively to Austria and England were of course closely analogous. The embarrassed poet sought further to fortify himself by a ponderous bit of irony, "Unionism and Crime" (the *St. James's Gazette*, May 6, 1887), signed "A Gladstonite", in which he pretends to bring charges of atrocities against the Primrose League. It is dull, heavy fooling.

found time to watch the poet and to meditate upon the defection of one of the band of advanced Liberals whom he had rallied under his editorial banner two decades earlier; and Swinburne's name may be read between the lines of a sentence in "The Life of Gladstone": "Distinguished men of letters . . . now choked with anger because they were taken at their word." That Swinburne was regarded as an apostate is evident from some verses which Rennell Rodd sent to Walt Whitman, in which it is said that Swinburne "has passed from the van to the rear-guard, forsaking the Ayes for the Noes." W. Robertson Nicoll's record of Swinburne's interest in William Hale White's essay on "The Alleged Apostasy of Wordsworth" is significant. Did he sympathize with a defence that might have been employed in his own case?

The verses against Home Rule are but one manifestation of the intense patriotism of Swinburne's later life. No longer cosmopolitan in outlook but arrogantly British, he anticipated in the jaunty jingoism of such pieces as "A Word for the Nation" the kind of jingle that became immensely popular in the years immediately preceding the Boer War. This is the sort of thing perpetrated by the author of "Songs before Sunrise":

> We have not, alack, an ally to befriend us,
> And the season is ripe to extirpate and end us:
> Let the German touch hands with the Gaul,
> And the fortress of England must fall;

And the sea shall be swept of her seamen,
  And the waters they ruled be their graves,
And Dutchmen and Frenchmen be free men,
  And Englishmen slaves.

England must therefore beware of the "French hounds" and her other neighbors.[1] This pride in England's by no means splendid isolation and this consciousness that she must hold herself above "the lesser breeds" are curiously Kiplingesque in sentiment, though in form below the level of Kipling's imitators. A final chance remained for Swinburne to prove that he was not a "lost leader." The Boer War came. True liberalism protested nobly against this excursion of British imperialism; but Swinburne chanted an imperialism as strident as that of Kipling, as blatant as that of Alfred Austin. The Boers are "fiends"; they are "hounds" and England is the "hunter" (as indeed she was); England must "scourge these dogs"; England stands sublime amidst "the recreant hate of envious knaves." When at last peace came he sang in "Astraea Victrix" his "pride in righteous work well done."

[1]Swinburne attacked France bitterly on several occasions. The printed but unpublished "Rondeaux Parisiens", prompted by French attacks on British hypocrisy following W. T. Stead's notorious articles on "The Maiden Tribute of Modern Babylon", are extremely truculent. In November, 1899, when English relations with France were much strained, Swinburne wrote "Lutetia" and "Meretrix Moribunda", both vituperative attacks on France which remain unpublished. Yet he did retain a certain measure of sympathy for France. A sonnet "After the Verdict" (*i.e.*, the temporizing verdict reached at the second, Rennes, trial of Captain Dreyfus) commends the "high souls and constant hearts of faithful men" who had sustained France's honor "with tongue and pen." Among these "high souls" was, it is interesting to remember, Swinburne's *bête noire*, Emile Zola.

The historian of English poetry who holds that in it are enshrined the noblest aspirations of the race must avert his eyes from the exhibition afforded at this time by Swinburne, Kipling, Payne, Austin, Henley, Newbolt and all the other celebrators of "the strength and splendour of England's war" and rest them rather upon Sir William Watson's "For England: Poems written during Estrangement."[1]

It is but just to Swinburne to close this unsympathetic notice of his patriotic verse with some reference to two poems which show that in this field he was capable of something better than versified war propaganda. One of these poems is "The Armada", celebrating the tercentenary of England's triumph over Spain. Selecting as the "keynote" of a new meter those verses of unknown antiquity —

They that ride
Over ocean wide
With hempen bridle and horse of tree,

and turning them into one line, intermingled with other stanziac forms, he produced a narrative lyric in which glorification of England's prowess is interwoven with descriptions of the battle. The vituperation of the Roman Catholic Church is shrill, absurd and extravagant; but other portions

[1] Mr. Drinkwater argues that Swinburne was incorrectly informed as to the facts of the Boer War and that he was not consciously disloyal to his early ideal of liberty. The excuse is at best a lame one. Professor De Selincourt, in "English Poets and the National Ideal", endeavors, unsuccessfully, to show that Swinburne's patriotism is a logical outgrowth of the cosmopolitanism of his early life.

of the poem are genuinely stirring, and in the final section the undercurrent of Imperialism may be pardoned for the fervid music of the verse:

England queen of the waves whose green inviolate girdle
  enrings thee round,
Mother fair as the morning, where is now the place of thy
  foemen found?
Still the sea that salutes us free proclaims them stricken, ac-
  claims thee crowned . . .

Mother, mother beloved, none other could claim in place of
  thee England's place:
Earth bears none that beholds the sun so pure of record, so
  clothed with grace:
Dear our mother, nor son nor brother is thine, as strong or as
  fair of face.

The sentiments will not carry universal conviction, but the ringing sincerity of the utterance strikes home. But this over-long and over-rhetorical piece fails where the less pretentious but more truly martial battle pieces of Campbell and Tennyson succeed.

"The Commonweal", in which Swinburne celebrated Victoria's fiftieth jubilee in 1887, is the finest of his patriotic poems. Mr. Nicolson finds in it only "studied platitudes"; but there have been other readers who estimate it at a higher rate. The poem would have been better had it contained fifteen stanzas instead of fifty, to which number Swinburne expanded it to conform to the number of years of the Queen's reign. Here are some examples of his sentiments on this occasion:

Hope, wide of eye and wild of wing,
  Rose with the sundawn of a reign
  Whose grace should make the rough ways plain,
And fill the worn old world with spring,
  And heal its heart of pain . . .

War upon war, change after change,
  Hath shaken thrones and towers to dust,
  And hopes austere and faiths august
Have watched in patience stern and strange
  Men's works unjust and just . . .

The morning comes not, yet the night
  Wanes, and men's eyes win strength to see
  Where twilight is, where light shall be
When conquered wrong and conquering right
  Acclaim a world set free . . .

The story of England's struggle for political and intellectual freedom is reviewed; and England's greatness, of which Victoria's reign is a sign and the sea the symbol, is sung:

The sea, divine as heaven and deathless,
  Is hers, and none but only she
  Hath learnt the sea's word, none but we
Her children hear in heart the breathless
  Bright watchword of the sea . . .

She, first to love the light, and daughter
  Incarnate of the northern dawn,
  She, round whose feet the wild waves fawn
When all their wrath of warring water
  Sounds like a babe's breath drawn . . .

She, loving light for light's sake only,
  And truth's for only truth's, and song
  For song's sake and the sea's, how long
Hath she not borne the world her lonely
  Witness of right and wrong.

In verses such as these the poet rises above the mere occasion for which they were written, and is not altogether unworthy to stand beside the greater poet who wrote the "Sonnets dedicated to National Independence and Liberty."

In 1903 Swinburne underwent an attack of pneumonia, premonitory of the end. In 1907 his seventieth birthday was the occasion of tributes of admiration.[1] Taken suddenly ill with pneumonia in April, 1909, he died on the tenth of that month.

[1]Swinburne's indifference to the achievements of younger men of letters during his last years has been the object of adverse comment. It is worth while recording some facts about this matter which I have been able to assemble. There are several cases on record of interest and encouragement. Thus, when John Davidson, provided with a letter of introduction from Nichol, came to "The Pines", Swinburne received him kindly, laid his hand upon his head, and called him "Poet." (Were there recollections of that far-off day when Rogers had in like manner passed on the succession to himself?) A decade later, Mr. Alfred Noyes, then just beginning to be widely known, experienced a like reception. For the poetry of John Payne and Lord De Tabley Swinburne showed some predeliction but no great enthusiasm. Wilfrid Blunt's work he knew, but from Blunt's connection with the Irish Nationalists he unwarrantably deduced the idea that Blunt was a Catholic fanatic, and though Morris printed the "Proteus" sonnets at the Kelmscott Press, Swinburne manifested no interest in them. I have seen Swinburne's copy of Sir William Watson's early volume of "Epigrams", in which he wrote Martial's line "*Sunt bona, sunt quaedam mediocria, sunt male plura.*" But he seems not to have known, or at any rate cared for, Watson's later and finer work. The poetry of the Celtic Revival developed in a world infinitely remote from Putney; Swinburne's only allusion to Mr. Yeats is harshly hostile. Yet he was attracted by the delicate work of Dora Sigurson and Mary Coleridge. There is no record of even the least expression of interest in Mr. Kipling. Stevenson did not attract him; and though he read some of the earlier novels of Mr. Moore his comments were not favorable. When Mr. Hardy sent him "Wessex Poems", he acknowledged the gift with courteous comments on the illustrations and some of the verses. He showed more interest in "The Dynasts", writing to the author about certain details and speaking of the epic-drama to his friends; but he expressed the hope that Hardy would not turn to poetry from his "great work in creative romance."

He was buried in the old churchyard at Bonchurch on the Isle of Wight beside members of his family.[1] Among the mourners were the second Lord Tennyson and Miss May Morris, representatives of two of the most illustrious of Swinburne's contemporaries. There was no public memorial or tribute. But among the floral offerings at Bonchurch were bunches of violets from the children who had known the poet during his daily walks on Putney Common; and a great wreath from Eton bearing Swinburne's beautiful line: "Still the reaches of the river, still the light on field and hill." The tone of the estimates in the press was generally condescending and half-hearted; but from Paris came this dispatch:

> The death of Mr. Swinburne touches the French literary world more closely than any loss which English literature has suffered for generations . . . [He was] the only singer of high rank who absorbed into his very nature the poetical genius, the spirit of the language of France . . . Like Byron he represented for the French a revolt from what are considered to be the narrower traditions of English

[1] Acting on Swinburne's own directions Watts-Dunton, himself too ill to attend the funeral, telegraphed the rector of St. Boniface's church, forbidding him to read the burial service. The clergyman wisely compromised by reading some sentences and by adding some simple words of tribute and explanation. An unpleasant controversy ensued, the only notable thing about which is a passage in a sermon delivered by this clergyman on the following Sunday, in which he said that "the Church of England was ever ready to receive all those who, whether at the gate of death, or even at the grave itself, came to her as a refuge." With the charity of these words a sermon preached on the same day by the Vice-Dean of Canterbury, bitterly attacking Swinburne's memory, was in marked contrast.

life, English thought and English literature; and he stood for the fraternization with the larger literary and political aspirations of the Latin peoples . . . From the political point of view it is legitimate to regard Swinburne as one of the heralds and harbingers of the *Entente cordiale*, for he sang of France and England as "sister stars" in the European firmament.

I have already in an appropriate context quoted extracts from the tributes in the Italian press. To the *Times* George Meredith sent a letter, the last he ever wrote, from which these sentences may be quoted:

Tomorrow . . . earth will take to her bosom the most spontaneous singer of all her English children. Song was his natural voice . . . Those who follow this great poet to his grave may take to heart that the name of Swinburne is one to shine star-like in English literature — a peer among our noblest.

Among the numerous verse tributes one may note Mr. Eden Phillpotts' sonnet, Mr. Noyes' elegy, "April whispers, canst thou, too, die?" and Mr. John Helston's more elaborate elegy. In 1910 Mrs. Leith, the cousin who had collaborated with Swinburne nearly half a century earlier, published "A Year's Mind"; and a little later Thomas Hardy composed his beautiful and impressive elegy, "A Singer Asleep."

Swinburne's grave is within sound of the sea; around it flit the swallows and sea-mews that he loved. The wish expressed long before in "Ex-Voto" has been almost literally fulfilled, for the poet

> hath made his everlasting mansion
> Upon the beached verge of the salt flood.

"He lacks thought" was the verdict which for a generation epitomized criticism of Swinburne. Tennyson gave it an epigrammatic turn: "He is a reed through which all things blow into music." Sir William Watson's lines "To a Certain Great Poet", though written with Shelley in mind, are applicable to Swinburne, whose strain is a mountain cataract lost in iridescence and spent in vapor. Critics who have made him the object of special study have generally treated his ideas as of secondary importance while they centered attention upon questions of prosody and style. Let the over-fluency of that style, the amount of repetition, the scanty variety of themes, the limitations of vocabulary and imagery, be admitted; the fact remains that the generation which first voiced the criticism that he was a mere juggler with words was one that ignored Meredith's poetry, that "compelled" Hardy to turn from poetry to prose, and was content to listen idly to Swinburne's music. His style, and especially the prevalence in it of anapæstic rhythms, could not but make the thought diffuse. The speed of his mental processes, the narrowness of his interests, and the complete control of his instrument led him to return often to the same general group of ideas. He makes large dependence upon the sympathy of the reader, imparting a mental impression by means of the suggestiveness of his rhythms. It is of course erroneous to hold that in poetry there can be no intellectual element apart from the logical development of ideas. John Addington Symonds' remark that in poetry "the application of ideas should not be too conscious, else the poet sinks into the preacher" is precisely to the point; and Pater speaks of "a certain suppression or vagueness of mere subject, so that the meaning reaches us through ways not distinctly traceable by the understanding." The poet, like the musician, need not, perhaps had better not, offer to his hearers a completely wrought-out chain of thought. He may take to himself the function of the natural world whose myriad sounds — the song of birds, the rustle of leaves, the murmur of streams — are harmonies accompanying the meditations of the listener thereto. He thus contributes the harmonies of the music, depending upon the reader to supply the first part: the melody, the theme, the thought. Through "the turnings intricate of verse", forms and substances present themselves with added glory.

During Swinburne's later life the world lost interest in him. The initial impression he had made left no novelty to startle people into new attention. It was not for him to charm them with the songs of respectability which till lately never failed to win an English audience. From the time of his first successes his instrument so perfectly suited his intents that he felt no inclination to experiment along novel lines of expression and thus did not avail himself of a means of awakening new interest. Meanwhile the drift of literary fashion, when not obscured by the neo-mysticism with which he had nothing in common, was in the direction of a realism he tried twice to imitate without success, but which was far removed from the romanticism of which he was the last important representative. He was thus left in lonely preëminence. Within his lifetime he had disciples a-plenty, but they were all *epigoni*. He founded no school. He was not, as his first admirers hailed him, the sunrise of a new era of poetry, but the flaming sunset of Romanticism.

His place among English poets whose work belongs exclusively to the second half of the nineteenth century is indisputably first. Rossetti offers no such "ample body of powerful work." Morris lacks intensity. Meredith's claim will be defended by but few critics. If we view the century as a whole, Wordsworth, Shelley, Keats, Tennyson and Browning stand above him. Coleridge, by the quality of a few poems, is immeasurably his superior, but in the mass of his achievement less impressive. Byron equals him in mass and surpasses him in strength, but as an artist is far below him. Arnold offers a special appeal to a limited number of minds. No one else can be brought into possible comparison.

He is not of the first order of poets nor, perhaps, even of second rank. Nowhere in his verse will be found a line or a stanza in which is concentrated the inmost spirit of poetry. "The light that never was on sea or land" comes to him by glimpses or not at all. That element which we find in the greatest verse and which we loosely describe as "mystical" — a yearning for something larger than this life affords, "an ampler ether, a diviner air", "beyond these voices", where

> Our noisy years seem moments in the being
> Of the eternal silence —

that element is rarely discoverable in Swinburne's poetry. The note is caught in:

> We are such stuff
> As dreams are made on, and our little life
> Is rounded with a sleep;

in:

> The One remains, the many change and pass;
> Heaven's light forever shines, Earth's shadows fly;
> Life, like a dome of many-coloured glass,
> Stains the white radiance of eternity;

in:

> Thou, silent form, dost tease us out of thought
> As doth eternity;

and in:

> A sense sublime
> Of something far more deeply interfused,
> Whose dwelling is the light of setting suns

Tennyson, commenting upon this last line, interprets the thought common to all these passages of verse: it is "the sense of the abiding in the transient." The positivist and secularist spirit is antithetical to this; the children of this world stand without the gates of Paradise. With them Swinburne belongs. Yet his survey of "life immeasurable and imminent love", the "natural force in spirit and sense", that expands and reveals itself in all nature, culminates in a vision well-nigh mystical in intensity, of the "serene Republic of a world made white." That goal is still far to seek. Between the lines of the "Prelude" to "Songs before Sunrise" we have read the disillusionment with which he regarded the established Italian monarchy. The "Ode on the Proclamation of the French Republic" was written, as he afterwards declared, "under the influence of a hope since so miserably deceived." Were he alive to-day his disillusionment would be deeper still, yet one may be sure that his confidence in man's high destiny would have remained unshaken by the events of recent years. He was not, as was Tennyson, a representative of his age; and a vanished epoch has not taken so much of him along with it. He was not committed to a Victorian point of view or hedged within insular boundaries. Nor was he, as he has been described, the mere herald of a political *Entente* or of a "Parliament of Man." He is the herald and trumpet of Mater Triumphalis, the Life Force working not only in the individual but in the social organism. Society cannot progress save through the exertion of conscience and reason; and it is this action, thus working, that Swinburne has in mind when he hails the coming Republic. It is a vision too fair perhaps for the twentieth century; but it belongs to the world of poetry, for, as Gissing says, "the Poet is indeed a Maker; above the world of sense, trodden by hide-bound humanity, he builds that world of his own whereto is summoned the unfettered spirit."

THE END

BIBLIOGRAPHY

The serious student will have access to Thomas J. Wise's "Bibliography of the Writings in Prose and Verse of Algernon Charles Swinburne." London: Printed for Private Circulation. Two volumes, 1919–1920. In revised form, but without the accompanying facsimiles of title pages and manuscripts, this is reprinted as volume xx of the Bonchurch Edition of Swinburne's Works. Mr. Wise includes in his work a section on the books devoted to the study of Swinburne's life and writings. In the following list I include, first the titles and dates of the poet's published volumes, and second, a list of authorities which does not pretend to be exhaustive but is to serve merely as a guide to further reading.

I

Swinburne's Works

The Queen-Mother and Rosamond. 1860.

The Children of the Chapel. 1864. [Contains "A Pilgrimage of Pleasure", not included in the Bonchurch Edition.]

Atalanta in Calydon. 1865.

Chastelard. 1865.

Poems and Ballads. 1866.
Notes on Poems and Reviews. 1866.
A Song of Italy. 1867.
William Blake. 1868.
Songs before Sunrise. 1871.
Under the Microscope. 1872.
Bothwell. 1874.
George Chapman. 1875.
Songs of Two Nations. 1875.
Essays and Studies. 1875.
Erechtheus. 1876.
Note of an English Republican on the Muscovite Crusade. 1876.
A Note on Charlotte Brontë. 1877.
Poems and Ballads, Second Series. 1878.
A Study of Shakespeare. 1880.
Songs of the Springtides. 1880.
Studies in Song. 1880.
The Heptalogia. 1880.
Mary Stuart. 1881.
Tristram of Lyonesse and Other Poems. 1882.
A Century of Roundels. 1883.
A Midsummer Holiday and Other Poems. 1884.
Marino Faliero. 1885.
Miscellanies. 1886.
A Study of Victor Hugo. 1886.
Locrine. 1887.
A Study of Ben Jonson. 1889.
Poems and Ballads, Third Series. 1889.
The Sisters. 1892.

Astrophel and Other Poems. 1894.
Studies in Prose and Poetry. 1894.
The Tale of Balen. 1896.
Rosamund, Queen of the Lombards. 1899.
A Channel Passage and Other Poems. 1904.
Collected Works: Poetry, six volumes; Tragedies, five volumes. 1904.
The Duke of Gandia. 1908.
The Age of Shakespeare. 1908.
Three Plays of Shakespeare. 1909.
Charles Dickens. 1913.
Posthumous Poems. 1917.
Complete Works, Bonchurch Edition. Twenty volumes. 1925–1927.

II

Authorities

Drinkwater, John. "Swinburne. An Estimate." London: Dent, 1913.

Gosse, Sir Edmund. "The Life of Algernon Charles Swinburne." London: Macmillan, 1917. [The latest revised edition forms volume xix of the Bonchurch Edition.]

Hake, Thomas, and Compton-Rickett, Arthur. "Letters of Algernon Charles Swinburne. With some Personal Recollections." London: John Murray, 1918. [These letters are not included in the Bonchurch Edition.]

Henderson, W. B. D. "Swinburne and Landor. A Study of their Spiritual Relationship." London: Macmillan, 1918.

Kernahan, Coulson. "Swinburne as I Knew Him. With some Unpublished Letters from the Poet to his Cousin, the Hon. Lady Henniker Heaton." London: John Lane, 1919. [These letters are not included in the Bonchurch Edition.]

Lafourcade, Georges. "Swinburne's 'Hyperion' and other Poems; with an Essay on Swinburne and Keats."[1] London: Faber and Gwyer, 1928.

Lafourcade, Georges. "La Jeunesse de Swinburne." Oxford: The University Press, 1928.

Leith, Mrs. Disney. "The Boyhood of Algernon Charles Swinburne. Personal Recollections. With Extracts from some of his Private Letters." London: Chatto and Windus, 1917. [These letters and extracts are not included in the Bonchurch Edition.]

Lucas, E. V. "At 'The Pines.' A Visit to A. C. Swinburne." London: Privately Printed, 1916.

Mackail, J. W. "Swinburne. A Lecture." Oxford: The Clarendon Press, 1909.

[1]At Oxford Swinburne wrote a "Hyperion" in continuation of Keats' poem. In it he reproduces cleverly the superficial qualities of Keats' style; but this bit of *pastiche* affords no evidence of fundamental sympathy with the elder poet. M. Lafourcade, who has published this piece for the first time, makes a study of Swinburne's changing opinions regarding Keats. He shows that the publication of the letters to Fanny Brawne was in large part responsible for Swinburne's low estimate of the poet in later years. Hence the inadequacy of the article on Keats in the "Encyclopaedia Britannica" in which I have commented on page 260.

Nicolson, Harold. "Swinburne." ["English Men of Letters Series".] London: Macmillan, 1926.

Reul, Paul de, "L'Œuvre de Swinburne." Brussels: Robert Sand, 1922.

Rossetti, W. M. "Poems and Ballads. A Criticism." London: Hotten, 1866.

Serner, Gunnar. "The Language of Swinburne's Lyrics and Epics." Lund, 1910.

Thomas, Edward. "Algernon Charles Swinburne. A Critical Study." London: Secker, 1912.

Welby, T. Earle. "Swinburne. A Critical Study." London: Elkin Mathews, 1914.

Welby, T. Earle. "A Study of Swinburne." New York: George H. Doran, 1926.

Woodberry, George E. "Swinburne." New York: McClure, Phillips & Co., 1905.

Wise, Thomas J. Bibliographies, as on page 307.

INDEX